Identity Studies in the Social Sciences

Series Editors: **Margaret Wetherell**, Open University, UK; **Valerie Hey**, Sussex University, UK; and **Stephen Reicher**, St Andrews University, UK

Editorial Board: **Marta Augoustinos**, University of Adelaide, Australia; **Wendy Brown**, University of California, Berkeley, USA; **David McCrone**, University of Edinburgh, UK; **Angela McRobbie**, Goldsmiths College, University of London, UK; **Chandra Talpade Mohanty**, Syracuse University, USA; **Harriet B. Nielsen**, University of Oslo, Norway; **Ann Phoenix**, Institute of Education, University of London, UK; and **Mike Savage**, University of Manchester, UK

Titles include:

Will Atkinson
CLASS, INDIVIDUALIZATION AND LATE MODERNITY
In Search of the Reflexive Worker

John Kirk, Sylvie Contrepois and Steve Jefferys (*editors*)
CHANGING WORK AND COMMUNITY IDENTITIES IN EUROPEAN REGIONS
Perspectives on the Past and Present

John Kirk and Christine Wall
WORK AND IDENTITY
Historical and Cultural Contexts

Janice McLaughlin, Peter Phillimore and Diane Richardson (*editors*)
CONTESTING RECOGNITION
Culture, Identity and Citizenship

Ben Rogaly and Becky Taylor
MOVING HISTORIES OF CLASS AND COMMUNITY
Identity, Place and Belonging in Contemporary England

Susie Scott
TOTAL INSTITUTIONS AND REINVENTED IDENTITIES

Ruth Simpson, Natasha Slutskaya, Patricia Lewis and Heather Höpfl (*editors*)
DIRTY WORK
Concepts and Identities

Margaret Wetherell (*editor*)
IDENTITY IN THE 21ST CENTURY
New Trends in Changing Times

Margaret Wetherell (*editor*)
THEORIZING IDENTITIES AND SOCIAL ACTION

Valerie Walkerdine and Luis Jimenez (*editors*)
GENDER, WORK AND COMMUNITY AFTER DE-INDUSTRIALIZATION
A Psychosocial Approach to Affect

Identity Studies in the Social Sciences
Series Standing Order ISBN 978–0–230–20500–0 (Hardback)
978–0–230–20501–7 (Paperback)
(*outside North America only*)

You can receive future titles in this series as they are published by placing a standing order. Please contact your bookseller or, in case of difficulty, write to us at the address below with your name and address, the title of the series and the ISBN quoted above.

Customer Services Department, Macmillan Distribution Ltd, Houndmills, Basingstoke, Hampshire RG21 6XS, England

---

Dirty Work

Concepts and Identities

Edited by

Ruth Simpson
Brunel Business School, Brunel University, UK

Natasha Slutskaya
Brunel Business School, Brunel University, UK

Patricia Lewis
Kent Business School, University of Kent, UK

and

Heather Höpfl
Essex Business School, University of Essex, UK

palgrave
macmillan

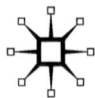

First published 2012 by
PALGRAVE MACMILLAN

Palgrave Macmillan in the UK is an imprint of Macmillan Publishers Limited, registered in England, company number 785998, of Houndmills, Basingstoke, Hampshire RG21 6XS.

Palgrave Macmillan in the US is a division of St Martin's Press LLC, 175 Fifth Avenue, New York, NY 10010.

Palgrave Macmillan is the global academic imprint of the above companies and has companies and representatives throughout the world.

Palgrave® and Macmillan® are registered trademarks in the United States, the United Kingdom, Europe and other countries.

ISBN 978–0–230–27713–7

This book is printed on paper suitable for recycling and made from fully managed and sustained forest sources. Logging, pulping and manufacturing processes are expected to conform to the environmental regulations of the country of origin.

A catalogue record for this book is available from the British Library.

A catalog record for this book is available from the Library of Congress.

10   9   8   7   6   5   4   3   2   1
21   20   19   18   17   16   15   14   13   12

Printed and bound in Great Britain by
CPI Antony Rowe, Chippenham and Eastbourne

Contents

Figures and Tables

Figures

Tables

Notes on Contributors

Gina Grandy is Associate Professor with the Commerce Department, Ron Joyce Centre for Business Studies at Mount Allison University, located in New Brunswick, Canada. Her research focuses on stigmatised occupations, competitive advantage, leadership, identity, organisational change and culture. She has published in *Gender, Work and Organization*; the *Journal of Management Studies*; *Qualitative Research in Organizations and Management: An International Journal*; *The Learning Organization* and the *Journal of Strategy and Management*.

Heather Höpfl is Professor of Management at the University of Essex, UK. A psychologist by training, she has worked in a number of different jobs and fields, including on design with a large engineering company, as an Economics teacher in a convent grammar school, as tour manager for a theatre company and as a researcher with the Department of Health and Social Security (DHSS). Her research interests are in aesthetics, embodiment and ethnography. Recent publications have been on theorisation and reflection, the incarnate consciousness, women's writing and dissolute magic.

Jason Hughes is Senior Lecturer in Sociology and Communications at Brunel University, UK. His current research interests include the sociology of emotions, the sociology of the body and health, sociological theory and organisational sociology. He has published in the areas of emotional labour and aesthetic labour as well as emotional intelligence and addiction. His first book, *Learning to Smoke*, was awarded the 2006 European Norbert Elias prize.

Geraldine Lee-Treweek is Principal Lecturer in Applied Social Studies with the Department of Interdisciplinary Studies, Manchester Metropolitan University (Cheshire), UK, where she runs the MA courses in Abuse Studies and Public, Community and Voluntary Sector Studies. She is currently researching racism in schools (funded by the Big Lottery Research Programme, UK, in collaboration with the Cheshire, Halton and Warrington Race and Equality Centre, UK) and the experiences of economic migrant communities in the UK.

Patricia Lewis has been Senior Lecturer in Management at the Kent Business School, UK, since October 2007. Prior to this she worked in the Brunel Business School, Brunel University, UK. Her research interests include gender and emotion, gender and entrepreneurship, entrepreneurial identity and the development and evolution of enterprise culture. She has published in *Gender, Work and Organization*; the *British Journal of Management*; *Human Relations*; *Work, Employment and Society* and the *Journal of Business Ethics*. She is an active member of the Gender in Management Special Interest Group of the British Academy of Management (BAM), London, UK.

Kate Mackenzie-Davey is Senior Lecturer in the Department of Organizational Psychology at Birkbeck, University of London, UK. Her research draws on discourse to explore the individual–organisation relationship and has examined boundaries and transitions in careers, individual values and organisational politics and bullying at work. She has published in *Gender, Work and Organization*; the *Human Resource Management Journal* and the *Journal of Occupational and Organizational Psychology*.

Sharon Mavin is Dean of Newcastle Business School, Northumbria University, Newcastle upon Tyne, UK. She has a sustained interest in women leaders and has published widely on women in management and leadership and gender research. Her work has been published in *Gender, Work and Organization*; the *British Journal of Management*; *Management Learning*; the *International Small Business Journal* and *Gender in Management: An International Journal*.

Robert McMurray is Senior Lecturer in Management at Durham University Business School, UK. Research interests include occupational identities, emotional labour, health care organisation, deeply processual notions of change and dirty work. Robert's research has been published in journals such as *Human Relations*, *Organisation*, *Public Administration* and *Social Science and Medicine*.

Alison Pullen lives on the Gower and works at Swansea University, Wales, UK. Alison's books include *Managing Identity* (2006, Palgrave), *Exploring Identity: Concepts and Methods* (2007, Palgrave), *Bits* *of Organization* (2009, CBS), *Organization and Identity* (2006, Routledge) and *Thinking Organization* (2006, Routledge).

Giulia Selmi holds a PhD in Sociology and Social Research from the University of Trento (Italy), where she is currently a member of the steering group of the Centre of Interdisciplinary Gender Studies and a member of RUCOLA (Research Unit on Communication, Organizational Learning and Aesthetics). Her research interests concern the social construction of sexuality and gender and embodiment in the workplace, with a special focus on the sex industry and its contemporary configurations.

Ruth Simpson is Professor of Management at Brunel Business School, UK. She is member and co-founder of the Centre for Research in Emotion Work and Employment Studies (CREWES), UK, and for several years was co-editor of the *International Journal of Work Organisation and Emotion*. Her research interests include gender and emotions as well as gender, work and careers.

Natasha Slutskaya is Lecturer in Organization Studies at Brunel Business School, UK. Her research interests can be divided into two broad areas: organisational identity and creativity and embodiment, in as far as they pertain to empirical and theoretical dilemmas in the field of organisation studies. She is a member of the European Group for Organizational Studies (EGOS) and BAM.

Liz Stanley is a consultant specialising in organisational change and employee engagement and a part-time PhD student at Birkbeck College, University of London, UK. Her research is a longitudinal, qualitative exploration of media positioning of investment bankers throughout the financial crisis and of individual bankers' positioning and identity work in response to this. She has a BA in social and political science from Cambridge University, UK, and an MSc in organisational behaviour from Birkbeck, London, UK.

Elaine Swan is Head of Academic Group at the University of Technology, Sydney, Australia. Her research interests include cultural representations of global elites in business media and magazine culture, critical visual pedagogy as well as critical whiteness and diversity studies. In 2009 Elaine published a book, *Worked up Selves: Personal Development Workers, Self-Work and Therapeutic Culture* (Palgrave).

Melissa Tyler is Reader in Management at the University of Essex, UK. Her research on emotional, aesthetic and sexualised forms of labour, on feminist organisation theory and on gender and subjectivity has been published in a range of international journals, authored and co-authored books and edited collections. Melissa's current research focuses on retail sales work in sex shops based in Soho, London, UK; on sales-service work in the children's culture industries; and on ageing and sexuality at the workplace.

Sheena J. Vachhani is Lecturer in Organisation Studies at the School of Business and Economics, Swansea University, Wales, UK. Her research interests lie in understanding embodiment, difference, ethics and the feminine in organisation. She concentrates on developing visceral perspectives on organisation by critiquing and investigating the relationships between language, bodies, identities and subjectivities. She has been published in scholarly journals such as *Organization, Culture and Organization* and *Creativity and Innovation Management*.

Paul White is Lecturer in the People, Organizations and Work research group of Swansea University's School of Business and Economics, UK. He has a broad interest in social, cultural and organisational theory and is currently attempting to formulate a vague understanding of what a cosmopolitics of organisation means.

1
Introducing Dirty Work, Concepts and Identities

Ruth Simpson, Natasha Slutskaya, Patricia Lewis and Heather Höpfl

Introduction

This edited book sets out a research agenda for the study of dirty work – generally defined as tasks, occupations and roles that are likely to be perceived as disgusting or degrading (Ashforth and Kreiner, 1999). Through the different occupational settings presented, it explores the identities, meanings, relations and spaces of dirty work and how the boundaries between 'clean' and 'dirty' are negotiated and defined. As Ashforth and Kreiner (1999) have argued, dirty work has been a neglected area within Organisation Studies, with theory and research failing to reflect changes in the nature of and demand for such work. This neglect is surprising given, within the context of the UK and elsewhere, the increase in the demand for 'dirty' work – including paid caring (Anderson, 2000), domestic work and low-level service (Noon and Blyton, 2007) and night-time work driven by the 24-hour economy (Hobbs, 2003) – as well as for areas of work performed by migrant labour.

One reason for this neglect might be that forms of dirty work are seen as 'out of step' with notions of modern 'clean' work (Bolton, 2007). 'Good work' not only signifies the absence of proximity to dirt, but routinely offers intrinsic rewards such as job satisfaction, engagement and opportunity for career advancement. As Bolton (2007) points out, while there is concern among policy makers about widening divisions in the labour market, they continue to propose a narrow vision of clean, high-skilled and 'better' work. Such work is not, however, open to all – and some people fail to gain access to the opportunities and benefits that are conveyed. Conditions in the West have undoubtedly improved, with few people working in unsafe or hazardous environments (though these persist in many parts of the world). However, the availability of 'good work' is still limited and many people end up in jobs that may be characterised by poor pay, limited opportunities for advancement and unsavoury working conditions. In fact, as suggested above, such work may have become more readily available as the better-off 'out-source' (Ehrenreich and Hochschild, 2003) personal services they do not want to do themselves – from domestic cleaning to childcare. 'Bad work' therefore is unlikely to disappear – though it may well take new forms.

Another reason for the neglect of dirty work may pertain to its largely invisible status. Dirty work can be seen to be invisible on several counts. Firstly, we try to create distance from the pollution of dirt and from those who deal with it. From this perspective, cleanness is about establishing boundaries, separating the pure from the contaminated and imposing a system on an 'inherently untidy experience' (Douglas, 1966: 85). Thus, we seek to withdraw from whatever bears traces of contamination and impurity. Secondly, work involving dirt or defined as 'dirty' is often undertaken by those at the lower levels of the hierarchy (Hughes, 1958), that is those at the margins of society. Such work can be spatially absent – undertaken in private homes (care workers, domestic cleaners) or temporally concealed (night-time work or work involving unsocial hours). Finally, work involving dirt may be visible (street cleaners, refuse collectors, vegetable pickers) but 'unseen', partly because it fails to conform to notions of modern 'clean value added work' (Bolton and Houlihan, 2009), as referred to above. Such work (and the workers) may therefore be characterised as having low cultural priority – overlooked in policy discourses and only coming into view under unusual circumstances, such as the plight of migrant cockle pickers who were drowned in Morecambe in 2004.

Conceptualising dirty work

One aim in this book is to render aspects of dirt and dirty work more visible. In doing so, we advocate an approach that takes into account its social and cultural meanings as well as its 'fluid' nature – how meanings may alter with different contextual conditions and how these conditions may be implicated in the way the work is experienced. We argue, along the lines of Dick (2005), that this orientation has been underplayed, allowing further potential, in the context of work and organisations, to uncover dirt's social, political and cultural aspects. These aspects may include how dirty workers are 'othered'; the significance of intersections with social divisions based on gender, race and class; and also how 'staining' is experienced. This suggests a need to go beyond the nature of the tasks and roles that make up what we perceive to be dirty work to include these broader implications.

Dirt as material and moral

From a largely anthropological perspective, early conceptualisations of dirt focussed on meanings associated with the physicality of contamination and pollution, for example from muck, slime and bodily fluids (Douglas, 1966). This foregrounds the materiality around dirt which relates to bodily sensations such as smell, touch, stickiness and slime that lead to feelings of repulsion and disgust (Dant and Bowles, 2003). Following Douglas (1966), a further orientation has been more symbolic – founded on perceptions of dirt and pollution as 'matter out of place', that is as arising when there are violations of cultural norms or of the social order.

Cleanliness and dirt are therefore not just material matters but can have social and moral significance, triggering with respect to dirt a desire to avoid or remove it and stigmatising those who are involved in it. In terms of the former, not all dirt is seen as equally polluting. Earth for example, while dirty, has meanings associated with life-giving properties, while bodily fluids represent a form of contamination that is more extreme (Ackroyd and Crowdy, 1990). With reference to the latter, as Dick (2005) points out, avoidance rules mean that occupations which deal with polluting, physical dirt are carried out by members of lower classes who are separated spatially and socially from other groups (e.g. 'untouchables' of the Hindu class system). Where higher-status occupations deal with dirt (e.g. doctors whose jobs involve aspects of intimate care), avoidance rules operate so that much of the work is delegated to those lower in the hierarchy such as hospital orderlies.

In this respect, as McClintock (1995) illustrates, discourses related to dirt and hygiene were one of the earliest to combine and condense the notion of class. She demonstrates how hands reveal one's class by expressing one's relation to labour. Historically, clean, smooth hands covered by gloves were the indication of 'good breeding' and financial standing (one could afford to buy the labour of others) so that middle-class women went to great lengths to clean their hands to remove staining, so disguising their work and erasing its evidence. In a more contemporary context, Skeggs (2004) argues that dirt and disorder serve as signifiers of class and as moral evaluations by which the working class are coded. Dirt is therefore tied up with a moral and social order and a set of norms that may shift over time and under different circumstances – linked to meanings around disease, staining and depravity and triggering public policies (e.g. public health regulations) to eradicate and contain it.

Physical, social and moral taint

The ability of meanings around dirt to capture both the material and the moral was highlighted by Hughes' (1951, 1958) foundational analysis of dirty work as being physically disgusting, a symbol of social degradation and/or counter to moral conceptions. As he argues, dirty work of some kind can be found in all occupations – if only because at some point the worker is likely to have to do something that undermines a sense of personal dignity or because the work involves some contact with a stigmatised group.

Building on Hughes' (1958) early conceptualisation, Ashforth and Kreiner (1999), from a social psychological perspective, categorise dirty work under three main headings. These include physical taint, namely occupations associated with dirt or performed under dangerous conditions (e.g. refuse collectors, miners); social taint, namely occupations involving regular contact with people from stigmatised groups or where the job is seen as involving being servile to others (e.g. prison officers, domestic workers); and moral taint, namely occupations regarded as sinful or of dubious virtue (e.g. debt collectors, prostitutes).

More recently, Kreiner et al. (2006) have, from a similar perspective, made reference to the 'breadth' and 'depth' of perceived dirtiness. Breadth refers to the proportion of the work that is dirty or the centrality of dirt to the occupational identity (a physician may occasionally deal with dead bodies, but a mortician always does so). Depth captures the intensity of dirtiness and the extent to which a worker is directly involved. For example, police officers deal mainly with criminals (high intensity), while security guards mostly deal with the public (low intensity). Some occupations may have high breadth and depth because of a single dimension (e.g. the moral taint of prostitutes, the physical taint of sewage workers). By contrast, other occupations may be low on both dimensions. This classification therefore captures a wider group of occupations or roles beyond the 'extreme' cases identified by Ashforth and Kreiner above.

Social and cultural processes of dirty work

The above typology has provided a sound starting point for the categorisation and identification of such work and has been foundational in framing and developing the field. However, while Ashforth and Kreiner (1999) position dirty work in social constructionist terms (e.g. highlighting the significance of attitudes of 'visceral repugnance' on the part of others towards such work), it has been argued that they nevertheless undertheorise the influence of social and cultural processes and their power dynamics (Dick, 2005; Tracy and Scott, 2006). Accepting the socially constructed nature of dirty work implies a need to recognise that meanings attached to such work may vary across occupations and may be dependent on those who are seen to embody such work and that norms of 'acceptability' may be temporally and culturally bounded, that is varying from group to group, at different points in time and across geographical/international space. For example, technology can lead to a rearrangement of job typologies so that previously rejected occupations become newly 'acceptable' to some groups. In this respect, Witz (1992) has described how a revised form of radiography emerged out of new technology in the 1920s and 1930s so that the profession became less tainted as 'female' and more acceptable to men. Some tasks and roles may be avoided by indigenous workers as undesirable but are taken up by migrant groups (see Lee-Treweek, this volume). These norms, however, may change with economic circumstances; for example, men made redundant in the de-industrialisation of the 1980s and 1990s considered 'feminised' service and caring roles, previously avoided as incongruent with traditional gender norms (Gregg and Wadsworth, 2003). Similarly, as Liz Stanley shows in this volume, the taint attributed to investment bankers did not predate their entry but emerged and intensified throughout the financial crisis. Other work in this volume explores the cultural meanings attached to dirt and purity in different contexts and how individuals negotiate the clean/dirty divide, highlighting experiences of abjection, emotions of fear and disgust and practices that relate to staining. This demonstrates the need to recognise the significance of different social and cultural processes that are involved in the meanings attached to dirt as well as to how dirty work is encountered and experienced.

Dirty work as gendered, classed and raced

As Tracy and Scott (2006) argue, concepts of taint, dirt and prestige are intimately connected to powerful social identity categories such as gender, race, class and nationality. However, these aspects are rarely explicit in the literature – perhaps because dirty work tends to be drawn on traditionally gendered, 'raced' or classed lines so that these are hidden within taken-for-granted assumptions and values. In this respect, the gendered nature of dirty work is partly manifest in the way such work often conforms to traditional notions of masculinity and femininity. Service and care, for example, have strong associations with the embodied dispositions of women, while other forms of dirty work (e.g. heavy manual labour, work involving risk or danger) are traditionally the domain of men. A body of work has accordingly explored the experiences of women as care workers or domestic helps (Anderson, 2000; Jervis, 2001) and as sex workers (Brewis and Linstead, 2000; Grandy, 2008). Other research has considered the physical taint of male mechanics (Dant and Bowles, 2003), male slaughtermen and butchers (Ackroyd and Crowdy, 1990; Meara, 1974; Slutskaya et al., 2009) and male firefighters (Tracy and Scott, 2006). However, with some exceptions (e.g. Bolton, 2005; Tracy and Scott, 2006), gender and the significance of broader gendered discourses remain peripheral to understandings of dirty work – implicit rather than explicit to the analysis – and relatively marginal in terms of how it is seen to be experienced.

These social divisions are complicated – both reinforced and undermined – by class, race and migrancy. As we have seen, dirty work is often undertaken by lower classes, both men and women, remaining invisible to those higher up the hierarchy. Race and nationality can add a further category of disadvantage and another layer to the hierarchical arrangement of such work. In the context of domestic service and pointing to the disproportionately high employment of racial-ethnic women, Duffy (2007) has shown that the gender typing of such work is not race-neutral. Black and migrant women have been found to be disproportionately employed in private, domestic cleaning, that is within the home. Migrant men, however, are often found within institutional cleaning, where, as Anderson (2000) argues, they are effectively 'de-gendered' by race and citizenship. These groupings accordingly challenge the gendered status quo, as migrant men, for example, take up work (such as institutional cleaning and food preparation) previously designated as female. Further, as Lee-Treweek (2010) notes, migrant men and women are often 'morally' tainted through perceptions that they are taking away jobs from indigenous workers, while at the same time enduring the physical taint of low-level and physically dirty jobs. The often low and marginal status of dirty work, the 'moral overtones' and stigma associated with such work and the desire by many to avoid or remove it, suggest that gender, race, class and migrancy are all implicated in work practices and workers' experiences.

The embodied nature of dirty work

The last section indicated some of the ways in which bodies are integral to how dirty work is understood. At a basic level, some forms of work involve bodily encounters, as in the sex industry, or extreme physical effort. Following our earlier discussion, some skills and attributes may be devalued depending on who practises and embodies them. Thus, with reference to levels of servility and deference captured by Ashforth and Kreiner's (1999) 'social taint' mentioned earlier, women are seen to 'naturally' deliver service in the workplace (Lewis and Simpson, 2007) i.e. certain attributes are perceived to be essentially feminine and hence devalued and invisible (Taylor and Tyler, 2000; Williams, 2003). Women's bodies are thus marked by servility and deemed appropriate for deferential displays. When men undertake service and caring roles, their untainted and authoritative bodies are out of place so that the work is re-valued and given new meaning (Pullen and Simpson, 2007). This complicates and disrupts the meanings attached to forms of dirty work when undertaken by bodies that are otherwise seen as untainted, unmarked and 'clean'.

Therefore, hierarchies are not only evident within the binary of 'clean' versus 'dirty' work but are manifest in the embodied characteristics and perceived dispositions of the worker. Cleanliness and dirt are accordingly inscribed onto particular bodies, affording them different levels of value. Elaine Swan, in this volume, points to how cleanliness and associated meanings of morality are commonly associated with 'whiteness' and with the white, middle-class body. Black and working-class bodies are marked as 'unclean' and routinely carry dirt's stigma.

A further embodied dimension relates to staining and the marking of the body through dirt. As Sheena Vachhani illustrates in this volume, staining through proximity to dirt is written on the body, leaving its mark through disorder and rendering dirt visible. Heather Höpfl highlights how to be contaminated is to be infected, polluted or dirtied in some way – often through touch as in a disease communicated from one body to another. Staining from physical taint can have affirmative effects. As Ackroyd and Crowdy (1990) and Slutskaya et al. (2009) show, while looking at the butcher trade, men can present marks made by blood and offal as a badge of honour and symbol of masculine endurance, mobilising feelings of disgust. These feelings, routinely aroused in connection to forms of taint, are also visceral, embodied experiences. Therefore while all forms of work have an embodied dimension – in the effort involved as well as in its pleasures and pains – dirty work may have particular bodily significance. Dirt not only represents and reproduces classed, raced and gendered divisions – divisions that are written on the body – but can also be spread through bodily contamination and be productive of body-marking stains. Further, dirt is productive of feelings (e.g. abhorrence, disgust) that are corporeally experienced.

These aspects indicate a complicated terrain in terms of how such work can be understood and experienced. In this respect, the typology of physical, social and moral taint has provided a sound basis for conceptualising such work and has been foundational in terms of shaping and developing the field. However, it may not sufficiently capture the diverse, contingent and fluid nature of occupational meanings or how contemporary implications and significances emerge. From a shared starting point that acknowledges the significance of social and cultural factors in understandings of such work, the chapters in this book go some way to test the boundaries of these definitional constructs and to incorporate at a deeper level other (e.g. social, cultural and corporeal) implications.

Dirty work and identity

As we have seen, dirt symbolises a contravention of social order – a transgression of particular boundaries – triggering a desire to avoid or remove it and stigmatising those who are involved in it. As Goffman (1963) has argued, dirt has potential to produce stigmatising conditions so that individuals are 'tainted' and disqualified from full social acceptance. In other words, society projects the negative qualities associated with dirt onto dirty workers, making identity management problematic (Bolton, 2005; Dick, 2005; Newman, 1999; Rollins, 1985; Stacey, 2005) and offering few status shields to challenge the identity imposed (Ashforth and Kreiner, 1999; Hochschild, 1983). This raises issues about how people manage job-related stigma (Bolton, 2005; Rollins, 1985) and how social validation is negotiated in order to, for example, create dignity at work (Bolton, 2007; Stacey, 2005).

Social identity theory and dirty work

This suggests a need to understand the processes underlying the intersection of dirty work and identity. Research indicates that people are acutely aware of the stigma attached to their work (Bolton, 2005; Rollins, 1985) and that this can make social validation problematic. Individuals may engage in normalising practices and processes

(Ashforth et al., 2007), thereby rendering the disruptive and problematic elements of the job seemingly ordinary. Through defensive tactics, such as 'gallows humour' or condemning those likely to judge the work negatively, individuals can actively counter the taint and render it less salient. Other work (e.g. Stacey, 2005) suggests that people can draw pride and satisfaction from their (dirty) work and that the nature of the work (e.g. unsocial hours which limit contact with outsiders) can facilitate the development of strong occupational and workgroup cultures.

Ashforth and Kreiner (1999) draw on social identity theory (Tajfel and Turner, 1985) to consider how taint is managed. They see identity as fairly stable, grounded in group membership and in the perceptions of others and oriented towards positive distinctiveness. In general terms, these perceptions constitute an ongoing threat to identity so, as they argue, there is often a preoccupation with outsiders and how the work is perceived. One strategy is accordingly to 'condemn the condemners' so that their views can be dismissed. Thus, as Rollins (1985) found, domestic cleaners often describe their employers as lonely and unfulfilled – this perceived deficiency serving to partially discount the servile, abject nature of the work.

A further strategy, in line with social identity's focus on the need to shape a positive identity, is to recast the work in affirmative terms. Some research, for example, has highlighted how demonstrating mastery of the dirtiest aspects of the job can be a source of value. Thus, care workers can find a source of distinctiveness, pride and moral authority in the ability to undertake work that others would be too 'squeamish' to perform (Stacey, 2005). As Ashforth and Kreiner (1999) argue, individuals can recast their dirty work in affirmative terms through occupational ideologies (e.g. around fortitude and toughness) that highlight group cohesion, articulating occupational identity in terms of 'us and them' and focussing on the specific demands of the job. This can be done by 'reframing' the meaning of dirty work by infusing it with positive value (e.g. seeing such work as a badge of honour or a mission); 'recalibrating', that is adjusting the perceptual and evaluative standards used to assess the work and thereby minimising the 'dirty work' component (e.g. hospital cleaners may introduce notions of patient care as integral to the work); and 'refocusing' through the shifting of attention away from the stigmatised to the non-stigmatised features of the job (e.g. refuse collectors may focus on the benefits of flexible hours and social solidarity). Overall, as Kreiner et al. (2006) point out, occupational stigmas may be particularly damaging to an individual's identity.

Individuals accordingly engage in a diverse set of cognitive, affective and behavioural coping strategies to deal with stigma at work.

The socially constructed nature of dirty work identity

As we have seen, while Ashforth and Kreiner (1999) position dirty work in social constructionist terms, it has been argued that they may have undertheorised the influence of social and cultural processes and their power dynamics (Dick, 2005; Tracy and Scott, 2006). The social and identity characteristics of the worker are accordingly given less priority in their accounts. The significance of these social dimensions, discussed above, was given some preliminary recognition by Hughes (1958), seen as foundational for conceptualisations of such work, in his assertion of the importance of social status for how dirty work is managed and experienced. Thus, dirty work undertaken by those of a higher standing (e.g. bodily care performed by doctors) can be 'integrated into the whole' – rendered less salient by being absorbed into the prestige-bearing role of the person who does it. For these well-positioned individuals, contact with dirt can be mitigated by other, more positive and socially privileged aspects of identity.

This suggests that identity management is likely to be dependent on the individual's ability to mobilise social and cultural resources to support (or resist) a particular sense of self. This indicates a view of identity that, rather than being relatively stable as in social identity theory, is fragile, emergent and ongoing (Ainsworth and Hardy, 2004; Pullen and Linstead, 2005), produced in interaction and through discourse. From this social constructionist perspective, identity is relational, processual and a 'doing' that highlights its fragmented, multiple and emergent nature. Thus, as Dick (2005) argues, the choice of strategy suggested by Kreiner et al. (2006) – for example reframing, recalibration, refocussing – can be context-specific and result in part from a hegemonic, discursive struggle among meanings as individuals negotiate subjectivity. Some individuals or groups may be able to mobilise resources to better manage the associated taint – for example by being able to draw on other, 'cleaner', aspects of the job and/or turn the work into a test of endurance or 'badge of honour'. Thus from Dick (2005), police officers were able to reconstruct occupational identity by bringing meanings of coercive authority into line with ideals of a liberal democratic society. They were therefore able to absolve themselves of personal responsibility for the use of force. Similarly, as Tracy and Scott (2006) found, firefighters could draw on discourses of masculine heterosexuality to reframe their work in preferred terms. From Bolton's (2005) study of gynaecology nurses, women were able to draw on essentialised notions of femininity as 'unique carers' to give value to their work and to create distance from men. This highlights the power of some groups to draw on and to mobilise privileged 'frames' in these ideological 'reconstructions', resisting the stain imposed, as well as drawing attention to the instability and contingency of the meanings conveyed.

This orientation also lends itself to an exploration of how categories of difference intersect in the management of taint – how proximity to dirt may impress differentially on identities and how gender, race, class and migrancy are likely to be implicated in workers' experiences. This helps us to explore how men and women manage the tainted nature of their work and how these negotiations are influenced by gender, class and race; how bodies are partly made through and marked by meanings around taint; the specific challenges that particular identity groups face; the meanings that individuals draw on to manage the dirty work component of their jobs; and how they position themselves in relation to other groups.

In summary, from this broad starting point, chapters in this book help surface the complexity, fluidity and contingency of dirty work – how occupational boundaries, work practices and the meanings around dirt and cleanliness are accordingly more fluid and subject to re-interpretation and change, rather than being fixed, stable and rooted in a job task or role. Through specific research sites and by drawing on innovative theoretical insights, the chapters explore different ways of conceptualising dirty work, the meanings afforded to cleanliness and dirt, how individuals manage and construct the 'clean/dirty' divide as well as how dirty workers negotiate taint in the management of identity.

Chapter summaries

In Chapter 2, 'Dirty Work and Acts of Contamination', Heather Höpfl looks at contamination as a form of disordered 'otherness' and practice that transgresses boundaries between the clean and the dirty. Drawing partly on Kristeva's (1982) work as inspiration, she examines the fear of contamination and the embodied dimensions of cleanness and dirt within aspects of work performance. Using Diderot's comparison between dramatic performances and prostitution – both involving the promise of intimacy while withholding parts of oneself – she explores the dirty nature of specific performances within a work role. As she points out, actors offer themselves in embodied performances that are regulated and ordered by organisational scripts and performance metrics – the latter regarded as having purity and worth based on authority and legitimacy. Through this regulation, the organisation designates what is 'proper' and 'clean' as well as what is 'dirty', dangerous and disordered. Here, she draws on Canetti's 'sting', which attaches to a command and causes repressed anger against authority, to explore some responses to being cast as 'other' and as 'dirty'. Through these powerful examples, she highlights how the performance requirements of organisational life can produce actors who are 'humiliated, debased and under-valued' and how the sting can, as an embodied response and deliberate act of contamination, take a physical form.

In Chapter 3, 'Stains, Staining and the Ethics of Dirty Work', Sheena Vachhani explores the theoretical potential of stains and staining as a productive way of conceptualising dirty work. Here she brings together analyses of the physical and ethical that invoke the material and symbolic relations involved. As she argues, on the one hand we seek to eradicate stains as disorder or 'corruption' from our bodies – a visible marker of dirt that arouses disgust; on the other hand, stains can be productive of knowledge and identity, as in the process of medical diagnosis and research and engagement with professional caring roles. The chapter engages in wider debates in feminist ethics – in particular a corporeal ethics concerning the sense of responsibility towards those who are displaced, marked or excluded as a result of physical, social or moral taint. By showing how stains and staining are both about exposure and vulnerability, presencing but also making absent, the chapter invites a new level of recognition of an other, other bodies and other stains. This generosity, she argues, can emerge through an understanding of the specificity of lived bodies that does not privilege a prescriptive ethics but is able to reflect on the social injustices perpetuated by moral order, maps of respectability and relations of classification. This underpins a more inclusive theory of staining that troubles the clean/dirty divide.

In Chapter 4, 'From High Flyer to Crook – How Can We Understand the Stigmatisation of Investment Bankers during the Financial Crisis?', Liz Stanley seeks to extend the models and typologies of dirty work by drawing attention to the importance of subject positions and positioning in the exploration of the dynamics and processes of stigmatisation, taint attribution and stigma management strategies. The chapter questions the existing taxonomy of tactics, suggesting that it adopts a relatively stable view of identity, favours the experiences of low-prestige workers and focusses on established taint, which is associated with stigmatised tasks. Here, Liz Stanley explores a high-status occupation such as investment banking that has been newly stigmatised – presenting the case for a more dynamic conceptualisation of taint. By shifting focus onto a more specific analysis of how well-established occupational groups, in situations of nascent taint, respond to identity threats, the chapter presents the case that the challenge of normalising and countering taint is a complex, messy and fluid identity project. Given the evolving and emergent nature of taint in this context, she argues for a focus on the processes of stigmatisation that can surface the confusion, contradiction and ambiguity in individuals' responses to a newly experienced form of taint, as boundaries of appropriateness are contested and redrawn. In this respect, she promotes the theoretical and analytical lens of subject positioning to prompt an exploration of how moral taint is constructed and conveyed.

In Chapter 5, ' "Glamour Girls, Macho Men and Everything in Between": Un/doing Gender and Dirty Work in Soho's Sex Shops', Melissa Tyler explores sales-service work in sex shops. Falling between research which focusses on sex workers and the more recent work on sexualised labour in sales-service work, the sex shop is an underresearched commercial entity. Her consideration of the experience of men and women who work in Soho's sex shops begins by drawing on Hughes' (1951) notion of dirty work, exploring the way in which the physical, social and moral taint of this sales occupation is managed. The physical taint of the job is associated with the intimacy inherent in selling sex products to and discussing them with customers, while the social taint is connected to the stigma that such work prompts, leading some of the respondents to conceal their occupation from family and friends. The close association between sex shops, sex work and stigmatised people means that working in such an establishment also carries a strong moral taint. Conventionally, considerations of 'dirty work' which are explored through Hughes' (1951) framework focus on how the taint associated with an occupation is managed, that is on how individuals deal with the repugnance that this type of work provokes. However, Tyler goes further and argues that for sales-service workers in sex shops the situation is more complex than just managing taint. Rather she suggests that there is a simultaneous attraction and repulsion towards the various taints attached to this type of work on the part of most of her respondents. On this basis she argues, drawing on the work of Kristeva (1982), that sales-service work in sex shops is better understood as abject labour, as this allows us to consider what it is about 'dirt' that attracts as well as disgusts the respondents in her study. Framing sales-service work in sex shops as abject labour allows us to not only consider the coping strategies of those involved in it, but also to understand the appeal that attaches to such work.

In Chapter 6, 'Doing Gender in Dirty Work: Exotic Dancers' Construction of Self-enhancing Identities', Gina Grandy and Sharon Mavin examine another underresearched form of work, that of exotic dancing. This occupation has tended to be subsumed within the broader category of sex workers, with the particular characteristics and issues of this form of work being concealed. In response to a recent call for research specific to this employment, Grandy and Mavin explore how dancers construct a favourable identity within a context where significant physical, social and moral taint attaches to the labour. Through their analysis they identify a number of positive and negative identity roles which exotic dancers construct. The positive identity roles constructed include those of the empowered, the temp, the good girl, the professional and the artist, while the negative ones include those of the lifer, the dirty dancer and the competitor. These identity roles are connected to issues of freedom, that is to control over their own work situations, the longevity of their dancing career and their behaviour in regards to nudity and drinking while working as a dancer. Two aspects of these identity roles and the characteristics that attach to them are notable. First, Grandy and Mavin emphasise that these identity roles are fluid and that it is possible that an individual can enact multiple, overlapping and contradictory identity roles. Second, those women who take up positive identity roles as a means of managing the taint attached to their occupation, do so through a process of othering individuals who are associated with the negative identity roles. This helps to establish distance from the stigma attached to exotic dancing as dirty work, while also enabling a favourable positioning within the complex, gendered sex and sex-industry status hierarchies.

In Chapter 7, 'Dirty Talks and Gender Cleanliness: An Account of Identity Management Practices in Phone Sex Work', Giulia Selmi explores the ways in which identity is managed by female phone-sex operators. Through her Italian study, she highlights the specific gender dirtiness of the work (e.g. through the 'whore stigma') as well as how gender is drawn on in the management of taint. Through the narratives of the women concerned, she highlights how women respond to the symbolic conception of commercial sex as a form of deviance or immorality and how they resist being so framed. Here, women draw on the commercial aspects of the interaction, aligning themselves with other call operators and downplaying the sexual element. Some women present themselves as caregivers, offering a unique service in this respect. Others position their male clients as deficient and as having violated norms of gender appropriateness – thereby allowing space for self-constructions that mobilise conventional norms of acceptable femininity. Through these practices and processes, she highlights how women respond to the symbolic conception of commercial sex as a form of female immorality by casting the work in socially acceptable terms. This 'identity cleansing' is deeply gendered and, as she argues, involves the strategic use of, as well as distancing from, symbolic elements of the whore stigma.

In Chapter 8, 'Embracing Dirt in Nursing Matters', Robert McMurray explores how constructions of nursing work have changed in relation to notions of dirt by tracing a shift from Nightingale's concern with sanitation to the development of Advanced Nurse Practitioners (ANPs) who claim jurisdiction as diagnosticians. In the former case the dirty work of nursing speaks of vital daily work with messy bodies, messier practices and unwanted populations. In claiming dirt and its management as part of nursing practice, the core of 'women's work', an occupational identity can be supported around possession of sanitary knowledge that demands recognition. The chapter considers the manner in which ANPs resist this positioning, by staking a claim to the medical knowledge that characterises professional status. Yet in making such claims – in challenging the livelihoods of doctors and the presumptive exclusivity that is at the heart of gendered notions of a profession – they themselves are rendered as 'dirt'. In Douglas's terms, they are seen as 'matter out of place'. In tracing this change, the chapter considers the potential for positive and negative meanings to be activated in relation to nursing's association with dirt. In doing so, it highlights the socially constructed nature of dirt, its multiplicity and historical contingency and how it is mobilised to support a particular occupational identity.

In Chapter 9, 'Dispersing of Dirt: Inscribing Bodies and Polluting Organisation', Paul White and Alison Pullen draw on the processes and practices of intensive care to explore the significance of the body as present and absent, invaded, pierced and managed through technologies of life support. Within the space of the ceremonial ordering of clinical work, they utilise notions of cleanliness and sterility as illusive 'matter in place' to highlight principles of organising as well as of dirt dispersal. Here, they discuss the cultural implications of the dispersal of dirt as an act of forgetting and deferment that leads to its eventual return. Through a series of evocative photographic and other images, they demonstrate how the (integrated techno-) body is made knowable and read – amenable to organisational manipulation and interpretation – and how the critically ill body is punctured, interpreted, manipulated, cleansed and spatially managed through technology. Further, they show how bodies are rendered legible through the ceremonial order of clinical work and how they are rendered visible via leakages as fleshy, carnal and unsanitised while also contained within technologies of intensive care. The body is shown to be an extension of technology and technology itself as it is transformed as a techno-body. Through this example, the authors make visible how the body of the critically ill is incorporated into the broader circuit of material, social and spatial relations as well as how any breach in this order amplifies dirt.

In Chapter 10, 'Gendering and Embodying Dirty Work: Men Managing Taint in the Context of Nursing Care', Ruth Simpson, Natasha Slutskaya and Jason Hughes explore the gendered nature of dirty work and how dirty workers manage taint. Through an Australia-based study of 16 male nurses, they draw attention to the gendered and embodied dimensions of dirty work and argue that notions of 'suitability' underpin understandings of such work. In particular, they show how men draw on gender as an active strategy to manage taint. With regard to physical taint, male nurses frame their work-based abilities in explicitly 'masculine' terms (e.g. around fortitude and endurance) as special qualities. However, in managing the moral taint associated with the sexualisation of men's touch in nursing care, they work to create distance from gender and masculinity, drawing instead on (more gender-neutral) norms of professionalism. Gender is thus drawn on in an active strategy to reframe meanings around such work. At the same time, men's bodies are seen as out of place in a nursing role, and the authors show how notions of embodied 'suitability' can underpin perceptions of dirt, 'disorder' and taint.

Much of the research on dirty work has focussed on individuals located at the lower end of the occupational spectrum, exploring the means by which they recast their work in positive terms by managing the taint and stigma attaching to it. In Chapter 11 entitled 'Cleaning up? Transnational Corporate Femininity and Dirty Work in Magazine Culture', Elaine Swan builds on this research by focussing on a group of elite workers, namely career women, who have been underrepresented and underresearched in the contemporary dirty-work literature. Focussing on a 2007 supplement of the magazine *Harper's Bazaar*, entitled 'Bazaar at Work', she explores how the magazine issue contributes to the creation and maintenance of an elite by acting as a tool for middle-class career women to draw upon. A key theme of the supplement is the management of time, with women being identified as a group of workers who face particular temporal problems due to the cultural expectation that they will take responsibility for family and domestic issues. The solution to time pressures is presented as lying in the adoption of appropriate strategies to enable the successful achievement and management of work/life balance. The contracting out of household chores, what can be referred to as 'dirty work', is vital to the achievement of the sought-after 'balance', with the service of other (non-elite) women being central in securing this. Through the imagery and text of such a supplement, she argues that a new version of femininity labelled 'transnational corporate femininity' is being constructed. Developing this notion, she argues that central to the achievement of this version of femininity is the cultural resource of cleanliness which is secured through the domestic labour of others, enabling elite career women to maintain a distance from any taint that attaches to domesticity. What emerges clearly from the analysis is that there is no 'pan femininity' across all women, rather the outsourcing of 'dirty work' as a strategy for career success contributes to the enforcement of hierarchical relations between femininities.

In Chapter 12, 'Managing "Dirty" Migrant Identities: Migrant Labour and the Neutralisation of Dirty Work Through Moral Group Identity', Geraldine Lee-Treweek explores how dirt and taint are managed among Polish migrant workers and how the work culture focusses inwards to manage dirty meanings. Building on UK-based ethnographic fieldwork, the chapter demonstrates how the work group appropriates ways of understanding and being and the moral values and cultural traditions they inherit as a form of resistance to negative meanings attached to their work. The chapter highlights the fact that though migrant workers are physically mobile they often find themselves 'stuck' in the old forms of self-definition and self-differentiation. Having very limited resources to redeem both the 'dirtiness' of their work and the precariousness of their newly occupied positions, they adhere to the ideas of 'traditional' Polishness, a good 'Polish worker' and 'proper' feminine behaviour. The lack of means to positively 'make the self' or perhaps (given the possibilities opened up by migration) to 'remake the self' in the workplace also reveals itself in the elements of racism, workplace bullying and intolerance to difference and alternative ways of living. By focussing on how identity is managed from within the group, as pre-migration identities are invested with worth to become a source of group membership, Lee-Treweek shows how despite geographical mobility, the relationship between past and present identity becomes non-fluid and definitive.

In Chapter 13, 'Post-feminism and Entrepreneurship: Interpreting Disgust in a Female Entrepreneurial Narrative', Patricia Lewis explores expressions of disgust within one businesswoman's narrative and considers the broader social phenomenon that such expressions represent. A central focus of a number of studies of dirty work is to explore how jobs designated as 'dirty work' taint the individuals who perform them, while also considering how those who do dirty work manage any associated stigma. In contrast in this chapter, Lewis considers the reactions and responses to those individuals whose presence in a particular job is perceived to taint an occupation which would not conventionally be labelled 'dirty work', while also exploring how these individuals and their perceived stigma is 'managed'. In particular she considers how women business owners who are deemed to be inappropriately feminine are rendered 'disgusting' as a means of establishing distance from them and reducing the impact of their perceived 'taint' on the entrepreneurial activities of other women. It is argued that disgust is an emotion which has been underresearched but which acts to establish divisions and distinctions between different types of individuals in general and businesswomen in particular. However, she further argues that these expressions of disgust are not only about establishing boundaries between individuals but are also a manifestation of what Gill (2007) refers to as a post-feminist sensibility which acts to prevent individual women from understanding their business experiences as connected to wider structural and cultural constraints.

2
Dirty Work and Acts of Contamination

Heather Höpfl

Contagion

The story of Mary Mallon is well-known. Otherwise known as 'Typhoid Mary', Mallon worked as a cook in New York from 1900 to 1907. She was the first known person to be identified as a healthy carrier of the typhoid pathogen, and it is thought that she infected some 53 people, though estimates vary, in the course of her employment: three died. In the households in which she worked, she left a trail of death and disease as successive families fell victim to contact with her. In her work as a cook, she infected the food she prepared and left her fatal mark on everything she touched (Brooks, 1996).

Contamination

Leaving aside for a moment the urge to begin with an account of the origins of the notion of dirty work, since these origins receive extensive attention elsewhere in this volume, this chapter is about contamination. As such, it takes its point of departure from the idea of what it is to be tainted, corrupted, infected, polluted or dirtied in some way by contact. The chapter is about contagion spread by touch: by contact with a physical or moral pestilence or disease communicated from one body to another body. It is about physical and moral corruption: about affliction, and in a figurative sense about communicable disease. Central to this is the idea of harm coming from contact: the fear of contamination, the need for immunisation and the urge to seek exemption from transmission. Etymologically, the word *contamination* is derived from the Latin *contamen* and is cognate with *tangere*, to touch. Hence, in this chapter, contamination is inexorably linked to the effects of touch. Not the fond touch of the carer – the parent, the lover, the nurse; the concern here is with the contaminating touch that brings infirmity, that mortifies.

To some extent, the notion of contamination is linked to a state of *disordered otherness*. This can be seen in the accusations and attributions which follow outbreaks of disease. The salmonella outbreak of 2009 was blamed on Spanish eggs but also on 'dirty' European practices, and one email to the *Daily Mail* (*Daily Mail* website) declared Spain as 'third-world'. According to a report in *Science Daily*,

> [The] Norovirus is the leading cause of acute gastroenteritis in the United States and is estimated to cause nearly 21 million cases annually. It is highly transmissible through person-to-person contact and contaminated food, water, and environmental surfaces. The results of an investigation of a 2009 outbreak on a cruise ship shed light on how the infections can spread and the steps both passengers and crew can take to prevent them.
>
> (25 March 2011)

In the main, these causes and remedies relate to poor cleanliness, inadequate hand-washing after using the toilet, superficial cleaning of toilets and a range of behaviours which might be regarded as 'dirty'. These disordered practices – 'dirty' behaviours – are what bring contamination. It is the touch of the dirty hand which brings disease and perhaps death. After the 1996 E. coli outbreak in Wishaw, Lanarkshire, in which over 1,000 people were affected and tested for the bacterium, 496 cases were confirmed, 21 people died in the outbreak and the butcher whose shop was the source of the epidemic, John Barr, was criticised in the subsequent enquiry for permitting *cross-contamination* between 'clean' and 'dirty' work areas. There are numerous examples of such stories in which there is an implicit and frequently explicit categorisation which determines some activities or behaviours as 'clean' and others as 'dirty'. Almost invariably there is a specific sense in which such behaviours and practices are embodied. It is the disordered body of the *other* which is the agent of transmission: the result of unhygienic habits, degenerate lives, filthiness and moral turpitude. Often this disordered otherness involves a literal contamination by the body of the other such as through bodily fluids and leakages – blood, urine, vomit – and via a notion of dismemberment – the synecdoche of the tainted hand, the infected breath, the bleeding wound – a literal and metaphorical contamination.

Dirty work

Of course, in the context of this book, it is necessary to give some thought to the nature of dirt from the perspective of occupational characteristics. Originally 'dirty work' meant exactly that. It meant work that involved getting your hands dirty, your clothes stained, your shoes wet. Dirty work required touching things that most people do not want to touch, handling unpleasant and unspeakable materials: bodily fluids; dead matter – people, animals, fish and poultry; cleaning up after other people; looking after toilets, excrement and waste of all kinds, human, animal and refuse. Dirty work necessitated touching both unspeakable materials and being exposed to obnoxious smells, abominable locations, appalling conditions. However, the concept has been expanded to encompass all forms of work which are regarded as socially undesirable. In this sense, dirty work is work that involves things which are untouchable and contaminating. The metaphorical use of the term dirty work has come to be applied to jobs such as tax inspectors, estate agents and, recently, bankers – to the extent that there is now a Facebook page dedicated to 'Dirty Rotten Bankers'. Amongst political activists, there is a derogatory term for the police, 'the filth', and in some quarters, the long-term benefit claimant is referred to as 'scum'. The argument presented here is primarily concerned with the original use of the term, albeit in a largely metaphorical sense, and considers how dirty work is both experienced and resisted. That is to say, the chapter is concerned with the ways in which definitions of dirty and clean can be applied to the specific demands of work performance and the implications of this for self-perception, resistance and response. Consequently, the concern here is less to do with how some occupations come to be characterised as 'dirty' than it is to do with the dirty and clean aspects of the work role.

The body and the law

In order to explore the relationship between 'dirty work' and the ways in which it is experienced, it is necessary to adopt some theoretical framework which is consistent with the perspective of the analysis. In this respect, this chapter draws on the work of Julia Kristeva and, in particular, on her discussion of the relationship between what she describes as 'the Body' and 'the Law'. This distinction which she makes in her book *Tales of Love* (Kristeva, 1987) opens up the space, the 'catastrophic fold-of-being', between the Body as embodied experience and the Law as authority and regulation (Kristeva's [1983] *Stabat Mater*, in Moi, 1986: 173). In *Stabat Mater*, she *breaks the body* of the text in order to allow her personal reflections on motherhood to enter and subvert the text, which is constructed to represent these two positions. Her writing on the Virgin Mary and on Bernard of Clairvaux as 'mother' of his community is set against her own reflections on motherhood: two columns running down either side of the page to represent, on one level, the Body on the left and the Law on the right. The Body speaks of rupture and tearing and blood. It is twisting and sensuous. 'Motherhood', Kristeva says,

Destines us to a demented *jouissance* that is answered, by chance, by the nursling's laughter in the sunny waters of the ocean. What connection is there between it and myself? No connection, except for that overflowing laughter where one senses the collapse of some ringing, subtle, fluid identity or other, softly buoyed by the waves.

(Kristeva, 1987: 255–6)

The Law speaks of regulation and representation, of rational argument and rhetorical trajectory. The Law is authoritative. It is rigid, right, upright: solid. In contrast, the Body is experiential: fluid.

Yet it must be acknowledged that both the Body and the Law are both *rhetorical* aspects of Kristeva's writing in her attempt to move between embodied experience and *mastery* of language. Her writing ruptures the Body of the text, rends the page. Her writing is 'dirty' in the sense that it is contaminated by the Body and as such it makes for uncomfortable reading. Set against the authoritative text on the right is the odour of the body, the ooze of breast milk on the left. It is as if the 'purity' of the authoritative text is contaminated by the leakages of the body. In this context, these ideas introduce a way of speaking about this relationship which is fruitful in thinking about dirty work and dirty practices. However, in a short account such as this, it is only possible to offer a brief introduction to Kristeva's work. A fuller account of Kristeva's writing can be found in John Lechte's book *Julia Kristeva* (1990) or in Toril Moi's *The Kristeva Reader* (1986). Here, the intention is to examine the conceptual possibilities which are presented by the separation of writing into the categories of authoritative and experiential and which can be further understood as 'abstract' and 'physical', 'pure' and 'impure' writing and 'clean' and 'dirty' expressions (see also Pullen and Rhodes, 2008).

Purity and the body

A further strand of ideas comes from Mary Douglas's well-known book *Purity and Danger: An Analysis of Concepts of Pollution and Taboo* (1966) and her celebrated discussion of dirt and pollution as 'matter out of place' (1966: 36). In one sense, it is the purity of an order which is violated by *matter out of place* and as such this raises the question of both liminality and what determines the proper order of a place. To keep an order, boundaries have to be drawn to protect one enclave from the incursion of another, to defend against contamination by the other and to quell a fear that order might be threatened by unruly bodies. So, taking Kristeva's distinction between the Body and the Law and Douglas's notion of 'purity' and 'danger' together, there is a sense in which the danger which is posed to the purity of order is that of the body itself. It is as if the body might leak into the text and disturb the proper order of things, might disrupt the supremely rational order with the anamnesis of the physical, as if blood, breast milk or urine might flood, over-flow and wash through the text. The fear of contamination is great.

A third strand of argument which draws this conceptual structure closer to occupational definitions of work and furthers the notion of the clean and dirty aspects of work can be found in Diderot's famous treatise on the acting profession, *Le paradoxe sur le comedien* (Diderot, 1949 [1773]). Here he says that the actor is like 'the whore who feels nothing for the man she is with, but lets herself go in his arms anyway as a demonstration of her professional competence' (Diderot, 1773, cited in Roach, 1985: 138). In other words, Diderot identifies a partial performance where some aspects of the self are withheld and, in doing so, he articulates both a response and a remedy to the performance requirements of work. Consequently, the next section attempts to analyse Diderot's conception of the actor's skills in relation to the construction of performance. In particular, it seeks to give attention to the ways in which *mere* (from the Latin *merum*, meaning 'pure') performance is required in the servicing of a role. When Diderot compares the actor's skill as similar to that of the whore, he is making reference to the way in which the nature of the relationship with the other – actor–audience, customer–client – involves putting merely a part of oneself into the role, into the performance, while other aspects of the person are held back. It is sometimes said that prostitutes will not kiss their clients. So, while they might offer themselves and their most physical intimacy to the client, they reserve the intimacy of the kiss for their partners. Of course, prostitution is one of the oldest service occupations and one which has long held the attribution of 'dirty work' (Arnold and Barling, 2003). Indeed, the term 'dirty whore' is in common parlance, and in several European Romance languages the word for a whore is thought to derive from the Latin *putidus,* meaning 'stinking'. Interestingly, *prostituta* was the Latin term for 'to be placed in front of' and so carried the connotation of being publicly exposed. This is perhaps a useful starting point for a comparison with the contemporary service role.

Performance and dissimulation

There are many day-to-day references to the experience of work as 'performance', and the notion of work as 'abuse' is not unfamiliar. Here the intention is to consider the relationship between performance and the emotional repertoire which is used in the service of such performance. Acting is a craft which requires the simulation of behaviour and emotion, a practised dissimulation, the 'professionalization of two-facedness' (Roach, 1985: 137). Consequently, it is the consummate counterfeit of experience. The word hypocrite in Greek means literally 'an actor' and hypocrisy, 'to play on stage'. Nothing is as it appears. Acting is performed hypocrisy. The actor's craft is primarily one of self-transformation. It is for this reason that the actor has, throughout history, been regarded with suspicion and unease. Indeed, actors were frequently excommunicated from the Church and their craft was regarded as degrading, deceitful, morally bankrupt and hypocritical. In effect, in the sense that the term is used in this chapter, acting was a dirty occupation.

So what does this add to an understanding of dirty work? In Kristeva's work there is an opening up of the space between the Body and the Law; in Douglas, a positioning of the relationship between 'purity' and 'danger'; and in Diderot there is a means of understanding the partial commitment of the 'actor', the performed synecdoche of the dramaturgical role. Taken together, these strands of argument provide a means of understanding something of the way that some occupational roles are taken on and performed. However, first a short discussion of performance as dirty work.

Contact with actors brings the fear of defilement. As has been argued above, the actor is considered to lack morality and to have no capacity for normal relationships and is thought to possess an unstable character. Yet, these very aspects of the actor intrigue the audience. Audiences experience both envy and moral superiority in relation to actors. Performance itself, in a dramaturgical sense, is regarded as glamorous. In a similar way perhaps, the essentially dirty work of airline cabin crew is elevated into glamour by make-up, costume and setting. Yet arguably, not all performance carries this allure. The fascination of the task is less so for the bank clerk, the car rental salesperson or the local office employment advisor for whom there are few theatrical props to glamorise the role and, this is perhaps why, in consequence, there is frequently a more insistent rendering of the role in such occupations – a more insistent and less improvisational interpretation. In the theatre, the audience is held in ambivalent thrall to the performance. On the one hand, spectators desire a furtive excursion backstage to marvel at the devices which produce theatrical illusion and show a considerable curiosity for the techniques of transformation; cabin crew retreat behind a curtain to separate their performance roles from their off-stage areas. On the other, the audience wishes to maintain a belief in the integrity of the performance. Behind the curtain is the territory in which the actor perfects his/her craft in order to enter and exit the role with practised facility. The actor knows the point at which he or she must 'enter' the role and the costs of surrender to it. The esoteric learning of stagecraft alienates the actor from the audience. Actors offer themselves for consumption in performance, yet despite appearances to the contrary they despise audiences who, they feel, do not and cannot understand the sacrifices which are demanded by the pursuit of their craft. Ashforth and Kreiner (1999) make a similar point about dirty work and argue that workers in 'dirty' occupations find solidarity and camaraderie in their work. They say that against external definition, such workers consolidate their position by making selective comparisons with other jobs and by transforming the meaning of dirty in order to moderate the perception of the dirtiness of their jobs. All jobs which require performance skills carry similar demands and require similar responses. The audience (or client) cannot appreciate how much the actor suffers. Only the other actors know this and find solace in their own company. Likewise, the manager who has not experienced the suffering of playing minor roles will not be credible to his/her staff and may lack empathy with them as actors.

Moreover, whereas consumers of the actor's performance might wish to see the backstage areas, they will often recoil from what they might see behind the dramatic mask, which maintains the essential purity of the performance uncontaminated by the 'realities' it conceals. The audience is discomfited by personal contact with actors per se. Spectators prefer to sustain the illusion of performance. There is some security in not knowing the person in the encounter, the person behind the mask – of dealing with the role rather than with the individual. In a similar way, the regulation of organisational behaviour by close reference to the text and the framing of organisational roles permit a reassuring regularity in the nature of interaction between organisational members and their audiences. Of course, this is the essence of bureaucratic anonymity.

Regulated by text

In the context of the theoretical concerns presented here, there are problems in terms of the way in which the body is permitted to engage with the text. The regulation of organisational behaviour is, in the first instance, external to the actor(s). It is, effectively, regulation by an anterior authority which provides the script for the performance, sometimes with associated metrics and the collaborative interpretation of this in performance. This anterior authority may be in the cultural norms, patriarchs or matriarchs of the organisation, traditions and the whole range of prevailing assumptions that might be brought to bear on the construction of a performance. It is proposed that the prevailing and preceding authority are the source, the producer, of a text that specifies what is to be brought to the performance. In other words, the performance is regulated by a text which specifies the right and proper behaviours appropriate to that performance and its enactment. Such a text, being the authoritative text, is regarded as having a purity which is the basis of its legitimacy. It protects itself from the incursion of the body, from contamination by flesh. It is entirely metaphysical in its representation of its dramaturgical function. It defines what specific dramaturgical skills are required by the performance and how they should be employed: the speeches, the costumes, the set. It marks the 'proper' order of the play. For the actor, it imposes the context and determines what is required in performance. Gouldner (1969) makes the same point, although in a converse way, when he argues that in the experience of work 'the individual learns... which parts of himself [*sic*] are unwanted and unworthy' (Gouldner, 1969: 349).

The elision of the role of the actor and that of the corporate actor is not a simple one. However, there are common issues related to the requirements of performance which can be identified. In order to examine the implications of these, it is necessary to give attention to the consequences of exclusion and the regulation of the body, to consider the ramifications of a concern for 'mere' or 'pure' performance and to ponder the likely effects of the conceptualisation of the physicality of the disordered, dangerous and contaminated other. Of course, this chapter situates these ideas in relation to the organisation as the putative source of order and regulation. In this context, the organisation provides the authoritative definition of the 'proper' role and designates 'proper' performance for employees and by doing so both demarcates what is 'clean' and 'dirty', permitted and not permitted in the performance of the role and more importantly, by the act of such definition determines that all work performed under the mandate of such definition is de facto rendered dirty. In simple terms, it is the very division of the actor into aspects of the role which are required in the service of performance and those which are not that denigrates the role, debases the actor and renders the possibility of performance merely partial. Via the disaggregation of the person in this way, the employee is not only rendered expendable – as a collection of mere attributes – but is also put into a position where aspects of the self which might be valued become regarded as potential agents of contamination to be excluded and feared. These aspects of the self become emblems of unworthiness because they are not valued in performance.

Several years ago, a friend who is a human resource development specialist was head-hunted for a new post with a major UK company, where she had responsibility for the global dissemination of corporate culture. Unfortunately, just three weeks into her new appointment, she encountered major problems in her personal life and the breakdown of her marriage. Being in a state of some distress, she asked for some consideration from her new employers and explained her changed circumstances to her line manager. She was told in no uncertain terms that she was not to allow her personal life to 'intrude' into her work. 'What is happening in your domestic life has no place in your work,' she was told, assuming she would be able to readily disaggregate herself into aspects of her life which were relevant to her job and those which were not. The purity of the role, it seemed, required the exclusion of the contaminating effects of the disorder in her domestic life. Of course, what this short vignette also demonstrates is that the categorisation of performance requirements at work go far beyond the more obvious application to front-line service roles. Like the chancel arch in the medieval church which separated the space for the clergy and the space for the laity, so a boundary is drawn between the 'sacred' and 'profane', the 'clean' and 'dirty' and the 'pure' and 'dangerous' aspects of performance. Under the imperative of such a categorisation, only work is sacred (the word hierarchy refers explicitly to a sacred structure), sanitary and safe. It might be profitable at this stage to consider the implications of this for the colonisation of all areas of life and the subsequent designation of all life as 'work'. However, this argument requires more attention than the space available here permits. Suffice it to say that the disaggregation of the employee into attributes of performance which are worthy and those which are not is demoralising, not to say mortifying. Consider a recent email I received from a young woman whose PhD I had examined five years ago. Her email was extremely distressing to read. She had received a notice from her university that if she did not improve her research output in highly rated ABS (Association of Business School) journals, her contract would be changed to 'Teaching Only'. I know the young woman's work. She is an excellent theoretician and a meticulous researcher – innovative and capable. However, her work is not 'clean'. She does not have a 'pure' performance indicator. She has potential – because good research takes time – but she does not have the 'sacred' signs which would mark her salvation. She is distraught because the imposition of such definitions renders her unworthy. In protecting itself from the contamination of her lack of performance, the university soils her reputation, her name and her career by its naïve faith in the validity of the metric that represents its delusionary commitment to the suspension of disbelief. In a different example but in a similar way, the practice nurse at my local doctor's surgery urges me to attend for an annual review because their practice income is dependent on achieving specific performance targets. In this case, it is preferable that I present myself to be judged well than to not turn up at all and assess myself as well by doing so. Put simply, I need to be purified by categorisation. The obsession with metrics and feedback, performance and appearances leads to a vicarious apprehension of the moment – a commitment to trajectory and self-evaluation. Attached to this is an implicit fear of contamination by the other, the body and material existence. There is a preference for taxonomy over tactility and an abstraction which at the same time requires the greatest intimacies of the individual in performance. Clearly, the relationship between the apparent purity of the abstract and the dangerous implications of embodied experience figure in a discussion of a wide variety of work experiences.

Canetti's sting

However, in the final part of this chapter, attention is given to some responses and resistances to such simplistic and surgical definitional impositions. This section draws on the work of Elias Canetti, the essayist, sociologist and playwright, awarded the Nobel Prize for Literature in 1981. His most influential work is *Crowds and Power* (1962 [1960]), which is a study of mass movements and disordered society. Canetti was interested in the behaviour of crowds and fascinated by the response of crowds to commands. In order to do this he drew on historical events, folklore and mythology. In his book, for example, he offers an illustration of the German people's response to the leadership of Adolf Hitler, the response to German hyperinflation and the treatment of the Jews. However, one of his most powerful concepts which is much examined in sociological literature relates to his conceptualisation of response to command. He came to the conclusion that one of the characteristics of command is what he famously termed the 'sting' which attaches to the imposition of a command and which accumulates in the individual, causing resentment and a repressed fury against authority. According to Canetti, individuals seek to free themselves of the stings that are laid on them and so seek opportunities in which they can reverse the original situation in which the commands were set, that is to say, in which they can return the sting (Cooper, 1990; Linstead, 1997; Linstead and Chan, 1994).

Canetti's work considers a range of reversal. He refers to 'the fear of being touched', to the moment where individuals feel threatened by the presence of other people and try to protect themselves from contact by creating a space around themselves to keep other people at a distance (Canetti, 1962 [1960]: 184). This fear of being touched is deeply seated. Yet, he argues, ironically it is frequently the case that a person loses this fear of being touched only when in a crowd. This is when the fear is reversed, according to Canetti, and this provides a measure of relief from the fear of contact and of contamination by the other (Canetti, 1962 [1960]: 185). Taking both this fear and its reversal and the notion of the reversal of the sting by the replication of the original conditions of command, what follows is a series of illustrations which consider the consequences of being categorised as 'dirty' and the suppression of the physical, embodied and experiential aspects of work, except where these are employed in the service of the objectives of the organisation. Thus, being rendered untouchable by contact with dirt and the body and with death and disorder inevitably results in the 'sting' of retribution. What is significant about the reversal of the sting is its symmetry with the command. In other words, where the embodied subject is repressed, the response comes in a physical form.

Pee soup

In 1978, when I was working on my PhD at Lancaster University, I had a number of friends working towards their Masters degree. One of them was ex-army and he told me of an occasion when he had been assigned to catering duties. One weekend when many of the recruits had planned leave, they received instructions that all leave had been cancelled, that the officers had planned a dinner party and that they would be required to cater for it. This was an order and it had to be obeyed. The soldiers were required to work into the night to make ready for the following day. The former soldier was brief in his account of his response and said: 'Peed in the soup'. According to the story, the sting of command was reversed by a physical act which returned the resentment that the young soldiers experienced. Their sense of being pinned down by the touch of command, since they had no power to resist the restrictions placed on their movements, was an act of physical contamination. At the same time, it could well be that the story is an apocryphal one, made up to say what they would have liked to do. At this remove it is impossible to say. However, this does not violate the notion of the sting. They gave back in kind.

A mephitic reversal

In the early 1990s I was working with Stephen Linstead at Lancaster University on a management development programme for a major UK company. As part of the programme, we explored issues of emotional labour and asked participants to provide examples drawn from their experiences of the workplace. One story concerned a newly appointed manager who was 'very full of himself'. This young man was apparently very quick to assume what he saw as the managerial role and this had obvious consequences for his staff who were expected to demonstrate appropriate deference to his self-importance. For about three weeks after his promotion they reluctantly and grudgingly gave him the approbation he demanded of them, but then they began to formulate a plan for revenge. One afternoon, this pretentious and narcissistic new manager had an important meeting in his office. One of the company's senior managers was coming to hear his plans for the development of his area. He was not to be disturbed at any price. He would go down to the reception himself to greet his guest. Did they all realise how important this was for him? He planned the visit with meticulous care. Reports and graphics were prepared, but he would present them. He did not want his staff to damage his opportunity to make a big impression on the visitor and he made this clear to them. He arrived in the morning smartly dressed, with a spring in his step and a confident air. Unfortunately, what he could not have anticipated was that his staff, now thoroughly disaffected by his posturing, planned to bring him down. His glass-walled office was beautifully ordered and polished, with fresh flowers on his desk. He responded to the call made to the reception to greet his guest; however, while he was out of the office, his staff arranged for a colleague with an unenviable but practised capacity for passing bodily wind to enter the office and emit a foul and noxious flatus. Then, the unsuspecting manager returned to his office, proudly opened his office door and ushered in his guest to be greeted by the fetid smell his staff had left for him. The glass walls of the office made a theatre of this event and as the new manager looked round at his colleagues he was met by their various faces regarding him with a strange mixture of affected innocence, contempt and satisfaction at achieving some degree of retaliation (Höpfl, 2004). Again, the reversal of the sting is a physical one.

Blood, sweat and excrement

In various periods of work with a number of commercial airlines, I have heard stories of such reversals. A male cabin crew member once told me that he would wipe his fingers in his armpit and then rub sweat around the rim of a cup when he came across a difficult passenger. Other crew have admitted spitting in food and even putting pubic hair into food. However, in these cases the revenge is turned against the customer rather than the company. Perhaps one of the most distasteful stories I have come across in my career was told to me by a woman who claimed to have posted excrement to her much-hated boss. I did not enquire whether or not this was human or animal, nor indeed whether it was a true story or a revenge fantasy. So accustomed to working with abstract accounts, I was shocked by the story – one might say contaminated by it. That said, there is no denying the physicality of the reversal and the calculated nature of the return.

Some concluding thoughts

The performance requirements of organisational life on all levels which affect a broad range of occupations have produced actors who are humiliated, debased and undervalued. Only fellow actors understand the sense of abuse which they share. The cult of the 'customer' has led to the expectation of increasing levels of service and high standards of performance from organisational members and yet they cannot appreciate the sacrifices required of the performer. The categorisation of some aspects of work as 'clean' and others as 'dirty' through the emphasis on performance metrics and abstract constructions of the employee have rendered all human experience that is not work 'dirty'. Human qualities of all varieties fall outside of such a definition and are either colonised or marginalised. The actor is left with the difficult reconciliation of the experience of degradation and defilement and the public production of virtue. The customer is led to expect continuity, regularity and, indeed, improvement. The contradiction of contamination and goodness produces in the actor a disdain which is thinly masked by the persona of professional competence. At the same time, the audience is not deceived by the counterfeit of performance and being now the consumers of grotesque counterfeit of service, they find a residual dignity in a scornful aversion to the actor's craft. The client as audience is aware of the minuscule movement which transforms the performance into ludicrousness. As a result, we are all sullied by this travesty of 'purity' and worth. There is a need to revisit the possibilities of resistance from the standpoint of embodied response. A number of writers have begun to consider the dynamics of such a response. Works that in one sense or another are concerned with the relationship between structures and resistance which they consider from the miniscule to the momentous inter alia include those by Fleming and Sewell (2002), Costea et al. (2005), Fleming and Spicer (2007, 2008), Stiernstedt and Jakobsson (2009), Gastelaars (2010), Ng and Höpfl (2011) and Hancock and Spicer (2011). However, a useful starting point for a re-conceptualisation of dirty work might be found in Burkard Sievers's (2000) paper, 'AIDS and the organization: a consultant's view of the coming plague offering', as it offers a way of understanding the dynamics of epidemiology and its implications.

3
Stains, Staining and the Ethics of Dirty Work

Sheena J. Vachhani

Introduction

This chapter focuses on the theoretical potential of stains and staining as a productive way of understanding dirty work, especially the physical, social and moral taint attributed to it (Ashforth and Kreiner, 1999; Drew et al., 2007). The concept of the stain can be understood through the ethics of dirty work, focusing on healthcare and the presence of the body as a key site through which staining and stains may be a rich theoretical resource. This may involve physical as well as emotional and symbolic staining, something that leaves its mark against the backdrop of domestic hygiene, cleanliness and order. The *Oxford English Dictionary* (2010) defines a stain as 'a discoloration produced by absorption of or contact with foreign matter; usually, one that penetrates below the surface and is not easily removable'. This chapter focuses on and takes up different themes related to the presence of stains as physical taint, understood through feminist analyses of bodily fluids that are written on the body, and the notion of moral taint (such as a stain on one's character) that implies an ethical relationship of a responsibility that has been left somewhat untroubled in research in the field. As such, I bring together analyses of the physical and ethical that invoke material and symbolic relations in dirty work. Using feminist ethics, in particular a corporeal ethics, allows us to explore more deeply how stains are written on the body and how this relates to an ethics which necessarily must recognise the stain. It is argued here that there needs to exist a generosity in this ethical relationship that inevitably circumscribes dirty work.

Borrowing from Douglas's work on pollution and taboo that is central to arguments of dirty work (Douglas, 1966), I attempt to expand the bases on which dirty work is discussed, not simply as a negotiation or construction of occupational taint but as an ethical responsibility. We may consider ways in which we ourselves or others may be seen as 'stained' and how this is related to cleanliness or the fear of being rendered dirty. Dirty work has been explored in terms of stigma (Goffman, 1986), for example, but has not been related closely to a corporeal ethics. One could argue that we are engaged in the consistent pursuit of remaining unmarked. In a physical sense, we routinely attempt to eradicate stains from our clothes and from our houses and from our teeth and from our skin. Whether these are bodily fluids or other stains, we secure identity through eradicating the negative impulse of the stain.

Furthermore, given the moralising discourse that circumscribes conceptions of dirty work, the main concern of this chapter is to explore bodily and corporeal vulnerability recognised as an ethical responsibility. This in turn provides a theoretical treatment of the ways in which the bodywork of healthcare involves 'negotiating the less attractive aspects of corporeal life' (Twigg, 2006: 135; Wolkowitz, 2006) through bodily substances, which can be situated in discussions of dirt and staining and the cultural significance these hold. Healthcare is a site where the visceral and corporeal come together and are negotiated, and where stains are written on and through the body, whether it be in the form of staining on the surface of the skin (from blood, for example) or bacterial staining that helps to form cartographies of the interiority of the body (Diprose and Ferrell, 1991). More broadly, however, in societal convention dirt is worthless but is also viewed as vileness or corruption which has moral significance (Douglas, 1966). This raises questions about the value of staining, of marking out and making present and of how it may relate to a generosity to the other, but also how it has the potential to conceal. There is ambivalence in this process of making present which defines but is never fully accomplished – the stain is also a shadow, as it is incomplete and concealing. Therefore, the aims of this chapter are to raise the question of the stain and by situating it as part of the dirty work agenda, to expose the tensions associated with it by unearthing its ethical implications.

Exposing the stain

Staining is considered here to be the physical presence of what is routinely termed taint. Stains leave their mark, scar and construct dirt as visible. However, in medicine, staining (such as the staining of bacteria) is also positive; it marks out disease – it locates pathology by naming poison and threat. Pigments used to stain bacteria, for example, expose the pathology of the body. These may be understood through pathogenesis that focuses on the mode of origin of a disease process or pathophysiology which looks at the physiology of disease or the disorder or derangement of function in the disease of susceptible tissues or organs (McPhee et al., 1995). Such staining is constructed as positive and is valued, and it allows us to distinguish good from bad or the malignant from the benign. For example, iron, melanin or bile may appear brown or golden-yellow by light microscopy which is vital for diagnosis. Excess brown pigment may reveal haemochromatosis related to iron or obstructive liver disease relating to bile (Lakhani et al., 1993).

The histochemical staining pattern of these substances varies – a Prussian blue stain is used to demonstrate the presence of iron, the Fouchet technique stains bile pigments blue-green and the Masson-Fontana technique stains melanin black (Lakhani et al., 1993). Such vivid colours as Congo red, crystal violet or methyl violet are used to mark out this threat. This type of staining offers comfort; it raises our knowledge about the abnormal and is valuable and valued. This form of staining interrupts and disrupts disease; it can be said to disrupt the disorder of disease. One could argue that this form of staining even brings *order to disorder*. These stains can be contrasted with the unsettling scar or mark of the stain that disrupts or brings *disorder to order* in the form of dirt. It is the relationship between these two in the construction of dirt that is most interesting if we consider stains as disrupting a physical order and, as I argue here, intersecting with how we conceptualise taint and the ethical responsibility associated with it.

So, on the one hand stains associated with filth, grime and muck pose a threat and trouble a moral order; on the other we see them as productive in marking out threat and troubling the invisible (in terms of the staining of bacteria). Through this conceptualisation that highlights the ambivalence of the terms, stains and staining begin to cast light on the hitherto limitedly explored theoretical questions that pervade the study of taint. We can begin to define stains and staining in these terms – as a marking out and creation of order and disorder. What is rendered clean or dirty is contextual and exists in relation to a system of cultural resources with positive and negative valences (Hamilton, 2007). Moreover, this interplay also makes the absent present. The stain is both a soiling or colouration of a substance through ruination, as it relates to dirt for example, and a process by which something is made to appear that makes structures visible, such as bacterial staining. This status of the stain relates to notions of cleanliness and uncleanliness and to symbolic disgrace and being marked, as I will now explore.

Pollution, transgression and staining

Most generally, stains pose the threat of pollution and this is manifest in the organisation of occupations. Dirt signifies transgression of a moral and often social order (Dick, 2005; Stallybrass and White, 1986), and professional identity is constructed through and between the cultural and symbolic deployment of dirt (Hamilton, 2007). There has been focus on the intersections between dirty work and identity, especially the occupational status of dirty work and the threats it poses to self-identity (Hughes, 1951, 1962) or the marking or staining of one's identity as tainted or dirty. By considering the symbolic value of dirty work, the transgressive capacity of grime has been enrolled into discourses of professional identity in which workers have reclaimed dirty work as affirmative. 'Dirty work may be an intimate part of the very activity which gives the occupation its charisma, as is the case with the handling of the human body by the physician' (Hughes, 1974: 344, cited in Emerson and Pollner, 1975: 243). The dilemma of dirty work has been associated with the societal privilege of cleanliness and goodness over dirtiness and badness so that dirt is constructed as threat and danger (Ashforth et al., 2007). This can be linked to conceptions of contamination and as Ashforth and Kreiner (1999) assert, even though people may view some forms of dirty work as heroic or noble, there is still a tendency to remain psychologically distanced and separated from the work. This presents dilemmas for dirty workers in how professional identity is secured. An ethics of dirty work intends to bridge this gap and addresses this dilemma.

Ashforth and Kreiner's (2002) work on normalisation serves to understand this dilemma and explain how workers go about negotiating occupational taint. One argument would be that this is a form of destabilising the power of dirty work as unusual, different and something to be actively countered or cast out. By rendering taint less unusual and less different, the dirty worker is able, in part, to lessen the burden of stigma, which, in this sense, is less an individual tragedy (Goffman, 1986) than a shifting and resisted social process (Harris, 2009; Parker and Aggleton, 2003). Thus, the stigma of dirty work can be understood through the social beliefs that ascribe value to (or devalue) its worth. Harris's (2009) study of hepatitis C stigma explores the processes and social beliefs that contribute to the stigmatisation of the disease. Harris (2009: 34) foregrounds the study by exploring her own body as a site of embodied stigma and focuses attention on how 'societal attitudes and regulations draw from and feed back into corporeal processes and experiences of

embodiment'. Such corporeal processes demonstrate the symbolic staining of disease as a contravention of social norms (such as the healthy,
or acceptably unhealthy body that does not relate to addiction) and are
related to material staining, namely the abjection of injecting and pierc-
ing the surface of the skin in order to make the interior 'appear' in the
form of blood. The latter as an example of physical staining invokes horror, making present the liminal and ambiguous borders of the body and
the condition of being a living being by disturbing identity, system and
order (Kristeva, 1982). As Mol and Law (1994) also note, blood disturbs
the spatial securities of anatomy.

Research has demonstrated how dirty work is sometimes recast with
a positive valence in the construction of professional identity (Ashforth
and Kreiner, 1999; Hamilton, 2007), such as in Bolton's (2005) study
of the gynaecology nurse. Such a positive valence may be construed as
an engagement with ethical responsibility for the other but also as an
attempt to secure professional identity in relation to the status hierarchy
of healthcare. In Bolton's study, gynaecology nurses demonstrate how
they actively construct collective identity by celebrating a distinct form
of dirty work. As Bolton (2005: 179) notes, the work of the gynaecology
nurse,

> Is physically tainted due to its association with the body, death
> and abnormality; socially tainted through the regular contact
> with unmentionable topics such as the termination of preg-
> nancy, incontinence, infertility and sexually transmitted disease, and
> morally tainted because what should remain private and invisible is
> made public and rendered visible.

In this instance, the gynaecology nurse in some sense acknowledges
the stain of the occupation. As Bolton notes, this association is used
as a means of emphasising difference, and 'the very reasons why their
work may be classified as tainted are used to justify and verify its
value' (Bolton, 2005: 177). Here there is a resistance of the stain, where
the significant and honourable (Ashforth and Kreiner, 1999) aspects
of the occupation are valorised and defended. The negotiation of the
stain is re-presented as skilled work, exalted and given positive valence.
In such studies, there is both a recognition of the responsibility associated with the tainted occupation in securing professional identity and a
negotiation of the vulnerability of the patients' trauma.

Central to Bolton's study is the negotiation of taint in relation
to proximity to bodily fluids. Relatedly, bioethics and responsibility

can be understood in terms of the body in medicine and healthcare (*cf.* Komesaroff, 1995), using Douglas's (1966: 2) idea that:

> Rituals of purity and impurity create unity in experience. So far from being aberrations from the central project of religion, they are positive contributions to atonement. By their means, symbolic patterns are worked out and publicly displayed. Within these patterns disparate elements are related and disparate experience is given meaning.

Bodily fluids have symbolic significance and can be said to mediate the realm between the sacred and the profane (or Kristeva's notion of the abject). In conjunction, stains relate to cleaning and atonement; thus to be stained is to be marked. Douglas's (1966) thesis on purity and danger and the inseparability of purity and impurity help us to conceptualise staining. In saying so, dirty work can be considered sites in which the abject, a relationship with an other, responsibility and vulnerability coincide. Bodily fluids become present, visible and 'matter out of place' (Douglas, 1966). Blood and sweat in particular accord a significance that marks the identity and viscerality of the worker. Stressing this physicality, Ackroyd and Crowdy (1993) demonstrate the status hierarchies, domination and aggression associated with being a slaughterhouse worker. Ackroyd and Crowdy explain the work-related behaviours of slaughter gangs, such as harassment and degradation. The authors explain one such activity as involving the filling of the slaughterhouse worker's boots with fresh blood of a particular temperature such that the recipient would not notice until a late stage (Ackroyd and Crowdy, 1993). Blood, as a significant element of the work process, was used as a means by which to exercise hierarchy and domination over other workers. In such an instance, blood is less matter out of place than a physical and symbolic resource used by workers. Such a reclamation of bodily mess and status is emphasised by Hamilton (2007), whose study explores the professional identity of vets in relation to the primal significance of muck such as blood, excreta and other bodily substances. Vets in Hamilton's study constructed dirt and proximity to dirt in terms of a visceral tolerance to particular types of muck in the pursuit of professional identity.

Conversely perhaps, 'medicine shares a long-established set of assumptions whereby status is marked by distance from the bodily, and there is a clear dematerialising tendency within which the work is organised' (Twigg, 2006: 85). Thus we can establish that the visceral presence of bodily fluids has different effects on the identity of the dirty worker. For example, dust and excrement have different symbolic meanings, especially in a healthcare setting. One could argue that dust is more 'out of place' than excreta in such a context. Ethical responsibility may be analysed here in relation to status and the fear and dread of defilement and hygiene (Douglas, 1966). 'In chasing dirt...we are not governed by anxiety to escape disease, but are positively re-ordering our environment, making it conform to an idea' (Douglas, 1966: 2). As Douglas (1966: 95) intimates, disorder spoils pattern but it also provides the material for pattern:

> Order implies restriction; from all possible materials, a limited selection has been made and from all possible relations a limited set has been used. So disorder by implication is unlimited, no pattern has been realised in it, but its potential for patterning is indefinite. This is why, though we seek to create order, we do not simply condemn disorder. We recognise that it is destructive to existing patterns; also that it has potentiality. It symbolises both danger and power.

The concept of dirt is further compounded by care for hygiene and respect for convention but this is evinced through context. In proposing a theory of staining, it is the unity of experience and the potentiality of disorder of which Douglas speaks which is of interest here. The stain forms a physical presence of that unity. The stain is part of a unity of purity and impurity; it is inseparable from the purity which is its shadow other. It could be seen as a transgression that changes the order of things rather than simply as a social category of taint. Central to the studies of dirty work discussed here is the proximity to bodily fluids that present the abject borderlands of work (Bolton, 2005; Harris, 2009) that is both material and written on the body. Stains find such physical and bodily expression in a variety of ways, and it is to this we now turn.

Written on the body

> The most visible boundary of all, the skin, is both the limit of the embodied self and the site of potentially transgressive psychic investments. In consequence, any compromise of the organic unity and self-completion of the skin may signal monstrosity.
>
> (Shildrick, 2002: 51)

In this section I consider the concept of the stain as a gentle rupture, between transgression and conformity, which can be conceived as written on the body. The body is thus an inscriptive surface (Featherstone et al., 1991; Grosz, 1994; Hassard et al., 2000) of zones and organs on which the stain is written and relates to what could be termed the veiling or exiling of flesh (Höpfl, 2010). Thus, we are interested in transgressing the divide between the inside and outside. Bodily fluids as stains are a physical embodiment of what may be routinely constructed as dirt. As Ashforth and Kreiner (1999: 415) describe, 'the common denominator amongst tainted jobs is not so much their specific attributes but the visceral repugnance of people to them'. Dirt remains contextual and involves a negotiation between the physical and moral relationships that circumscribe it. As I have discussed, stains can be considered a way by which structures or substances are made visible. They may be said to destabilise order while also making it present. This status has relationships to cleanliness, pollution and taint through what is made present and absent. A stain is, therefore, both matter out of place and also a process of presencing by which substances are made present, and the value of this presencing is subject to the rules of social life and the negotiation of taint.

As Grosz writes, 'inscriptions on the subject's body coagulate corporeal signifiers into signs, producing all the effects of meaning, representation, depth within or subtending our social order' (1994: 141). Stains such as sweat and blood are written on the body (Harris, 2009; Street, 2009) and provide a physical reminder of its interiority without making its material fleshiness present. This liminal space may be constructed as an abject space which signifies one's mortality; however, the stain allows us to go beyond a reading of the abject. One could infer from Shildrick's work on monstrosity (see also Thanem, 2006) that the stain is written on the body, not just on the surface of the skin but at the heart of how we draw divisions and boundaries between inside and outside, good and bad or monstrous and non-monstrous. Influenced by feminist work on embodiment, this may be linked to a corporeal generosity (Diprose, 2002) which allows further focus on the ethical relationship between workers and work that negotiates but also troubles the clean/dirty divide. Höpfl (2010) explores how flesh is exiled in the pursuit of organisation: 'Organizations then, as expressions of collection expectations and abstractions, render physicality "dirty" corrupting and, by implication, to be excluded' (Höpfl, 2010: 47). In this sense, the stain as conceived through the body may be constructed as 'dirty' and always incomplete. However, if we take the stain as a sign of presence, that which is a manifestation and re-presencing of the excluded, then we can begin to consider an active engagement with staining as a productive process. While some stains written on the body, such as birthmarks (for example, port wine stains often present at birth), may present the urge for rituals of concealment that exemplify constructions of an errant body, rituals such as tattooing have the potential to bear a more positive relationship with the urge to stain. Body tattoos are examples of staining underneath the skin and bear relationships to self-marking and community but also to coercion. As Grosz (1994: 140) writes, drawing on Alphonso Lingis,

> Cicatrizations and scarifications mark the body as a public, collective, social category, in modes of inclusion or membership; they form maps of social needs, requirements and excesses. The body and its privileged zones of sensation, reception, and projection are coded by objects, categories, affiliations, lineages, which engender and make real the subject's social, sexual, familial, marital, or economic position or identity within a social hierarchy. Unlike messages to be deciphered, they are more like a map correlating social positions with corporeal intensities.

Such corporeal intensities open up the ambivalence of the stain. Grosz demonstrates how the incisions and body markings in Lingis' study of primitive inscriptions create erotogenic surfaces of different libidinal intensities. The site of corporeal inscriptions presents uneven zones of sensations, pleasure and pains of the body. Far from keeping the body configured, confined, constrained and regimented, such stains and marks distribute libidinal value through the body as an inscriptive surface. However, these values may also be coercive, as Grosz (1994: 142) also writes,

> Less openly violent but no less coercive are the inscriptions of cultural and personal values, norms and commitments according to the morphology and categorization of the body into socially significant groups – male and female, black and white, and so on. The body is involuntarily marked, but it is also incised through 'voluntary' procedures, life-styles, habits and behaviors. Makeup, stilettos, bras, hair sprays, clothing, underclothing mark women's bodies, whether black or white.

Such staining signals zones where bodies are contested and organised (Holliday and Hassard, 2001). In considering this ambivalence, stains may be seen as a break or rupture in the controlling urge of organisations understood through embodiment (Weiss and Haber, 1999). 'Thus, the embodied subject speaks of division, separation, rupture, tearing, and blood whereas the text of the organization speaks of regulation and representation, of rational argument and rhetorical trajectory' (Höpfl and Kostera, 2003: xix). Such 'sterile perfectionism' eschews the fleshy, leaking materiality of the body in pursuit of containment. Staining may, therefore, on the one hand break this boundary of containment but may simultaneously also make such a boundary present through inscription and different cartographies of the body, as Grosz points out.

Corporeality and staining

> Body fluids flow, they seep, they infiltrate; their control is a matter of vigilance, never guaranteed. In this sense, they betray a certain irreducible materiality; they assert the priority of the body over subjectivity.... In our culture, they are enduring; they are necessary but embarrassing.
>
> (Grosz, 1994: 194)

As we have established, stains find expression in many ways. Building on the notion that stains are related to the body as an inscriptive surface that marks out difference, we may extend this debate to a bodily reading of fluids as stains that allows us to explore the interplay between the ambivalence of the abject and the productivity of bodily inscription. The abject, drawing on Kristeva (1982), is that which disgusts and horrifies; it renders the certain uncertain. Stains in the form of bodily fluids such as blood and sweat, rather than being seen as compromising, may be reconceived as productive, as we see in such studies on professional identity such as Bolton (2005), Ackroyd and Crowdy (1993) and Hamilton (2007). Feminist enquiry has long since reflected on how the body, understood through fluids, among other aspects, may be a productive way by which to reimagine an ethical relationship (Diprose, 1994; Irigaray, 1993; Kristeva, 1982).

Shildrick's work on the leaking body suggests that we are unable to appreciate the unbounded subject, one that leaks and presupposes a relationship with fluids. Focusing on Douglas's (1966) work on pollution linked to the idea of fluidity, viscous fluids (such as sexual fluids) are viewed with horror because of their stickiness and indeterminacy as neither solid nor liquid (Linstead, 2000: 32):

> The presence of dirt then signals a threat to the system of order, whether individual or social, and remains a mark of the vulnerability of the system. Anywhere dirt is found is therefore dangerous to the system.... Anything which moves, or flows, across such boundaries, is a potentially dangerous substance.

Some have argued that this may be aligned with a fear of the feminine (Creed, 1993; Irigaray, 1985; Vachhani, 2009), such that clinging viscosity is associated with 'the horror of femininity, the voraciousness and indeterminacy of the vagina dentata', for example (Douglas, 1966; Grosz, 1994: 194; Vachhani, 2009). For Grosz,

> Body fluids attest to the permeability of the body, its necessary dependence on an outside, its liability to collapse into this outside (that is what death implies), to the perilous divisions between the body's inside and its outside.... They attest to a certain irreducible 'dirt' or disgust, a horror of the unknown or the unspecifiable that permeates, lurks, lingers, and at times leaks out of the body, a testimony of the fraudulence or impossibility of the 'clean' and 'proper'.
>
> (1994: 193–4)

The necessary permeability of the body suggests more expansive possibilities for understanding transgression and staining. Drawing on such literature, one is able to propose a theory of staining that does not reinscribe the dualistic poles of dirt/cleanliness, but locates the experience of an ethical stain as a corporeal encounter. Influenced here by Kristeva and Shildrick (as well as by Merleau-Ponty; *cf.* Crossley, 1996), the body is a lived, affective agent intimately entwined with social, historical and cultural processes (Harris, 2009). Staining, much like stigma, takes shape through processes of categorisation, ordering and differentiation as well as in culturally specific contexts of power (Parker and Aggleton, 2003). Thus, the body is able to be thought of as corporeal, lived and inscribed (Blackman, 2007; Harris, 2009), where bodily fluids, understood through the leaking body, may invoke a normalising urge of containment but also a recognition of the marking or staining of the body as a productive encounter. If dirt is constructed as disorder and contravention of rules such as hygiene, the stain presents a way by which to demarcate and draw different zones of corporeality given 'the "horror" or intense discomfort felt in response to the leaking, permeable and absorptive feminine body, in which boundaries between inside and outside and self and Other are constantly blurred, constituting "a formlessness that engulfs all form, a disorder that threatens all order" (Grosz, 1994: 203)' (Schmied and Lupton, 2010: 26).

A corporeal ethics of staining

> Ethics can be defined as the study and practice of that which consti-
> tutes one's habitat, or as the problematic of the constitution of one's
> embodied place in the world.
>
> (Diprose, 1994: 19)

A focus on ethics in this section raises the concept of moral taint associated with dirty work and further exposes the theoretical relation-ships that underpin commonly held interpretations of what moral taint means in relation to dirty work and staining. If dirt renders the system vulnerable, then dirt may also be read as constitutive of vulnerabil-ity and marks an ethical relationship. Here I turn to a feminist ethics or ethical feminism, firstly due to the prevalence of women in many dirty work occupations and secondly, due to its orientation towards embodiment and exclusion which attends to the fictive divisions in dualisms such as inside/outside (Anderson, 2000). Most broadly, fem-inist ethics seek to unearth marginalised, excluded and subordinated positions, and it can be argued that this necessitates consideration of an ethico-political engagement with tainted embodiment given the inter-twining and inseparability of mind/body. Meta-ethics and normative ethics, as Shildrick (1997) notes, have aimed to operate from a position of detachment and have respectively attempted to clarify and comment on terms such as the good and justice and to compare and contrast the ordering of competing ethical systems. Given this aim, the applica-tion of such theories intends to promote 'particular forms of behaviour as constitutive of morality' (Shildrick, 1997: 1). Such a discourse cir-cumscribes problematic assumptions with regards to what constitutes dirty work.

By questioning this mode of ethical enquiry, feminism, as Cornell (1995: 79) writes, presents a kind of endless challenge to the ethical imagination, one that questions a fully determinable morality always at risk of excluding 'the crucial task of re-imagining our own standards of right and wrong'. As Whitford (1991: 149) intimates, 'An ethics of sexual difference, that is, an ethics which recognises the subjectivity of each sex, would have to address the symbolic division which allocates the material, corporeal, sensible, "natural" to the feminine, and the spiritual, ideal, intelligible, transcendental to the masculine.' As Borgerson (2007) also asserts, 'Feminist ethics articulates, theorises and works to understand modes of exclusion, subordination and oppression – and the damage inflicted by these processes and practices – often against the backdrop of traditional ethical theories' marginalization of females generally.' Against the backdrop of common gender-neutral or essentialist readings of the 'feminine' in business ethics, for example, I argue for and draw out the fecundity of an approach that draws on morality and its relation to dirty work as a corporeal encounter rather than as a set of prescriptive rules and normative demarcations. Diprose (1994) suggests that behind this inquiry lies the conviction that a moral code can and should maintain our social order, protecting it against transgression and disintegration. 'Corporeal ethics is not about passing judgements as it is about *disrupting* the taken for granted means through which judgement is violently imposed' (Pullen and Rhodes, 2010: 243–4, emphasis in original). As such, 'responsibility can be considered as a horizon of possibility that, while demanding vigilant attention, is not something that can be achieved once and for all in the administrative arrangements of the here and now' (Rhodes and Pullen, 2009: 353). For Diprose, an understanding of generosity moves beyond the economy or aporia of the gift (that Derrida writes) and lies in a corporeal encounter:

> If generosity can only do its work if it goes unrecognized, then it is not governed by conscious intention, deliberation, or reflection, at least not primordially. Generosity operates at the level of sensibility (carnal perception and affectivity). The openness to otherness that characterizes generosity is ... carnal and affective, and the production of identity and difference that results is a material production.
>
> (2002: 9)

It is argued here that attention needs to be paid to the body in such ethical thinking in contrast with more disembodied ethics that one may find in areas of normative ethics or ethics as the nature of moral judgement to secure either a rational or universal basis for a decision. This is not least because there is asymmetrical evaluation of different bodies, 'some bodies accrue value, identity, recognition through accumulating the gifts of others and at their expense' (Diprose, 2002: 9). There is increasing belief that morality in the sense of value of and between bodies is often oppressive in its practice (Benhabib, 1995). Sex work, for example, can be said to define and commodify the body as a sexual object. This has direct consequences for dirty work as an embodied encounter that begins to understand morality, or moral taint, in more expansive terms. An embodied ethics addresses blindness to the oppressive function of an ethics directed towards maintaining social order, an order that does not recognise the lived specificity of different bodies. If we consider that dirty work involves some form of vulnerability on the part of the worker (and the worked upon) who is subject to its ambivalence, then a recognition and invitation of a corporeal generosity is necessary in order to recognise the face of the other (Pullen and Rhodes, 2010). If we consider ' "ethical" to indicate the aspiration to a non-violent relationship to the Other and to otherness in the widest possible sense' (Cornell, 1995: 78), then a corporeal ethics of generosity may have more potential for understanding staining not only as marking out and potentially discriminating but as a more inclusive set of possibilities.

Rather than advocating a restricted economy of generosity of bodies that are valued and exchanged, the corporeal dimension of generosity exposes the operation of social injustice and an openness to stained bodies. Social discrimination and normalisation operate through and impact on bodies (Diprose, 2002), especially given the social constitution of sexual difference. Biomedical discourses, for example, mask the constitution and regulation of bodies (Diprose, 1994; Komesaroff, 1995).

> Not only is generosity most effective at a carnal level, rather than as a practice directed by thought or will, but the injustice that inflects its operation is governed by the way social norms and values determine which bodies are recognised as possessing property that can be given and which bodies are devoid of property and so can only benefit from the generosity of others, and which bodies are worthy of gifts and which are not.
>
> (Diprose, 2002: 9)

What is argued for here is a generosity towards the stained body. In healthcare particularly, to be sick or in pain is to be dependent and vulnerable to others (Oakley, 1993). Cleansing rituals, such as the careworker bathing the patient or the Salvation Army cleaning the feet of the homeless, expose an openness to vulnerability which may be reimagined as a productive space in which the ethics of dirty work may be reconceived. Staining is subject to the exposure and vulnerability of those who are marked and depend on another. If we situate an ethics of the stain as responsibility towards these issues, staining may be reconceived as part of a productive process. Such recognition, understood through a corporeal ethics, would facilitate an openness to others that may help to overcome social injustices. The vulnerability to another also exposes the visibility of the stain amidst a desire for invisibility (Simpson, 2010). While I have discussed that staining invokes such a desire for invisibility or erasure – to be rendered stain-free and clean of staining for example – we also see the productivity of marking, of the positive valence of certain bodily differences over others. Staining with a positive valence may be reconceived as bringing flesh out of exile. So, while the stain may also be a form of erasure in itself, concealing and eschewing the individual, we may understand staining as a re-presencing of what has hitherto been excluded and begin to expose the stain as a productive process of presencing, of making the excluded present in a manner that allows us to reflect on social and cultural norms and rules.

Concluding remarks

Throughout the course of this chapter I have problematised the ambivalence of the stain as it may be applied to dirty work's associations with the body and bodily fluids, and brought together the ambivalence of its physical and ethical relationships, debates that hitherto remain limited in the study of dirty work. The chapter has provided a theoretical treatment of the symbolic values of the stain and of how it may presence but also conceal order and disorder. By way of concluding, what is advocated is an 'ethics understood as the openness and generosity to the uniqueness of the other and revealed as unknowable' (Pullen and Rhodes, 2010: 247). It is argued that the ethical relationship to staining, identity and the corporeal is most productive when understood through generosity. As such, bringing staining and generosity together enriches the research agenda for dirty work, such that we may pay further attention to the ethical role of the responsibility and vulnerability that is central to it. Such a focus allows us to deconstruct the moralising discourse that circumscribes dirty work occupations and explore the assumptions that underpin moral, material and symbolic relationships. Stains are present in both positive and negative ways and bring together different dimensions of a theoretical engagement with marking out and making present. The aim here is to develop a bodily ethics that incorporates and shows generosity to the stain given that 'one's body is not an objective body in objective space. Rather, as the place of one's engagement in the social and material world, the body institutes a spatial unity' (Diprose, 1994: 105).

If dirty work is commonly associated with disrupting a moral order, then an ethical responsibility of recognition and care for the other is a central concern. The stain concerns both material and symbolic relationships, discussions which may be brought together by considering the ways in which stains and staining are both about exposure and vulnerability, presencing but also making absent. Who is displaced through this moral order, for example? Through the marking out and making present of the stain, there needs to exist a generosity of recognition that understands the specificity of lived bodies, one that does not privilege a prescriptive ethics but one that is able to reflect on the social injustices perpetuated by a restrictive economy of ethics. The vulnerability of the ethical relationship means the necessary recognition of an other, other bodies and other stains. Stains will always exist, despite our best efforts to eradicate them. What one can argue for is work that is inclusive of stains and the potential for identifying the material and symbolic repercussions of such taint. If we are to imagine dirty work as located between and beyond the precarious space of archetypal dualisms such as dirty/clean or good/bad, then we are also able to imagine a generous and more inclusive theory of staining that engages with the physico-ethical demands placed on dirty work as an occupation.

4
From High Flyer to Crook – How Can We Understand the Stigmatisation of Investment Bankers during the Financial Crisis?

Liz Stanley and Kate Mackenzie-Davey

Introduction

> I was quite proud of it because your, it was, the connotation of working in investment banking was that you were a high flyer. Now that, on the street there's a connotation that you're a crook or rather you know, you're public enemy number one because you know you are spending the tax payers' money.
>
> (Darren, investment banker, October 2009)

The hostile UK media portrayal of investment bankers has been a striking feature of the financial crisis that occurred in 2008. The occupation, previously feted for its wealth creation and its attraction of business and capital to London, has become severely and widely morally tainted. The media stigmatisation has been widespread, with vituperative comments and headlines not confined, as might be expected, to the tabloids, but also appearing in broadsheets, including the *Financial Times* – for example 'Shoot the bankers, nationalise the banks' (Stephens, 2009). As the quote from Darren above highlights, bankers are aware of this hostility and of the dramatic change in public perception of them and their industry. Our research interest lies in trying to understand how bankers make sense of such high-profile stigmatisation of their occupation (of the rapid change from 'high flyer' to 'crook'), and this chapter explores the theoretical challenges associated with such an endeavour.

Despite acknowledging the depth and breadth of Ashforth and Kreiner's pioneering work (Ashforth and Kreiner, 1999; Ashforth et al. 2007; Kreiner et al., 2006), we will argue that it does not adequately account for the kind of stigmatisation experienced by bankers during the financial crisis. It is weighted towards low-prestige occupations facing an established taint that revolves around specific tasks within a job and that predates the individual's entry into the occupation. In contrast, investment bankers are high-status workers, facing an emerging and intensifying taint that post-dates their entry into the occupation and that surrounds their personal values, behaviours and remuneration. To explain this, Ashforth and Kreiner's occupational ideology-driven model (1999, 2007) would need conceptual elasticity in three areas: accommodating an individualistic rather than a collectivised approach to taint management, encompassing the taint surrounding behaviours and values as well as tasks and job content and allowing for development in the nature, direction and strength of reactions to taint.

While recognising the very significant contribution of Ashforth and Kreiner's work, we will argue that Dick's social constructionist exploration of how individual police officers discursively account for the parts of their role which are socially perceived as 'dirty' (Dick, 2005) provides a more fruitful approach for theorising the recent stigmatisation of investment bankers. Its emphasis on the 'socially located nature' (Dick, 2005: 1365) of the concept of dirty work draws attention both to the fluid and contingent nature of taint and to the process of how such taint is constructed, attributed and contested. In the context of an emerging and developing taint this process is likely to become more salient as the lack of well-established and entrenched concepts and boundaries surrounding the tainted occupation provides greater scope for creatively constructing and contesting what is deemed to be dirty. As Dick summarises: 'Dirt, whether physical or moral, is essentially a matter of perspective, not empirics' (Dick, 2005: 1368). We argue that it would be useful to explore this matter of perspective further – to extend an exploration of dirty work from identifying tactics for normalising taint to examining both how taint is constructed and attributed and how stigmatised individuals contest that taint, how they argue with it, question its legitimacy, undermine its validity and advance alternatives.

Recent work on the stigmatisation of corporate elites suggests that society's arbiters engage in a dynamic and value-laden process through which they discursively construct and attribute taint differentially, depending on context (Wiesenfeld et al., 2008). This is useful in highlighting both the dynamism and the subjectivity of the process. But we also want to emphasise the idea that taint and stigma are likely to be contested, not just managed. This foregrounds the notion of argumentation and 'the dynamic and responsive manner in which, in a specific context, our talk presents and justifies a particular perspective on reality to an audience, thereby arguing against other (implicit or explicit) perspectives' (Symon, 2000).

We therefore propose that the stigmatisation of investment bankers during the financial crisis can fruitfully be conceptualised as a rhetorical, dialogic process. The media constructs tainted subject positions for bankers and deploys a range of rhetorical strategies to render these convincing. Individual bankers equally deploy rhetorical strategies in response to such attempts to position them; they seek to undermine the legitimacy of the stigmatisation and to position themselves differently. We conclude that many of the tactics for taint management conceived of by Ashforth and Kreiner could usefully be reconceptualised as rhetorical strategies used in specific social contexts by those being stigmatised to undermine the legitimacy and force of the taint being attributed to them and to position themselves more favourably. Detailed rhetorical analysis could therefore enable us to 'better explore those micro-processes through which different "reframing" techniques (Ashforth and Kreiner, 1999) are mobilized and rendered effective' (Dick, 2005: 1385).

The limitations of existing work

Ashforth and Kreiner's groundbreaking work (Ashforth and Kreiner, 1999; Ashforth et al., 2007; Kreiner et al., 2006) has brought the experiences of stigmatised workers to the attention of social psychology and organisational scholars globally and paved the way for a great deal of empirical research on dirty work. However, when seeking to apply it to the stigmatisation of investment bankers during the financial crisis, we were confronted with three major limitations concerning the nature of the workers, the nature of the taint and the nature of the process of stigmatisation and taint management.

(1) The nature of the workers

The research on dirty work to date has tended to focus on low-prestige occupations, perhaps because of the view that the lack of any 'status shield' (Ashforth and Kreiner, 1999; Stenross and Kleinman, 1989) for low-prestige workers intensifies the challenge of dirty work. However, one could equally argue that it is high-prestige dirty workers who face the more intense challenge because the stigma attached to their work is in sharp contrast to the prestige and status they otherwise enjoy, thereby creating a dissonance that may be difficult to reconcile. While some studies (Ashforth et al., 2007; Kreiner et al., 2006) have included high-prestige occupations such as those of abortion clinic medical staff and personal injury lawyers among a wide range of occupations researched, these have not been examined in any great detail. More detailed studies of high-prestige occupations, such as Arluke's ethnogrophy of scientists involved in animal experiments (Arluke, 1991), are rare, and the balance of empirical research remains weighted towards either a range of occupations or in-depth studies of low-prestige occupations (Emerson and Pollner, 1975; Grandy, 2006; Hood, 1988; Tracy et al., 2006). The voice of high-status workers is therefore largely absent. Such an imbalance means there is a danger of making assumptions about high-prestige workers that are based on the experiences of low-prestige occupations. The lack of in-depth studies means that there is a risk that differences may be glossed over within as well as between such occupations: even if the tactics used to counter taint are shared between occupations, precisely how and when people mobilise them may vary significantly within occupations. Personal factors such as age, social class, career stage and marital/family status could all influence an individual's reactions to working in a tainted occupation.

With the conclusions drawn from the empirical focus on collectivised, low-prestige dirty work comes a view that reactions to taint are driven by shared occupational ideologies. Ashforth and Kreiner's focus is on the collective nature of responses to taint – a focus rooted in the view that 'typically, although not always, attributions of dirtiness arise not because of the organizational membership or personal characteristics of individuals but because of their occupational membership. Thus it is the occupational group that is seen to be directly threatened, and it is as a group that the members typically respond' (Ashforth and Kreiner, 1999: 419). So agentic power is placed largely in the hands of the group; it is collective agency that effectively challenges and manages the stigma of dirty work through the deployment of collective occupational ideologies. However, this orientation may not translate easily into contexts such as investment banking. This is a highly individualised occupation, with significant competition for rewards and no history of unionisation or collective action. It may not therefore be relevant to look at investment bankers' experiences of taint primarily from the standpoint of their membership of an occupational group. Ashforth and Kreiner suggest that their model 'may unfold in a more muted way' (1999: 430) for high-prestige workers. On this basis, greater education and job complexity mean that high-prestige dirty workers are likely to undergo extensive socialisation under the auspices of professional organisations. Thus, they may benefit from and be able to draw on institutionalised ideologies which can equip them to deal with stigma more effectively. This appears to be a rather careless linking of high-prestige occupations with professions which does not hold true in all cases. It is questionable whether investment banking, while undeniably high-prestige, is actually a 'profession'. While it shares some of the characteristics of professional services such as being knowledge-intensive and involving discretionary effort by service experts (Lowendahl, 1997), other fundamental features are missing (*cf.* Cook, 2008). In particular, it lacks the proscribed and narrowly focused pre-career education path and closely corralled postgraduate training central to other professions such as law or medicine, which are likely to be a key vehicle for occupational socialisation. In investment banking, occupational learning is largely 'on the job' (Whimster, 1992), and organisation and industry-wide training is largely limited to regulatory compliance requirements. We cannot, therefore, be confident of using a diluted version of the occupational ideology-driven model derived from studying predominantly low-prestige workers to understand the experiences of high-prestige dirty workers.

(2) The nature of the taint

The dirty work literature encompasses a wide range of taint, based on Hughes' definition that dirty work may comprise tasks that are physically, socially or morally tainted (Hughes, 1958: 122). Ashforth and Kreiner (1999) expand this by offering two criteria for each of these three types of taint. Thus physical taint applies to work that is either directly involved with actual dirt, such as death, blood and rubbish (e.g. funeral directors, pest controllers or refuse collectors), or is seen as being performed under dangerous or noxious conditions (e.g. firefighters, soldiers or miners). Social taint applies to work that is either directly involved with stigmatised individuals or groups (e.g. prison officers, social workers or psychiatric nurses) or where there appears to be a servile relationship between the worker and others (e.g. maid or chauffeur). Finally, moral taint applies to work that is seen as somewhat sinful or dubious (e.g. pawnbroker, casino owner or erotic dancer) or where the worker is thought to use deceptive, intrusive or confrontational methods (e.g. tabloid reporter, bailiff or private investigator) (Ashforth and Kreiner, 1999). However, when exploring the stigmatisation of investment bankers it became clear that this breadth masks the fact that in all the occupations explored to date the taint focuses on the tasks carried out in execution of the work. The theoretical concepts and the tactics identified for dealing with taint are therefore focused squarely on the work's itself being dirty and the people who do that work being stigmatised as a result. Despite Dick's assertion that when an occupation is morally tainted that taint carries over to the individual (Dick, 2005), there has been little exploration of how this may happen or of what its impact might be.

This focus on tasks limits the immediate applicability to the experiences of investment bankers in the financial crisis, because here the stigmatisation has been more about the bankers themselves than about the tasks of banking. While there are elements of banking – subprime mortgages, Collateral Debt Obligations and structured and highly leveraged finance – which have been particularly criticised, much of the media, political and public condemnation of bankers has focused more on the way bankers have behaved and how they have been rewarded for this than on the actual tasks of banking. The taint thus surrounds bankers' values (greedy and reckless) and their remuneration (excessive and unwarranted), and it is not clear how, or even whether, the cognitive and behavioural tactics identified by Ashforth and Kreiner (1999; Ashforth et al. 2007) to normalise taint associated with tasks would be deployed by bankers to deal with this much more personal, value-based taint.

The taint attributed to investment banking may also differ from that in the extant literature because the stigmatisation appears to be more indiscriminate. Little attempt is made to distinguish between bankers working in the type of transactions blamed for the financial crisis. Instead, investment banking as a whole has become tainted and this means that the stigmatisation is by indirect association, more than by direct implication, in tainted aspects of job content. This can be seen as an example of courtesy stigma (Goffman, 1963). Neither the personalised element of the taint nor the taint by association is adequately accounted for in Kreiner et al.'s typology (2006) which maps breadth and depth of taint and offers four types of stigma: pervasive (high breadth–high depth), diluted (high breadth–low depth), compartmentalised (low breadth–high depth) and idiosyncratic (low breadth–low depth). The closest fit seems to be in the compartmentalised stigma cell, in that only some of the tasks are strongly stigmatised. However, this still assumes that all occupation members are involved in those stigmatised tasks. Another key feature of the taint surrounding investment bankers during the financial crisis was its visibility, but the typology (Kreiner et al., 2006) does not accommodate this characteristic either.

As well as being more personal, broader and visible than the taint studied to date, there is a fourth critical difference in the taint surrounding investment bankers. The dirty work research carried out to date examines occupations where the taint is fixed, static and predates the individual's entry in the occupation. While this does not negate the stigmatisation they experience, it does suggest that at the very least they entered the occupation with their eyes open. In contrast, the taint attributed to investment bankers emerged and intensified throughout the financial crisis. While there are historical examples of taint attached to banking (the taint of usury for example), in a contemporary context investment banking has been glamorised and the taint attributed during the financial crisis was, if not completely new, at least significantly more widespread through its promulgation by the media. Such a dramatic and high-profile shift in perceptions is not accounted for in existing literature on taint management, other than in Kreiner et al.'s mention in the idiosyncratic taint category of their typology of accountants following the Enron scandal (2006) and in Gendron and Spira's exploration of the identity work conducted by former employees of Arthur Andersen, also following the Enron scandal (2010).

This leaves a significant gap in understanding taint management. As highlighted above, Ashforth and Kreiner (1999) argue that occupational ideologies – defined as 'a coherent perspective ... that details the nature of the relationship between the occupation and its members with other types of work as well as with the larger society' (Dressel and Petersen, 1982: 410) – form the basis for taint management. Yet it surely takes time for such a 'coherent perspective' to emerge, coalesce and then become disseminated and shared so that it can enable occupation members to quash and nullify the taint they encounter. What happens when an occupation becomes tainted for the first time? When the stigma is new and perhaps unexpected, there may not be an occupational ideology to fall back on. Or there may be an occupational ideology but one that does not readily furnish the kind of tactics that help to rebut taint, because such taint has never before been ascribed to that occupation. It may be that the experience of stigmatisation fosters the very swift development of such an ideology, but there could be a period at the beginning of the stigmatisation when there is a vacuum. This suggests that to understand reactions to a new stigmatisation it would be more fruitful to look at individual rather than at collective taint management approaches.

(3) The nature of the process

The dirty work literature's heritage of Social Identity Theory (SIT) and the realist ontology which underpins it casts identity as an essentially stable phenomenon fashioned from the congruence of the organisational, occupational and individual identities, and may therefore overlook more dynamic processes of taint management and identity formation. The orientation can be seen to fit into a 'militaristic' model of 'attack–defence'. In the face of 'attack' to identity through attribution of taint by others, individuals draw from an arsenal of 'weapons' created by their shared occupational identity to defend and preserve their preferred, self-esteem-enhancing, positive self. This orientation may be problematic in situations of nascent taint. Here, individuals may encounter taint for the first time and the taint itself may be shifting and evolving in nature, content and intensity. For example, before the start of the financial crisis there was no coherent, consistent view of investment banking as dirty work. The moral taint associated with the occupation has materialised and coalesced into a widely held articulated opinion over time in tandem with events in the economic context. This suggests a complex, messy and fluid process that sits uneasily with the 'attack–defence' model of earlier accounts.

Following from the above, Kreiner et al. (2006) do introduce an element of movement into their discussion of the 'identity dynamics' involved in dirty work, integrating SIT with Systems Justification Theory (SJT). In expounding SJT, Jost et al. (2004) criticise the assumption that all stigmatised groups are actively trying to rebut taint, claiming that history shows a great deal of evidence to the contrary and that stigmatised groups are in fact more likely to accept taint and stigma than to challenge them. They reject the assumption of what they call 'group justification theories' that people are driven by ethnocentric motives to build group solidarity, and argue that research evidence suggests that members of disadvantaged groups often have negative opinions of their own group members and positive views of more advantaged groups (Jost and Burgess, 2000). While accepting that people want to hold favourable attitudes about themselves, SJT argues that individuals have a general ideological motivation to justify the existing social order, because people also want to view the social and political systems which affect them positively. This can lead to the internalisation of inferiority among stigmatised or disadvantaged groups (Jost et al., 2004). They cite examples where the status quo is legitimised, upheld and even reinforced at the expense of personal and group interest (Jost and Banaji, 1994).

Kreiner et al. (2006) have integrated SIT and SJT, arguing that rather than competing, the two theories can in fact complement each other to provide richer insight into the experiences of living and dealing with taint and stigma. They argue that perceptions of legitimacy which are fundamental to SJT could be as much an outcome of SIT-related attempts to counter taint as an alternative. If an individual tries but fails to counter taint through the SIT-related processes, it may convince him/her that the taint is in some way deserved and lead to acceptance and legitimisation of the taint and stigma. This introduces a dynamic element to the model for understanding stigmatisation. However, it is possible that change works in the other direction – that is, that people begin by accepting the taint but later resist it. In this respect, there is likely to be confusion, contradiction or ambiguity in people's reactions to taint so that individuals may simultaneously accept and fight it, feeling both that it is deserved and yet also trying to minimise its impact on self-esteem and identity. Further, the realist assumptions about identity as something people 'have' leads to a focus on identifying the things they 'do' to protect their identity and on the outcomes of stigmatisation – identification, dis-identification or ambivalent identification (Kreiner et al., 2006) – rather than on an exploration of the process of stigmatisation and taint management. Following Dick (2005), this suggests an undertheorisation of the socially constructed nature of taint and, we argue, its attribution.

Emphasising the socially located nature of taint and stigma

Building on the work of those who have explored taint and stigma from a social constructionist perspective (for example Dick, 2005; Gendron and Spira, 2010; Grandy, 2008) and on recent work on stigmatisation (Paetzold et al., 2008; Wiesenfeld et al., 2008), we argue that understanding the stigmatisation of investment bankers during the financial crisis requires an acknowledgement of the broader social processes at play to account for how taint is constructed and attributed within the specific cultural and historical context. Stigma, or taint, is a social construction produced by interaction between two parties which means that it is open to change, development and flux, depending on the context and the specific interaction (Paetzold et al., 2008).

Similarly, Dick argues that what is seen as dirty work within an occupation is 'up for grabs' rather than being fixed or predetermined. This understanding helps to provide a map of an occupation's ideological landscape, highlighting the ideological boundaries within which people construct their professional identities. She claims 'the active construction and defence of these boundaries illustrates that the meanings that attach to the tasks carried out within any given profession are neither universal nor monolithic; they are situated within specific social and ideological contexts, open to contestation and dispute, and requiring continuous negotiation' (Dick, 2005: 1369). So rather than 'attack–defence', the attribution of and reactions to taint can be cast as a debate, as a negotiation of the boundaries of what is and is not socially acceptable or as an open-court hearing of evidence for and against the charge of moral taint. Conceiving of the process in these terms highlights its duality, for there is a dynamic interaction between those conferring taint and those on whom it is conferred. The existing models do not sufficiently acknowledge this, focusing on one side of the process (the tactics to counter a relatively undefined and all-encompassing notion of 'dirt' or 'taint') and neglecting the other (how taint is conferred).

Addressing both sides of the equation

Instead, we need to address both sides of the equation: how taint is constructed and conferred and the reactions of stigmatised workers to that. First we need to explore the construction and attribution of taint: how it is worded; what specifically is deemed 'dirty' and how that is conveyed and how such a perspective seeks to persuade us of its legitimacy and validity. This moves us towards a more contextualised conception which offers an understanding of not only the characteristics of taint but also of its function in society. As Dick argues: 'Dirt in its social sense is, therefore, related to ideological beliefs in societies. Such beliefs operate to produce and maintain the moral order, in which the appropriateness and "correctness" of social action and practice are clearly demarcated and bounded' (Dick, 2005: 1368). Similarly, Paetzold et al. (2008) argue that stigmatisation can contribute to social and organisational control by attaching disapproval and censure to certain behaviours. In the case of investment banking the boundaries of appropriateness and 'correctness' are developing, moving and crystallising in the particular social and historical context of the financial crisis. The demarcations have shifted, new boundaries are being established, new taint constructed. In such a state of flux it would be interesting to explore where the boundaries are being drawn and what they are anchored to – socially, culturally and historically – but to do this we need to conceptualise a dynamic, fluid process of stigmatisation and reactions to it.

Wiesenfeld et al.'s (2008) work on the stigmatisation of corporate elites describes this kind of fluid process for the first half of that equation, that is for the creation and attribution of taint. They propose that society's social, legal and economic arbiters engage in a dynamic and value-laden process through which they construct and attribute taint differentially, depending on context. The model offers three key insights of value in a situation of broader stigmatisation than that of individual leaders of failed companies: the crucial role of society's arbiters, the influences affecting those arbiters' judgements and the potential differences involved in the stigmatisation of elites.

Primarily, the model serves to highlight the critical role of society's arbiters in defining, attributing and disseminating the stigma or taint to an individual or an occupation. This process is simultaneously simple and complex. Its simplicity lies in the fact that the public's appetite for information is generally limited to straightforward questions of cause, effect and responsibility. What complicates it is that members of the public are not able to answer those questions for themselves and must instead rely on arbiters to provide the answers (Wiesenfeld et al., 2008). Thus arbiters are the lynchpin in the stigmatisation process; their role is pivotal and should be scrutinised empirically.

Secondly, the model exposes the inherent subjectivity of arbiters' assessments. Arbiters engage in 'constituent-minded sensemaking' (Wiesenfeld et al., 2008: 232), through which they seek to anticipate the expectations and biases of their stakeholders and accommodate these, as well as their professional norms and biases, into their judgements. In other words, they read the mood of their constituents and their decision-making is guided by that interpretation; they play to the gallery and seek to reflect public opinion as much as to shape it. Arbiters' judgements are also influenced by professional norms (for example journalists wanting attention-grabbing headlines and stories with relevance to the everyday lives of readers) and by the pronouncements of other arbiters. This dynamic can be seen in the financial crisis. For example, the media reports politicians' criticisms of bankers and politicians also anticipate and respond to the views of the electorate, partly conveyed to them via the media which they tend to view as a proxy for public opinion. So the diffusion of the stigma becomes mutually reinforcing and the censure escalates. The dynamic is also evident within one type of arbiter such as the media; for example, specialist financial writers may report a phenomenon such as the seizing up of inter-bank lending in early 2008 and as this story builds in volume and significance, it may be taken up by the news and headline writers, until the coverage and interest reaches such a level that it becomes the subject of editorial opinion and/or feature pieces. Thus the stigma becomes more widely disseminated and more deeply reinforced. The argument that arbiters' assessments are intrinsically subjective resonates with Dick's argument, highlighted above, that dirt or taint is a matter of opinion and perspective, not empirics (Dick, 2005: 1368), and underlines the need to examine in detail how such opinions and judgements are developed, conveyed and justified.

Thirdly, the model offers a rare insight into the stigmatisation of high-status individuals. Most of the research on stigmatisation, as also in dirty work research, focuses on low-status individuals and groups. Drawing on empirical research by Feather (1994; 1999; Feather and Sherman, 2002), Wiesenfeld et al. argue that in the case of high-status individuals, *schadenfreude* – enjoyment of others' adversity – is likely to emerge, particularly when previous success is seen as undeserved (Feather and Sherman, 2002; Wiesenfeld et al., 2008). They argue that *schadenfreude* may also encourage more generalised fault-finding, with focus moving away from perceived business-related deficiencies towards condemnation of personal values and morals, such as 'the CEO's ostentatious lifestyle or womanizing' (Wiesenfeld et al., 2008: 241). This in turn is influenced by the social and economic context; in times of economic hardship, such as during the financial crisis, 'the general populace and its various institutions (including the press) are on edge and in search of villains, then schadenfreude will prevail. In their own pain, observers will relish the pain of the once lofty' (ibid.: 240). This again emphasises the importance of the social context in determining the shape and strength of taint and stigma and suggests that understanding stigmatisation requires detailed exploration of this.

Drawing on these three insights from the process outline by Wiesenfeld et al., together with Dick's arguments (2005), we conclude that when seeking to understand dirty work, it is instructive to look first at how taint is constructed and attributed to a particular occupation at a particular moment, before exploring the reactions and responses to it by occupational members. This directs analytical attention towards the specifics of how texts/conversations/media coverage create taint and confer it on occupations and towards how these relate to the wider socio-cultural and historical context. So, in the case of investment bankers, we might usefully focus on social arbiters and analyse how taint is developed concerning investment bankers in media coverage and/or records of political debate about the financial crisis. This would involve exploring both what is construed as tainted and how the taint is attributed to bankers as well as how this evolved and changed throughout the financial crisis. Analysis of this kind would contribute to our understanding of dirty work by helping to reveal the socially constructed boundaries of acceptability and legitimacy and of purity and impurity (Douglas, 1966), and illuminate how these boundaries are proposed, modified, changed or reinforced as a particular episode of history unfolds. It would also help us to understand how the creation of these boundaries and the portrayal of bankers as having infringed them (and therefore as tainted) positions individual bankers and investment banking as an occupation (Just, 2006).

But that is only half the story. Taint may be constructed and conferred by society's arbiters but that does not necessarily mean it is accepted and managed or 'normalized' (Ashforth et al., 2007) by those on whom it is conferred. As Dick argued above, it is open to debate and dispute and involves ongoing negotiation (2005). Similarly, Törrönen argues: 'The agent that a cultural text tries to interpellate into a specific subject position has experiences with alternative subject positions and thereby holds power over the siren-signing of discourses' (2001: 315). In other words, individuals have the capacity to reflect and to choose. Positions need to be taken up (Davies and Harré, 1990). It is not enough that they are offered or conferred; 'a difference exists between the offer of an identity position and the take-up of that offer' (Just, 2006: 116). We suggest that the taint attributed to investment bankers during the financial crisis is likely to be hotly contested for two reasons. Firstly, it post-dates their entry into the occupation and they therefore experience the transition from, in Darren's words, 'high flyer' to 'crook', an experience which is likely to be contested and resisted. Secondly, the taint is personalised and surrounds their values and behaviours. That is, it attacks who they are and not simply what they do, and we believe that this is likely to strengthen reactions to it and increase the likelihood that the taint is questioned, resisted or rejected. Just as we have argued for a detailed exploration of how taint is constructed and attributed, so we propose that understanding stigmatisation requires a thorough study of how tainted individuals contest their stigmatisation to undermine its validity and advance alternative opinions.

This draws attention to the centrality of argument and persuasion in stigmatisation and dirty work. Society's arbiters need to convince that their construction and attribution of taint is justified and accurate, and tainted individuals dispute this and seek to provide a more convincing argument that the taint is invalid or unwarranted. This process of argumentation highlights rhetoric as a vehicle for persuasion. Rhetoric has been defined as 'discourse used to bolster particular versions of the world and to protect them from criticism' (Potter, 1996: 33), as 'discourse cal-culated to influence an audience toward some end' (Gill and Whedbee, 1997: 157) and as 'justification for the taking of a particular position on an issue or a particular view of reality and criticism of counter-positions' (Symon, 2000: 479). We propose that the stigmatisation of investment bankers during the financial crisis can fruitfully be conceptualised as a rhetorical process in which society's arbiters construct and confer taint on bankers and deploy a range of rhetorical strategies to render these convincing and in response individual bankers deploy rhetorical strate-gies seeking to undermine the legitimacy of the stigmatisation and to position themselves differently. This results in an ongoing negotiation of the boundaries and legitimacy of taint, contingent on social context, a negotiation in which 'every attitude in favour of a position is also, implicitly but more often explicitly, also a stance against the counter position' (Billig, 1991: 143). Examining the rhetorical process which sits behind the 'antagonistic relationship between versions' (Potter, 1996: 108) requires detailed analysis of the tactics and strategies used to con-vince and persuade on the one hand and undermine and invalidate on the other.

Since Billig's (1996) groundbreaking integration of rhetoric into con-temporary organisational studies, the interest in using rhetorical anal-ysis in empirical studies has mushroomed. There is a growing body of rhetorical research into topics as diverse as resistance to techno-logical change (Symon, 2005), multiple organisational identities and legitimacy (Sillince and Brown, 2009), the positioning of qualitative research (Symon et al., 2008) and identity and citizenship (Gibson and Hamilton, 2011). Symon defines rhetorical analysis as 'a kind of dis-course analysis that concentrates on analyzing linguistic strategies of argumentation as individuals seek to convince an audience of a con-struction of reality congruent with their interests (through justification) yet undermining of others (through criticism)' (Symon, 2008: 78). Con-sequently, what these studies, and others like them, offer is a detailed and thorough analysis of the content and form of argument, reveal-ing how individuals exercise what Billig calls 'witcraft', that is the skill 'needed to invent excuses and accusations' (Billig, 1996: 113) to estab-lish that their account is valid, true or factual and that alternative accounts are unreliable, inaccurate or biased. As Potter states, 'the pro-cess of fact construction is one of attempting to reify descriptions as solid and literal. The opposite process of destruction is one of attempt-ing to ironize descriptions as partial, interested, or defective in some other way' (Potter, 1996: 112). For example, Clayman (1992) reveals how television interviewers use rhetorical strategies such as citing others to create a sense of neutrality or personal distance, and Dickerson (1997) has built on this work to argue that politicians go one step further, citing others to provide apolitical, expert and counter-interest endorsement of their opinions. By doing this they seek to manage 'stake', that is the potential criticism that some form of vested interest is driving the stance they take and that it is therefore not a question of fact but of opinion (Potter, 1996). Dickerson also found that politicians declare themselves initially sceptical but now convinced, a tactic which voices the potential criticism and alternative view but quashes them at the same time, because the idea of the 'conversion' both demonstrates that the stronger argument won and protects the individual from the charge of vested interest – what Potter calls 'stake inoculation' (Potter, 1996).

In the context of dirty work, adopting a rhetorical approach means reconceptualising the taint management tactics identified by Ashforth and Kreiner (1999; Ashforth et al., 2007) as rhetorical strategies, employed both by society's arbiters in creating, defining and conferring taint and by tainted individuals seeking to rebut such stigmatisation. For example reframing, conceived by Ashforth and Kreiner as neutralising the negative value of the work and infusing it with positive value, could equally be conceived of as undermining the argument of one group and positioning one's own counter-argument as the 'truth', and refocusing, which they explain as emphasising the non-stigmatised aspects of the work, could be seen as ontological gerrymandering (Woolgar and Pawluch, 1985), where 'just as in electoral gerrymandering, where the vote is biased by drawing boundaries in the most efficacious way, the defence is shored up by drawing the rhetorical boundary around the most advantageous issues' (Potter, 1996: 184–5). Rhetorical analysis would allow us to take the taint management tactics identified by Ashforth and Kreiner and examine how they are accomplished and to explore what it is that individuals do in their talk and texts in their attempts to reframe, refocus and so on. At a micro-level, it enables us to understand how these outcomes are achieved (Dick, 2005).

However, rhetoric is not deployed in a vacuum and the focus on the detailed, micro-level of talk and text must not let us neglect the wider social context within which stigmatisation and reactions to it occur. We must also be alive to the 'argumentative context' (Symon, 2008), that is the initial issue at stake (Gill and Whedbee, 1997), the context in which it has arisen, the implicit counterarguments it is addressing (Billig, 1996) and the audiences at whom it is targeted. Rhetoric is deployed 'in a manner consistent with broader myths, narratives and cultural accounts' (Suddaby and Greenwood, 2005: 59), and understanding its essentially socially located nature means paying attention to this macro-context as well as to its micro operation.

Conclusion

Despite encompassing many different occupations in empirical research and offering typologies to cover different forms of taint, on closer inspection the existing dirty work literature does not adequately explain the stigmatisation of investment bankers during the financial crisis. In particular the experience of high-status workers is neglected in existing research, which means that there is a danger of generalising about their experiences from data based on low-status workers. In addition, existing research focuses on taint which predates the individual's entry into an occupation and which revolves around specific tasks and aspects of jobs which are seen as dirty. It does not include taint that is focused not on tasks or job content but on the values and morals of the individuals, nor does it explore taint and stigmatisation which arise after an individual has entered an occupation. It also offers a rather one-sided examination of dirty work, focusing on the reactions of tainted individuals but not on the construction and attribution of that taint.

Instead we have argued for an approach which explores both sides of the equation. Drawing on Wiesenfeld et al.'s mode of the stigmatisation of corporate elites (2008) and on Dick's social constructionist approach to the discursive construction of dirty work designations (Dick, 2005), we stress that not only is taint socially located but also that it is likely to be contested. We suggest that this foregrounds the role of argumentation and the importance of rhetoric. A focus on rhetoric enables us to explore arbiters' delineation of the boundaries of legitimacy and acceptability at a micro-level to examine how an occupation becomes tainted and how the opinion of it as tainted is packaged and conveyed to convince of its legitimacy and validity. In addition it encourages us to dig beneath the umbrella tactics – such as reframing, refocusing and recalibrating – defined by Ashforth and Kreiner (1999), and examine how individuals use these in their talk to undermine the legitimacy of the taint being conferred upon them and to offer alternative accounts. We believe that such an approach provides a fruitful theoretical and methodological approach to understanding how an occupation becomes stigmatised and how individuals like Darren contest such stigmatisation, and their change in status from high flyer to crook.

5
'Glamour Girls, Macho Men and Everything In Between': Un/doing Gender and Dirty Work in Soho's Sex Shops

Melissa Tyler

Introduction

This chapter draws on ethnographic research carried out in sex shops[1] located in London's Soho, an area that has been at the heart of the capital's sex industry for over 200 years. As a place of 'backstreet industry and below stairs debauchery' (Richardson, 2000: 57), the sex industry dominates both the actual and perceived character of Soho. The area occupies only a square mile of London's West End, yet its political, economic and cultural reach is considerable, and the area continues to have a global association with commercial sex. As one of the participants who took part in the research put it, 'you don't go to Soho to buy a pair of shoes do you?' As a place to live, work and consume, Soho has throughout its history been something of an abject space, maintaining a long-standing appeal as simultaneously alluring and threatening, at the same time as carefully nurturing its reputation as a place of bohemian indulgence offering a warm embrace and a sense of belonging in the heart of an otherwise anonymous urban environment. As Judith Summers (1989: 190) puts it in her monumental history of Soho and its people, the area's 'inherent tolerance has always offered the unconventional, the eccentric, the rebellious and the merely different a chance to be themselves'. In this respect, Soho is a particularly interesting place to consider some of the ways in which gender is simultaneously un/done (Butler, 2004) in and through work, in a place, an industry and an occupation often regarded as 'dirty' in a number of distinct but interwoven ways.

The discussion begins by reflecting on the historical evolution of Soho and its association with the sex industry, before giving a brief account of the methodology underpinning the research on which the chapter is based. It will then discuss the various ways in which sales-service work in sex shops constitutes 'dirty work' as described by Hughes (1951), in so far as it carries physical, social and moral taints, reflecting on how these taints are lived and experienced in a range of gendered ways by those who work in sex shops. The final part of the chapter borrows from both Julia Kristeva (1982) and Judith Butler (1988, 2000, 2004) to argue that what the former describes as the 'power of horror' – the alluring capacity of that which repels to simultaneously fascinate and ultimately seduce us – can be discerned in the performance of dirty work discussed here, a power that manifests itself in a coexistent attraction and repulsion to the sector and particularly to Soho as a place of work and as a place through which gender is perpetually (often consciously, as will be argued below) un/done. For many of those who took part in the study, the very attraction of the place, the sector and the job is precisely its 'dirt' – physically, socially or morally – and the opportunity that performing 'dirty work' accords for un/doing gender, that is for both shaping the compulsion to perform gender in a particular (in this case hegemonic) way, and at the same time providing opportunities to perform gender differently, to make 'trouble' with gender, as Butler (2000) put it. It will be argued here that this attraction to the 'dirt' associated with the job, the sector and the place therefore involves a positive reaffirmation that cannot simply be reduced to a strong organisational or occupational culture, as Ashforth and Kreiner (1999) outline in their discussion of the taint management techniques deployed by those who undertake dirty work. With this in mind, the discussion concludes by exploring the potential of moving the study of dirty work forward by drawing attention also to the performance of what might be termed 'abject labour' in order to capture this perpetual un/doing, as it is shaped by a simultaneous sense of attraction and repulsion and an apparent desire not to 'clean up' dirty work, but rather to revel (at least metaphorically speaking) in its filth.

Sales-service work in the sex industry

Within the social sciences, particularly in sociology and geography, there is a well-established body of literature on sex work (the term used here to refer to prostitution), much of which draws attention to the stigmatisation of those who provide and consume sex in exchange for money (Brewis and Linstead, 2000; Sanders, 2005, 2008a; West and

Austrin, 2002) as well as to the association of sex work with particular places and spaces (Day, 2007; Hubbard and Sanders, 2003). In addition to this emphasis on stigmatisation and location, research on sex work has also highlighted the need to study the 'supply side' of the industry, 'including ancillary industries that support sex markets in the shadow economy' (Sanders, 2008b: 704). Alongside, but not necessarily in dialogue with this literature on sex work (although much of the former has drawn attention to the emotional and aesthetic labour and body work required of sex workers), is an emerging body of research focusing on sexualised labour in sales-service work, much of which emphasises the sexualisation of, particularly female, employees' appearance as a central component of the exchange that takes place (Adkins, 1995; Filby, 1992; Warhurst and Nickson, 2009). Yet comparatively little attention has been paid to work that is carried out between these two alternatives, that is to those occupations in which the boundary between sex work and sexualised labour is relatively blurred and in which important emotional and aesthetic aspects of the sales-service encounter are arguably heightened. This intensification of the encounter is largely because the performance and consumption of commercial sex (in all its many guises, ranging from sex work to sexualised labour, to work such as sales-service work in a sex shop, as described here) transgresses boundaries generally considered to be necessary for the maintenance of the social and moral order (see Douglas, 1966), the latter involving the containment of sex to the private sphere (and space) of intimate relations, rather than to its enactment within a commercial transaction between relative strangers, and in the case of a sex shop particularly, in a relatively open, public environment.

In terms of the gendering of sales-service work in a sex shop, while 'traditional' sex shops such as those that continue to dominate the sector in London's Soho – largely perceived as 'a no-go area for women' (Smith, 2007: 169) – are deemed to be spaces of hegemonic masculinity from which women either exclude themselves (see Storr, 2003) or from which they should be protected, retail sales-service work at the same time (and through a related process) has historically been socially constructed as 'women's work'. In particular, the relatively high demand for emotional labour within sex shops – Malina and Schmidt (1997: 356) for instance note how exploitative pricing strategies in traditional sex shops rely on people being ashamed and embarrassed about sex – also further genders it as feminised. Hence, the gender construction of sales-service work in sex shops is interesting as, on the one hand, important elements of the work have traditionally been associated with skills attributed to women in the labour market, particularly in terms of the performance of emotional, aesthetic and sexualised forms of labour, while on the other hand, sex shops such as those that are characteristically associated with Soho tend to be perceived as distinctly male preserves, unsuitable 'for a lady', as Richard, one of the participants in the research discussed here, put it. Arguably, this means that those men who are employed in the industry are perceived, according to the terms of the heterosexual matrix (Butler, 2000), as hyper-masculine (as Michael, another participant stated, 'working here, people assume that you're always up for it'), while those women who work in the sector are either regarded as sexually deviant or as objectified by the industry and by their male co-workers and customers (see Malina and Schmidt, 1997 for a discussion). So where does this leave those men and women who work in Soho's sex shops, in terms of the ways in which they perform gender and experience the stigmatisation and stereotyping of their work and of themselves as workers? How are they perceived by others and how do they perceive themselves as workers within the industry and the setting in which they are employed? What attracts them to working where they do, and what difficulties do they encounter? It is to questions such as these that we turn in this chapter as we explore the work experiences of men and women employed in this relatively neglected sector and setting through the analytical lenses of 'dirty work' (Hughes, 1951), abjection (Kristeva, 1982) and gender performativity (Butler, 1988, 2000, 2004).

While organisational scholars have paid little or no attention to the work experiences of those employed in sex shops,[2] a steady stream of research has emerged from geography, ethnography and marketing on the sector more generally. Social geographers and sociologists have focused particularly on the regulation of sex shops, largely through an examination of strategies such as licensing and zoning (Coulmont and Hubbard, 2010; Edwards, 2010; Hubbard et al., 2009; Manchester, 1986; Ryder, 2004). Ethnographers have provided rich and detailed accounts of consumption practices in sex shops (Stein, 1990; Tewksbury, 1990), documenting the negotiation of stigma, and particularly of gender performance on the part of customers (Berkowitz, 2006; Tewksbury, 1993; McCleary and Tewksbury, 2010). In recent years, this research has established links with a growing interest in sex shops amongst retail marketing academics, focusing on the increasing presence of stores that market sex-related products primarily to women, such as the UK-based chain Ann Summers or *Sh!* in London. While some have argued that such stores challenge traditional notions of sex shops as male domains, describing shops that have a strong feminine aesthetic, or a female-only admission policy as 'gynocentric playspaces' (Malina and Schmidt, 1997: 352), promoting a 'hedonistic femininity' (Smith, 2007: 167), others have reflected more critically on this development, questioning the extent to which a feminised sexual consumerism genuinely disrupts the sexual objectification of women (Attwood, 2005; Storr, 2003). Retail marketing scholars have also emphasised the increasing 'gentrification' of the industry, noting the relatively recent proliferation of designer products and stores, with some commentators arguing that this combination of feminisation and gentrification has served to 'clean up' the industry and render it more socially acceptable (Kent and Berman Brown, 2006), by minimising the various physical, social and moral taints with which the industry is associated. Of course these twin processes are very much dependent upon the continued existence of an Other within the sector – that is, a retail sex industry that is perceived as dirty and dangerous because of its residual gender and class associations or because of its geographical location, a role that arguably continues to be filled by those shops based in London's Soho, described by Smith (2007: 169) as an area 'abandoned to sleaze and inadequacy'. It would be very easy therefore to contrast Soho as a phallocentric space with the gynocentrism of more feminised sectors of the retail sex industry, yet the research on which this chapter is based suggests that such a comparison would be an over-simplification and would fail to do justice to the gender multiplicity that can be discerned in the work experiences and identities of those employed in Soho discussed below.

With this in mind, the analysis of the findings presented here turns to Butler's account of gender as a perpetual process of un/doing in an effort to understand the lived experience of this multiplicity and its relationship to sales-service work in Soho's sex shops as 'dirty work' (Hughes, 1951). While the ontological basis of gender analysis within work and organisation studies has shifted in recent years towards a processual understanding of gender as a situated social practice (Bruni et al., 2005; Poggio, 2006; Pullen, 2006b), Butler's emphasis on gender performativity as a perpetual process of un/doing (Butler, 2004) has yet to make a significant impact on the study of work and organisational life, this despite the recognition that her writing has 'profound implications for organization theory' (Borgerson, 2005: 64). Mindful of this, the discussion here seeks to make sense of the empirical material presented on the lived experience of gender and dirty work in this particular sector and setting by extending the inroads that both Kristeva and Butler's thinking have made into feminist organisation studies, and in doing so, to further extend the conceptual analysis of dirty work by framing the performance of sales-service work in Soho's sex shops as a form of abject labour.

Soho and the sex industry

Described by Quentin Crisp (2007 [1968]: 199) in the first instalment of his autobiography, *The Naked Civil Servant*, as 'a reservation for hooligans', Soho occupies a relatively compact geographical area but constitutes something of a 'glocalized space' in terms of its disproportionate social, political, economic and cultural impact, primarily as a result of its global association with commercial sex and its reputation as a 'night-time economy' (Roberts and Turner, 2005) or 'nocturnal space' (Houlbrook, 2005). But Soho is also a vibrant workplace and thriving residential community, an urban village in the heart of London's West End. It is 'a place of dazzling contrasts...both homely village and red-light district, a place of work and a place to forget it', as Summers (1989: 5) puts it. Stephen Fry (2008) describes it in a similar way in his Foreword to Bernie Katz's collection *Soho Society* – 'Soho's public face of drugs, prostitution and seedy Bohemia...has always hidden a private soul of family, neighbourhood, kindness, warmth and connection'. A 'hybrid and heterotopic site' (Mort, 1998: 891), shaped by a number of intersecting yet differential histories, Soho's multi-faith culture means that it is home to a range of religious and spiritual as well as political groups, many of which take an active involvement in the maintenance of the area as a place of openness to the Other. Unsurprisingly therefore, Soho is also notably home to London's main gay village, based around Old Compton Street. The area's characteristic sexual and legal liminality, coupled with gay male social and recreational opportunities and the assimilation of the area into a fashionable mainstream (in a vein similar to Manchester's gay village – see Binnie and Skeggs, 2004) all characterise Soho as the UK's 'gay capital' (see Andersson, 2007; Collins, 2004; Mort, 1998).

Since the 1980s Soho has undergone considerable transformation, most recently as part of a pre-Olympic 'clean up' campaign (Hamilton, 2009) – a project that has been somewhat counterbalanced by a local branding initiative called 'I Love Soho', sponsored by local businesses concerned to retain the 'heart' of Soho through the skilful marketing of its café culture. Soho has a long history of migration, with large French, Greek, Polish, Italian and Chinese communities, and (partly because of its culinary and cultural eclecticism and cheap rents) is a fashionable place for intellectuals, writers and artists, as depicted in the Carnaby

Street 'Spirit of Soho' mural and the many 'blue plaques' and other artefacts of the tourist gaze with which the area is replete and which constitute what Frank Mort (1998) calls its 'symbolic geography', all of which give the area a feeling of being something and somewhere significant. As Summers (1989: 193) states, Soho has been 'much written about, and much romanticized... It is almost a legend. But like all legends it has its dark side', and the latter relates primarily to the area's long-standing associations with commercial sex.

As documented in Barbara Tate's (2010) autobiographical account of the working lives of 'West End Girls', before the introduction of the Street Offences Act in 1959, sex workers solicited outside on the streets and in the many 'courts' and alleyways between the larger buildings, and there were nearly 100 strip clubs in Soho in its heyday. Since then, sex work has been driven, at least formally, indoors – 'into the nether regions of bare, dimly lit staircases' (Summers, 1989: 208). On the one hand, this has made Soho a (relatively) safer place for sex workers through the use of CCTV and other security devices, which enable them to screen potential clients before admitting them onto the premises. However, what this Act (nicknamed a 'pimps' charter') has also meant is that as sex workers have moved off the streets, pimps and drug dealers have moved in to take their place. The 1959 Act also brought with it a proliferation of hostess bars (or 'clip joints'), strip clubs, saunas and massage parlours as premises where sex workers and their clients could be brought together, often by means of an overpriced non-alcoholic drink so that the bar owners could stay within the law while generating huge profits for themselves and their landlords.

In the last two decades or so however, Soho has undergone something of an urban renaissance, shaped by a combination of entrepreneurial activity, artful urban branding, local community initiatives, economic revival relating to the area's long-established links with the film industry and particularly the expansion of businesses specialising in new media and communication technologies. By the end of the 1980s, purges of the Vice Squad, along with the introduction of licensing regulations, began to 'clean up' Soho (a process that had actually been going on for at least 100 years or so). Sex work is still widespread though, and premises deemed suitable for sex-related businesses command inflated rents, a process that has effectively squeezed out many local traders not connected with the sex industry. Binge drinking and especially drug dealing are rife; there are many sex shops remaining, most of which are licensed and regulated by trading standards and licensing inspectors, but many of which are not, and the area continues to be associated primarily with commercial sex. While some have argued that the twin processes of gen-trification and corporatisation have sanitised the area, Soho retains an 'edge' to it that makes it unique as a place to live, work and consume. As a recent (and rare) paper on sex shops in the *Journal of Management History* claimed, there is 'no other concentration of specialist erotic retailing comparable to London's Soho, which remains a uniquely-themed neighbourhood' (Kent and Berman Brown, 2006: 201). It is on the experience of working in this 'uniquely-themed' setting that the research on which this chapter is based, and to which we now turn, focused.

Researching sales-service work in sex shops in Soho

As Frank Mort (1998: 901) argued in his discussion of commercial sex and the 'cityscape', 'ethnographic work delivers insights into the relationship between identity and place which cannot be supplied by the formal maps of the consumer city'. With this in mind, the approach taken here was driven by the conviction that ethnography could bring into focus the ways in which 'dirty work' is enacted and experienced within the context of a specific locale, focusing on the relationship between identity and place to which Mort refers and thinking about how this relationship shapes and is shaped by the performance and perception of gender and 'dirty work' by those who undertake it. This ethnographic dimension was important because it provided an opportunity to reflect on how sales-service work in the retail sex industry is lived and experienced by those working in the industry, in their own words and from their own perspective.

The research I undertook included observational fieldwork carried out in and around Soho, specifically in 12 (licensed and unlicensed) sex shops between May and July in 2009. This observational research was broadly carried out along a continuum, along which my role shifted from participation as a potential customer (in shops where I had yet to interview or where I had not planned to interview) or as an assumed employee (when the staff but not the customers were aware of my role as a researcher – although I had no direct involvement with customers, other than to exchange passing greetings) to entirely non-participant observation, when I spent time at the counter in the shops with a note-book and tape recorder out and was therefore clearly identified as an 'outsider'.

In addition to carrying out observational research inside the shops, I observed and made field notes on the spaces in and around the shops, and in Soho more generally, covering all of its main streets, side streets, courts and alleyways. I took over 300 photographs and

made notes on what I had photographed and why, making connections between the different photographs and the observational data
I had gathered and, whenever possible, asking those I interviewed to
do so as well. I also took photographs in and around the shops where
I undertook interviews and observational research, often in collaboration with interviewees. My role was therefore something of a research
'flaneur', consuming the place and the space, rather than its products
or services (although I did on occasion consume the latter). During the
course of the fieldwork, I undertook a total of 14 semi-structured interviews, guided by an interview schedule that I continually refined, with
people working in licensed and unlicensed sex shops (for full details,
please refer to Appendix 5.1). With one exception, these were tape-
recorded and transcribed and subject to thematic analysis at various
intervals. Data collection and analysis were therefore part of an ongoing,
iterative and often interactive process, as I discussed interim findings
after each visit with friends and colleagues as well as with the research
participants.

Of the 14 interviews, three took place in local cafes, sometimes over
several meetings during the participants' break times or after work; one
was undertaken (as part of an ongoing narrative discussion carried out
over two interviews and several email exchanges between and since) on
a bench in Soho Square; another was conducted initially through email
exchanges and then over two meetings in a small office at the back of
the shop floor (above the sex shop in the basement); the remainder
took place at the sales counter (by the tills) on the shop floor where
the participants worked, during their working hours, or while they were
on informal breaks during quiet periods. This meant that (much like
Sanders' interviews with sex workers that were also undertaken *in situ* –
see Sanders, 2005b) the flow of the conversation was often interrupted
by customers, or by co-workers, and that audibility was sometimes difficult due to the background music or noise from the pornographic
DVDs that are played in most of the shops. However, it also meant that
interviewees were able to talk candidly and often very animatedly about
their work and their work environments, giving examples and recall-
ing incidents as something in the shop itself triggered recollections or
prompted thoughts that they might not otherwise have had. Because
most of the interviews were undertaken with my tape recorder resting on
the sales counter at the front of the shop and because most of the shops
have at least one and many several screens on the shop floor playing
DVDs that are on sale, the majority of interviews were carried out while
hard-core pornographic films played on screens next to the counter and
at various other points throughout the store. Initially this made me feel

very self-conscious, particularly if I was the only (other) woman in the shop, but I quickly became accustomed, even immune, to it and this in itself gave me an interesting insight into the work experiences of those employed in the shops. As Shirley, one of the four women who took part in the interviews put it, 'after a while nothing fazes you, nothing at all, not in this business' (Shirley, June 2009).

This leads me to reflect on another interesting aspect of the field-work and of the project more generally, and that is the extent to which researching 'dirty work' becomes dirty work in itself, so that the research (and the researcher) carries the same physical, social and moral taints as the subject matter. Throughout the duration of the fieldwork both my (male) partner and I received comments questioning why I would want to carry out fieldwork in an area like Soho and why I would want to study a sector of work with such a 'seedy' reputation. Many of these comments appeared to be gendered in nature, displaying the kind of protective paternalism described in Morgan and Knights' (1991) study of women's exclusion from field sales work in the insurance indus-try. In a vein similar to the gendered assumptions made about Brewis' (2005) work, my interest in sales-service work in sex shops also provoked comments about my being either sexually obsessed or naïve (although many of these comments were light-hearted in nature). And to be fair, there were certainly instances during the fieldwork when I questioned my decisions and on one or two occasions felt notably uncomfort-able, almost to the point of abandoning my plans (at the beginning of the research) or being relieved that the fieldwork was coming to an end (on the last day), when I interviewed a man who worked in a store specialising in the sale of schoolgirl-themed 'spanking' equipment and pornography. The latter was the only participant who refused to allow me to record the interview, although he did permit me to take notes during our discussion and seemed keen to be interviewed, while emphasising that in his view Soho, and the shop in which he worked in particular, was 'no place...for a lady'. In the main, however, the ethos described above – one of openness and generosity – characterised my experience of the research process throughout my time in Soho, and most of those who took part were extremely welcoming and will-ing to share their time, thoughts and experiences (and often also their workspace) with me. Everyone I spoke to had interesting stories to tell, and before long and as I got to know them better, patterns began to emerge in their accounts of working in sales-service work in sex shops, and particularly in Soho. Many of the interviews, even though they were carried out in the shops themselves, continued over a couple of hours, and almost all were at least an hour long, generating rich, detailed and reflexive accounts of people's work experiences.

As indicated above, the analysis of the observational, visual and interview data to which we now turn combines Hughes' (1951) 'dirty work' typology and its subsequent development in the work of Ashforth and Kreiner (1999) with the anthropological concept of abjection and also Butler's (2004) performative analysis of gender as a perpetual process of un/doing, in order to make sense of what – for many, if not for most of those who took part – was a simultaneous sense of repulsion and attraction to their work, particularly their place of work and the gender performances it both compelled and enabled.

Performing 'dirty work' in Soho's sex shops

Hughes (1951: 319) defines dirty work as work that carries a physical, social or moral taint; dirty work 'may be simply physically disgusting. It may be a symbol of degradation, something that wounds one's dignity. Finally, it may be dirty work in that it in some way goes counter to the more heroic of our moral conceptions'. As Ashforth and Kreiner (1999) outline in their more recent development of Hughes' analysis, physical taint occurs when an occupation is associated with that which is thought to be dirty or disgusting in a material sense or when it is performed under what are perceived as particularly 'dirty' conditions. Social taint occurs when a job involves sustained contact with people who are stigmatised or where the worker has a particularly servile relationship to others. Moral taint occurs when an occupation is regarded as sinful or of dubious virtue or where the workers employ methods (being deceptive, intrusive or confrontational, for instance) thought to be immoral.[3] In his original typology, Hughes (1951) emphasises that what constitutes 'dirt' is very much a social construction, the common denominator being not the attributes of the jobs themselves or the assumed character of the people who perform them, but rather the reactions they provoke. Drawing on Douglas (1966), Ashforth and Kreiner (1999) also emphasise that the boundaries between the three forms of taint with which dirty work is associated are relatively blurred, and many occupations of course carry multiple taints – sales-service work in sex shops perhaps being a case in point.

With this in mind, the following section draws on Hughes' (1951) typology to examine the various ways in which sales-service work in sex shops is physically, socially and morally tainted. Following Hughes, it then seeks to extend the analysis of dirty work, much of which emphasises the deployment of 'taint management' techniques (Ashforth and Kreiner, 1999; Bolton, 2005; Tracy and Scott, 2006) and the desire to 'clean up' dirty work in order to cope with the stigma with which it is associated, by considering not only the repulsion but also the attraction of dirty work for those who undertake it, focusing particularly on the opportunities working in a sex shop in Soho accorded for those who took part in the study to 'do something different' with gender and sexuality, as one particular participant put it. It is in this respect that the analysis emphasises that integrating Hughes' typology with Kristeva's concept of abjection and Butler's performative gender ontology helps us to elucidate some of the potential pleasures, as well as the pains, of performing gender and dirty work in this particular sector and setting.

The physical taint of sales-service work in sex shops

In contrast to the manual labour performed by building workers in Thiel's (2007) study of dirty work and physical capital, sales-service work in sex shops is primarily dirty in a symbolic rather than a physical sense (although as with any retail work, aspects of the job such as unpacking and stacking or shelving stock, merchandising and cleaning the store involve the performance of manual labour). Aside from the performance of what might on occasion be relatively physically dirty manual work there are other important physical elements to the 'dirt' involved. The physically intimate nature of the products on offer means that the job often involves handling 'dirt'. Shirley for instance described her own reluctance to touch products that have been used by customers:

> You have people trying to return products that have been used in personal areas because they don't think they do what it says on the packet and they're trying to give me something that's been in certain parts of their anatomy and wonder why it's like 'Whoa!' you know?
>
> (June 2009)

This handling of dirt extends not just to the products on offer, but also to the services provided, including the intimate nature of the advice that customers ask for and often the performance of customers themselves within the stores. Nathan summed up what most respondents told me about their role in dispensing advice about the products on sale and their possible uses:

> Some people do ask you some of the strangest things, like you're a sex therapist or their doctor even. They come out with such

personal stuff...I mean I get stunned sometimes by the honesty when people ask because they're just perfect strangers and they just ask us anything...Yeah, you do get asked weird and wonderful things every week.

(May 2009)

Evoking the locale twice in his account, Michael described how being able to accept the presumed intimacy that characterises everyday inter-actions between staff and customers in sex shops as simply 'part of the job' was something of a rite of passage for him:

Some of the locals [regulars], they come in and speak to me as a local sex therapist! 'Oh, I'm having a bit of trouble with this'...One day a man walked over with his penis out in the shop. You do get that...that was one of my first breaking moments in the first two months on the job. When I say breaking moment, as in 'If I can handle this I'll stay'.

(May 2009)

Many of those I interviewed reflected on how, increasingly it seems, the job comes close to sex work, and several of those I spoke to accepted this as part of the job, relating their role as service providers to meet the expectations of customers resulting from the long-standing association of Soho with commercial sex. As Toby put it,

You get people coming onto you all the time. It doesn't matter if you're a boy or a girl, if you're 16 or 60. You know everyone gets that in this job...I mean you just have to deal with it...It's the wrong shop, and the wrong area to work in if you don't like that sort of attention.

(May 2009)

However, even for Toby, who accepted what others might regard as sexual harassment simply as an aspect of the job that 'you just have to deal with', certain customers transgressed what he perceived to be acceptable, leaving him feeling physically 'dirty' and violated. Here for instance, he recounts how he felt after one particular customer had smelt him:

That made me feel sick...I had a good two-hour shower after that...It just made me feel so dirty. Just like the idea of someone smelling you...Fair enough if you put your hand on my shoulder and I can push your hand off, but the idea of someone...It's really intimate. Oh, it was horrible.

(May 2009)

Indeed, following the closure of many of Soho's remaining clip joints and sex cinemas as part of Westminster City Council's current 'clean up' campaign, the increasing demand for private viewing booths means that the job is potentially becoming more like sex work for many of those who perform it, shifting further along a continuum between sexualised labour and sex work. The physical implications of this were clearly of concern to some of the people who took part in the research. Nathan, for instance, described how some customers were becoming increasingly voyeuristic, even predatory: 'they come in just to look at the screens and I find that increasingly uncomfortable. I really do' (May 2009). Alluding to customers who use the shops as places to experience sexual pleasure, Michael described how:

There are some that come in that we know why they're here...you see them and you get to know them after a couple of months. It's the same people...It's mainly since the cinemas have gone...They used to go in the cinemas and pay their £1.50 and they were happy with that, but now they haven't got that. So they come in here. They come in here and they'll just go round the back and just stand in a corner.

(June 2009)

Julie, who worked in one of the high street stores that market their products primarily to women, also recalled how some male customers ('the odd pervert') would come into the store specifically to get the female staff to talk about and demonstrate the products on display: 'I won't deny we get the odd pervert in, but it's nothing we can't handle' (June 2009). Although women like Julie suggested that such sexual objectification was nothing she could not 'handle', many of the men I interviewed and observed, particularly those employed in managerial or supervisory roles, displayed a protective paternalism towards female staff (similar to that which I experienced as a researcher), an approach that men such as Nathan for instance articulated through the way in which they encouraged an explicitly desexualised presentation of self on the part of female staff. As he put it, 'you really, really don't want people turning up for work looking sort of tarted up, not in this place and not in this industry' (May 2009).

The physical taint with which retail work in Soho's sex shops is associated relates not simply to the physicality of the products on sale or to the nature of staff-customer interactions, however, but also to the broader social materiality of the work and to its spatial context, particularly to the meanings associated with the place where it is carried out. Echoing the broader social assumptions underpinning the regulation of sex shops in places like Soho and the paternalistic practices of store managers such as Nathan, Shirley rationalised her decision not to tell her 80-year-old father where she worked as a reflection of a kind of 'mutual protection' strategy (involving her protecting him from knowing something about her working life, particularly her place of work, that she felt would undermine his desire to protect her as his daughter). As she put it:

> He lives up in Scotland and he hasn't been in this neck of the woods for 30-odd years. He would still remember Soho as cheap and dirty and he would be worried – not because of what I'm selling; more worried about me being in Soho.
>
> (June, 2009)

The materiality to the taint with which Soho is associated can also be discerned in its spatiality. Many of the (especially unlicensed and 'specialist') shops in Soho are located in dark, dingy and relatively physically dirty alleyways and 'courts' (small semi-enclosed spaces in between the sides and backs of larger buildings). Those on the main streets tend to be located in basements and so have something of an 'underworld' feel. As Mark, who worked in a sex shop located in the basement of a lifestyle store explained, 'we take turns down here. It's just, you know, it's like a cave down here, there's no light, so it's just nice to rotate the staff so you're not stuck down in this hole all day long' (June 2009). Dirt is also present in an olfactory sense; the archaic drainage system in central London means that many of the shops – which are below street level, often in the basements of remainder bookshops or 'lifestyle' stores – lack both natural light and fresh air. Hence, many of them (particularly following heavy rain), smell of a combination of latex and drains – 'the downside is the smell!' as Stewart (who worked in a basement store) put it.

The social taint of sales-service work in sex shops

Sales-service work in sex shops also carries a social taint for those who provide and consume the goods and services on sale – commercial sex, particularly in a retail environment constitutes 'matter out of place'. Nathan for instance described how even long-standing customers seemed conscious of the social taint attached to frequenting a sex shop: 'I've seen some regulars who've been coming in the shop for years since I've been here and they will never, ever pay on credit card even now...It's stigma stuff because of what we are, a sex shop' (May 2009). Michael alludes to the impact of this stigma on other people's perceptions of those who work in the shops, describing how a woman came into the shop where he works with a friend and started chatting to him, but when he asked her if she might like to meet for lunch one day, he recalls how 'she wouldn't do it, and she was really honest. She was like "I'm a bit put off by where you work" ' (May 2009). In a similar way, Toby connects customers' own discomfort with frequenting a sex shop with the social taint attached to working in one: 'it's like if you're embarrassed to be in here, what does it make me to work here? Do you know what I mean? You feel they're judging you by being embarrassed' (May 2009).

Largely as a reflection of the social taint with which commercial sex is associated, and in a vein similar to the sex workers described by Sanders (2005) in her study of sex work, many of those who took part confessed to leading 'double lives'. While Shirley suggests a protective paternalism at stake in her decision not to tell her father that she works in Soho, amounting to something of a relationship of reciprocal protection, as she felt he would worry about her safety and security, perceiving Soho to be 'cheap and dirty', other women had decided to conceal the place and nature of their work because of its assumed transgression of gender roles and expectations. As Julie explained:

> I'm proud to work at this store. The only place I wouldn't really adver-tise it so much because I'm a mum of two is at school because it's still very taboo. So, there's some sort of boundary there that I wouldn't want to cross.
>
> (June 2009)

For others the decision to conceal their work seemed to be grounded largely in educational and class aspirations. As the very well-spoken Stephen put it when asked about how he responds when people inquire about what he does for a living:

> I tend to lie, you know! I say publishing or media or something...my friends know and they think it's funny, but I have a Masters degree

and I'm very conscious...I'm very conscious of the fact that it's all gone a bit tits up really [laughter]...Actually, my family don't know...I think they'd be a little disappointed. I tell them I work in a bookshop. I'm so bad!

(June 2009)

The moral taint of sales-service work in sex shops

The very nature and location of sales-service work in sex shops in Soho means that it also carries a strong moral taint, largely because of its association with relatively stigmatised people engaging in what are generally perceived to be immoral, possibly illegal activities. As Hubbard (2000: 201) puts it in his analysis of the moral geographies of commercial sex, urban spaces associated with prostitution, pornography and perversion tend to be perceived as 'immoral landscapes'. For the people working in the sex shops in Soho, most customers are regarded as perfectly 'normal' and 'ordinary':

> People have got an image of the sex shops that you're going to get old men coming in in dirty raincoats and it's not like that at all. You can get anyone from an 18-year-old couple to an 80-year-old couple and everything in between.
>
> (Nathan, June 2009)

Customers who are generally perceived to be outside of this 'norm', deemed to be predatory or perverse and to violate the strong moral code that characterises the place and sector are a regular and potentially increasing feature, however. Stephen explained the effects of the moral taint associated with these types of customers on his experience of the job and on his perception of self as someone employed within the industry:

> You just get certain types. You get the browsers, you get the people that are wanting to buy stuff. You get collectors, ...and then you get the occasional perv, which isn't pleasant. That's really not pleasant...Sometimes they touch themselves, or...but you're kind of immune to it...I can put on my very polite face and smile and do whatever because I work on commission. It's when you get the perverts, the ones that ask for really nasty stuff...mainly kiddie stuff, and animals ['What do you do? How do you cope?'] 'Sorry, out'. Done...I just feel a little bit degraded by stuff like that.
>
> (July 2009)

Amongst those people I interviewed, there is a strong feeling of community based on the one hand, on a sense of belonging together, sharing both the pleasures and the pains of the job, and on the other, on the exclusion of those deemed not to belong, namely those who request or supply the kind of material that Stephen says makes him feel 'a little bit degraded'. Others echoed this sentiment, connecting it to the locale and to the assumption that because of Soho's long-standing association with commercial sex an 'anything goes' ethos prevails. As Nathan put it,

> Everyone is different, but to me, to come in here and ask me for that [child or animal pornography] insults me. It insults all of us doesn't it? Because they do think because of where we are, and because we're in a sex shop they can ask for whatever they want, which they do.
>
> (May 2009)

Indeed, in a later interview, when asked about what aspects of the job he enjoys least, rather than talking about the travelling or the long hours we had been discussing, Nathan returned to our earlier discussion of those customers who ask for 'under the counter' material: 'I'd say people asking for kiddie stuff or animals, which you get asked a lot…That's the down side for me. I hate it' (June 2009). For those 'others' working in the sector – that is, for those who request or supply material, or have facilities such as private viewing booths (as several do) that are deemed to be particularly 'dirty' (as in, morally tainted) – their abject status is largely the outcome of what is seen as a violation of Soho's moral code. The essence of this code, one that I encountered time and again throughout the fieldwork, is that 'anything goes' *provided* it is between consenting adults. In practice this means that those who are known or believed to supply child or animal pornography or those who operate unlicensed premises or one of the few remaining 'specialist' shops are relatively ostracised. Richard, the only person I interviewed who would not consent to me tape-recording the interview, told me:

> We're a specialist shop [specialising in school girl pornography]. We don't have any contact with the other shops. We keep ourselves to ourselves…Some of the unlicensed shops are not as seedy as they used to be. But we make much more money because the licenses are so expensive.
>
> (June 2009)

Dirt, desire and un/doing gender: From dirty work to abject labour

Despite the relatively ostracised position of 'outsiders' such as Richard, without exception those who took part in the research were also concerned about a creeping 'sanitisation' of Soho and a residual fear that as the area is becoming physically, socially and morally cleaner, it is in danger of losing precisely what makes it attractive to customers and to the staff themselves as a place in which to work and consume, namely its 'edge'. It is important, therefore, in order to understand the richness of the working lives of those people who contributed to the research, to make sense not only of the various taints with which their work and their place of work is associated, but also to recognise what Kristeva (1982) describes as the 'power of horror' for those who work in Soho's sex shops, that is to also capture the alluring fascination with aspects of the job, and the place, that also repel or repulse those who work there.

As Judith Summers (1989: 2) has argued, 'Soho may not always be pleasant, but it is never dull', and for many of those who took part in the research, the very attraction of the place, the sector and the job is precisely its 'dirt'. Hughes (1951) himself hints at the attraction of dirty work when he notes, in a somewhat passing fashion, how dirty work may be an intimate part of the very activity that gives an occupation its charisma. But it is the concept of abjection, associated most closely with the work of Julia Kristeva (1982), that enables us to understand more fully the simultaneous attraction and repulsion that characterises the way in which most of the people I spoke to seem to feel about their work, particularly their place of work. Julie for instance echoed the sentiments of many others when she described her need to 'do something different'. She explained to me how she had taken what seemed to her to be a very predictable and parentally driven path through life, attending a well-respected girls' school and then university to study for a career in marketing, describing her decision to apply for a job in a sex shop in Soho as a conscious act of rebellion on her part. On being asked if she thought she had made the right decision, Julie's response was resoundingly affirmative, emphasising how she felt she had been successful in deviating from the very gendered path that had been set out for her: 'I need variety, to be doing something a little bit different...and I think I've captured that working here...There's always something going on, so there's always an atmosphere, always a buzz' (June 2009). Toby went into more detail, reflecting on his attraction to working somewhere that is both 'disgusting' and 'really exciting', as he put it:

> I like the idea of working somewhere that's...you know, you get to meet...the sort of people you wouldn't really want to meet in an ideal world...and they're really interesting. They've got stories to tell. You can't trust them as far as you'd throw them, but to chat to they're interesting...That's another thing about Soho – I always keep a watch in case you miss something! There's so much to watch. I love it... I feel more at home here than I do where I live. Because it's so intimate. It's quite a small area. Because all the shops we know each other, we all look after each other...as a place to work it wakes you up and it gives you stories to tell. It's living isn't it?
>
> (May 2009)

When Michael described how he felt when he was told he was being transferred from another branch of the shop where he worked to the Soho store, he said, 'I'd been asking for so long [for a transfer to Soho]...I was so ecstatic' (May 2009). Alluding to her own sexual interests, Davina described how much she also loves working in Soho, a place with which she identifies and which she finds 'inspirational':

> It's similar to my own universe of interest [here]. I'm very much into fashion, I'm especially into [antique] lingerie...I'm a collector of it. And I'm also into performance art...It's a similar universe to me here. It's an inspirational place to work in. Yes, it's seedy and it has an edge but that's what makes it exciting. It's what makes it what it is.
>
> (May 2009)

Developing the concept of dirty work by teasing out this sense of excitement associated with a sector and place of work deemed to have an 'edge' that is both seedy and inspirational, as Davina articulates it, we can begin to conceive of sales-service work in sex shops as it is described here as a form of abject labour; that is, as a form of labour in which there is a simultaneous attraction and repulsion to the various taints with which it is associated. In what is perhaps the most sustained theoretical discussion of abjection to date, namely Kristeva's (1982: 1) *Powers of Horror*, abjection (from the Latin *ab-jicere*, meaning 'to cast out') is defined as that which 'disturbs identity, system, order'. It is that which simultaneously fascinates and repels, threatening lines of demarcation and containment between what is 'pure' and what is 'dangerous' in

Douglas's (1966) terms. It is a fascination with what is tainted or perceived as a threat to the established moral order – what Kristeva describes as 'the power of horror' – that seems to characterise the experiences of those who took part in the research described here. In sum, the experiences described above suggest, in this respect, both an identification with the place, the sector and its people that goes beyond simply reframing, recalibrating or refocusing dirty work in order to manage the taints with which it is associated (Ashforth and Kreiner, 1999) and which instead seeks to retain the 'edge' with which their work, and crucially, their place of work, is associated, at the same time as being repelled, even repulsed by certain aspects of it. This is why, for those who took part in the research, Nathan's summation seems a particularly apt way of capturing the complexity of feelings, experiences and identifications that might be described as abject labour in this particular sector and setting: 'It's the best job in the world, and an absolute nightmare, usually in the same day. It's fascinating, really fascinating... but yeah, there are things about it that I absolutely hate' (May 2009).

This then leads us to the question of what it is about the 'dirt' that attracts the men and women I interviewed, and whose thoughts and experiences are described here. For many, it seemed, it was the opportunity, as hinted at by Julie, Michael and Toby (above), to 'do something different'. While many of the people I interviewed were acutely aware of the extremely hegemonic gender and sexual performativity that characterises the sex industry as it is materialised in a commercial setting such as Soho, they were also conscious of an ethos of openness to the other and of a generosity and humility that strongly attracted them to Soho and to the working community that constitutes the sex industry within this particular locale, at the same time as they were repelled, even repulsed, as Nathan suggests, by certain aspects of it. Mark, for instance, was among several of the men I interviewed who described the importance to them of working in Soho as a place where they were accorded a sense of recognition. As he put it:

> It's a kind of second home in a way because... with it being the gay village. You kind of feel safe here because there are others like you around, you know. So there's a kind of recognition... You know, there's a sense of belonging here that I've never had before
>
> (June 2009)

Echoing Mark's emphasis on recognition, others such as Michael talked about the ways in which those who 'do something different' with

gender and sexuality, that is those who perform their gendered and
sexual identities in ways that deviate from the terms of intelligibility established by the heterosexual matrix (Butler, 2000), 'get a lot of
courage' from Soho:

> Lots of people round here wear clothes that I would not have the
> courage to wear – you know, like huge leopard skin fake-fur coats
> and really, really tight black jeans and loads of lipstick; and he's a
> really gorgeous bloke and I think 'I'd love to have the courage to
> wear that because it does look really good and it works around here'.
> I mean if Walthamstow had that sort of person walking down the
> road, you'd have people pointing and laughing, but here it's the other
> way round and people like that rule here . . . I think it's great and this
> is the only stretch . . . where you actually see men and ladies walking
> hand in hand and kissing and I think that's really great . . . It's almost
> like it gives people . . . Some people get a lot of courage from around
> here. I really do believe that [Have you felt that yourself]. Oh yeah.
> Definitely. It's opened me up'.
>
> (Michael, May 2009)

For Stewart it was precisely its gendered and sexual multiplicity that
attracted him to Soho, and it is this which sustains his fascination with
the place and its people. As he put it,

> We get everything and everyone in here [the shop where he works].
> All walks of life. I love the madness of it all, absolutely love
> it . . . We get them all in here. Glamour girls and macho men and
> *everything* in between, and I mean everything. What's not to love?
>
> (June 2009, original emphasis)

And it is in trying to make sense of these experiences and their connections to the performance of dirty work, or what we might term 'abject
labour', that I would like to turn to Butler's performative ontology of
gender.

Emphasising the importance of understanding what she calls 'the
scenography of production' (that is, the relationship between gender
performativity, materiality and signification) in the performance of
gender, Butler (2004) emphasises both the agentive capacity of the subject and the constraints that compel particular performances. In her
discussion of the latter, she focuses explicitly on the dialectical interplay between 'what it might mean to undo restrictively normative

conceptions of sexual and gendered life' (Butler, 2004: 1) and the matrices of cultural intelligibility that compel the performance of gender in particular, hegemonic ways, namely those that are accorded recognition according to the terms of the heterosexual matrix, as a process of 'becoming undone' (Butler, 2004: 1). Crucially for Butler, this perpetual process of un/doing 'imposes a model of coherent gendered life that demeans the complex ways in which gendered lives are crafted and lived' (Butler, 2004: 5); to put it simply, the condition of cultural intelligibility (and by implication, ontological and therefore social, political and economic viability) is that the 'everything in between' so adored by Stewart and his colleagues becomes a simple either/or. What dirty work, framed as abject labour, as it is described in the particular circumstances discussed here potentially allows for is a reclamation of this complexity and, for those who took part in the research on which this chapter is based, this opportunity for reclamation which working in Soho accords (one which does not preclude recognition of one's cultural intelligibility and therefore ontological viability) constitutes a highly seductive force. Butler's account of gender as a perpetual process of un/doing, combined with Kristeva's concept of abjection (as a simultaneous attraction and repulsion), therefore helps us to understand some of the possibilities of tainted work for those who undertake it as a mechanism for challenging the heterosexual matrix, or what Butler (2004: 186) has more recently called 'presumptive heterosexuality'. For the men and women I interviewed and observed during the course of their everyday work experiences in sales-service roles in Soho's sex shops, the opportunity to 'do something different', as Julie puts it, or to 'make trouble' with gender, to paraphrase Butler (2000), explains at least in part their attraction to dirty work and their desire not to 'clean' it up through the coping strategies outlined by Ashforth and Kreiner (1999) and others – that is, to make their work or their place of work more socially acceptable or credible, but also to revel in its (metaphorically) 'filthy' and therefore alternative, cultural associations.

Concluding thoughts

In sum, then, this chapter has drawn on insights borrowed from Kristeva's and Butler's writing in order to develop Hughes' 'dirty work' typology, shifting the analytical focus away from dirty work towards an appreciation of the performance of 'abject labour' as a way of capturing some of the important gendered aspects of sales-service work in Soho's sex shops. Shifting the analytical focus towards abject labour has arguably allowed the drawing of attention to the importance of this particular sector and setting as a site on which to un/do gender (Butler, 2004). In their expansion of Hughes' (1951) original typology, Ashforth and Kreiner (1999) effectively argue that the various taints associated with dirty work result in a denial of recognition of dirty workers themselves and of the work they perform. This lack of validation is particularly true, they note, for dirty workers in low-prestige occupations. Nevertheless, their account emphasises how dirty workers are able to create and sustain positive work-role identities, largely, they believe, as a result of the resources provided by strong organisational or occupational cultures to reframe, recalibrate and refocus the meaning of dirty work, that is 'to foster enobling ideologies' (Ashforth and Kreiner, 1999: 428). Yet their focus on work role and identity leaves the question of workplace relatively neglected. In the research discussed above, the place of work was found to be particularly important both to the taints with which sales-service work in sex shops is associated and also to the simultaneous attraction and repulsion experienced by those employed in Soho's sex shops. A focus on the place itself also shifted the analytical concern away from the physical, social and moral taints of dirty work, enabling us to tease out the pleasures with which it is associated and to reconceptualise sales-service work in sex shops, as it is explored here, as a form of abject labour. This potentially offers a more comprehensive theoretical lens through which to understand the process of un/doing gender and the performance of dirty work in a neglected sector and setting of employment, one that seemingly cherishes its 'glamour girls, macho men and everything in between'.

Appendix 5.1 Interviewees

ANDY had worked in Soho (in an unlicensed store selling mainly DVDs) for about ten years. I interviewed him at the sales counter in a store for about an hour.

DAVINA AND PHOEBE both worked in a couture lingerie store. I interviewed them together. Both were in their late twenties. I interviewed them in their store for about half an hour.

JASON was the creative director and co-owner of a gay lifestyle store, incorporating a licensed sex shop in the basement. I interviewed him for about an hour and a half in his office at the back of the shop floor.

JULIE is in her late twenties and works in one of the 'high street' sex shops (described somewhat disparagingly as 'novelty' shops by some respondents) ,whose products are aimed mainly at female customers.

Julie had worked in other branches of the company and in Soho for about eight years (she had taken two periods of maternity leave during this time and returned to working in Soho following both periods of leave). I interviewed her for about 45 minutes in her store.

MARK worked part-time in a gay lifestyle store (I interviewed him while he was working a rotational shift in the licensed sex shop in the basement for about an hour and a quarter on a Monday morning). He is in his forties and had worked in the store since it opened (seven months earlier).

MICHAEL is in his mid-thirties and had worked in Soho for eight months (but for the company for four years). He had been asking for a transfer to Soho for ages and was 'ecstatic' when he was offered a job in Soho. I interviewed him on a bench in Soho Square for about an hour, and we corresponded by email afterwards.

NATHAN was in his forties and was working as an area manager in the South East for a large multinational chain of licensed sex shops. I interviewed him in the Soho branch, for which he has overall responsibility. He is married with two daughters, and had worked for the company for eight years. I interviewed him at the counter in the store for about an hour and a half.

RICHARD is semi-retired, in his late sixties, and works part-time in a specialist schoolgirl-spanking, unlicensed shop. He had no contact with other people in the sector/place, and was the only respondent who would not allow me to tape-record our (30-minute) interview. He was very keen to talk to me, partly it seemed, to emphasise that there was 'nothing wrong' with their shop/business.

SHIRLEY was a fascinating person to talk to. In her mid-fifties, she had been headhunted by a recruitment agency to manage a licensed store in Soho, where I interviewed her. She had been in the post for about six weeks. I interviewed her in-store (at the counter) for about an hour and a half (excluding breaks while she served customers).

STEPHEN was in his early twenties and had worked in a licensed shop (where I interviewed him for about 40 minutes) for just over 12 months.

STEWART is in his thirties and worked in a well-known gay lifestyle store, in the sex shop in the basement, which is where I interviewed him. He was joined by MATT about two-thirds of the way into an hour-and-a-half-long interview, and Matt took over the responses towards the end, when we talked more about Soho and the sex shops generally. Stewart had worked in the licensed shop for about three years. Matt did not work there but was a regular customer who helped out sometimes when the store was busy and who also wrote regular reviews of products on sale there for a website he edits. Matt and I exchanged several emails after the interview.

TOBY was the youngest participant at 19. He had worked in a licensed store for about 12 months. I interviewed him in a café near the store where he worked for about an hour, and kept in touch with him by email afterwards.

Notes

1. While, as Coulmont and Hubbard (2010) note, there is considerable legal ambiguity in the definition of what actually constitutes a 'sex shop', allowing for 'the emergence of shops whose legal status remains unclear but which adhere to certain shared styles of management', the term is generally taken to refer to

   > Any premises, vehicle, vessel or stall used for a business that consists to a significant degree of selling, hiring, exchanging, lending, displaying or demonstrating sex articles or other things intended for the purpose of stimulating or encouraging sexual activity or acts of force or restraint which are associated with sexual activity. (*Local Government Miscellaneous Provisions Act*, 1982, Schedule 3, Paragraph 4, cited in Coulmont and Hubbard, 2010: 193)

2. See for a notable exception Loe's (1999: 705) study of co-workers or owners of the 'pro-sex feminist business' Toy Box in the United States.
3. An interesting example of the latter is provided by Godin's (2000: 1396) study of mental health nurses, which describes the chemical, administrative and legal techniques used to constrain patients who are perceived as a nuisance or as dangerous as 'the dirty work of coercive control'.

6
Doing Gender in Dirty Work: Exotic Dancers' Construction of Self-Enhancing Identities

Gina Grandy and Sharon Mavin

Introduction

Exotic dancing and other types of sex work (e.g. prostitution, pornography) hold a low position in the hierarchy of paid work (Price, 2008) and other social hierarchies. These occupations are viewed as dirty work (Hughes, 1958) – physically, morally and socially tainted. Individuals who work in these occupations must manage the stigma associated with the work and in turn the stigma associated with being 'dirty workers' (Ashforth and Kreiner, 1999). It has been argued that the construction and maintenance of positive, affirming identities in this context are complex and problematic (Grandy, 2008). Price (2008) notes that constituents of exotic dancing establishments (e.g. club owners, managers, disc jockeys, clients, bar workers, dancers) re-produce gendered stereotypes of dancers – wild, easy, untrustworthy, immature, unreliable, expendable and promiscuous. Exotic dancers also ' "reinforce the gender hierarchy (Acker, 1990) within the club by reasserting "appropriate" ways of "doing gender" (West and Zimmerman, 1987)' (Price, 2008: 381). Our position in this chapter is that exotic dancing is a form of dirty work and that exotic dancers 'do gender' within socially constructed sex and stigmatised hierarchies. Here we explore how exotic dancers present favourable self-identities when doing gender within dirty work.

Penttinen (2008) contends that exotic dancers are a forgotten group whose voices are assumed to be the same as those of other sex workers. Responding to Penttinen's (2008) call for more research specific to exotic dancers, we interviewed exotic dancers employed in a chain of UK gentlemen's clubs to explore how they engage in identity construction processes. Our research objectives included: (*a*) to explore the identity roles of women exotic dancers when doing gender, as they construct favourable self-identities within stigmatised work and within sex hierarchies and in doing so, (*b*) to surface heterogeneity within, and between, sex work(ers).

Our findings reveal that the exotic dancers engage in a number of self-enhancing identity roles to present favourable identities and position themselves differently from other exotic dancers and sex work(ers). In doing this, our contribution is two-fold. First, drawing on the identity roles constructed by the dancers, we offer a gendered hierarchy of Good and Bad Girls within stigmatised work, to further our understanding of women's self-identities. Second, we conceptualise the heterogeneity of exotic dancers doing gender in dirty work, to further our understanding of sex and gender in organisations. We begin by outlining the gendered hierarchy of sex work(ers) and their identity construction within dirty work. We present our case-study research approach, followed by a discussion of the identity roles which comprise a gendered hierarchy of Good and Bad Girls within stigmatised work.

Doing gender

For the purposes of this research we use a social constructionist approach to gender to explore how exotic dancers enact cultural notions of what it is to be a woman and adopt a view of gender as 'patterned, socially produced distinctions between female and male, feminine and masculine' (Acker, 1992: 250). We are interested in exploring how women are marginalised and the accepted practices and identities that must be enacted in order to 'fit into' boundaries of organisations. Our specific concern is what happens when sex work(ers) become the lens through which work and organisations are understood.

West and Zimmerman (1987: 126) contend that '"doing gender" involves a complex of socially guided perceptual and interactional and micro-political activities that cast particular pursuits as expressions of masculine and feminine natures'. Doing gender remains a 'situated social practice producing different outcomes in different social and cultural contexts' (Van den Brink and Stobbe, 2009: 453), while gendered performance in organisations remains pervasive and taken for granted (Ridgeway, 1997). That women exotic dancers 'do gender' is not contested and we start from a position that doing gender is a part of doing sex work. We contend that doing gender, however, is linked to various discourses which influence and direct how exotic dancers *choose* to do gender.

Discourses and gendered sex hierarchies of sex work(ers)

There are key discourses which illuminate the positioning of sex work(ers) in the organisational world (Brewis and Linstead, 2000). Hollway (1989) offers three discourses: the 'male sex drive' discourse, positing male sexual libido as uncontrollable and the prostitute's role as necessary but stigmatised to satisfy their sexual desires; the 'have–hold' discourse which emphasises the marital bond and patriarchal family, placing women who provided sex outside of marriage to be 'condemned' as morally tainted in public; and the 'permissive discourse', whereby the sexual freedom of both sexes is embraced and sexuality is not limited to heterosexuality or even penetrative intercourse. Rubin (1993) provides further discourses to explain the restrictive notion of sexuality accepted in society and in organisational life; the 'Victorian morality' discourse where prostitution, masturbation, images and literature, birth control information and public intimacy were subject to various social, medical and legal enforcement; the 'sex offender' discourse describing those partaking in violent, illegal, moral and physically tainted activities (e.g. child molester, rapist); and the 'child porn panic' discourse, which appeals to protect children through attempts to eradicate and repress particular notions of sexuality.

The capillary effects of these discursive junctures extend to various aspects of our lives, both private and public; they inform our attitudes about what constitutes acceptable and unacceptable sexuality, including what acts are normal, where 'it' is to be conducted and even with whom it is appropriate. In considering discourses of sex work, there remains a rigid sex hierarchy which underpins fixed notions of good sex – that which is private, non-commercial, monogamous, martial, reproductive and heterosexual (Brewis and Linstead, 2000; Rubin, 1993) and which leaves sex work(ers) subject to dualist notions of sex, sexuality and gender.

Rubin (1993) argues that the underlying criminality and moral taint of sex-oriented businesses keep them marginal, underdeveloped and distorted, similar to other sexual preferences that are deemed abnormal. Brewis and Linstead (2000) surface the place of sex work as both bad work and bad sex, arguing that some discourses within the sex hierarchy are more persuasive than others. Here we argue that sex work(ers) crosses both avenues of what constitutes abnormal or bad sexuality and illegitimate or bad work, leaving the women involved in sex work perceived as bad girls (Kong, 2006) in dirty work.

Kong (2006: 427) argues that 'within Rubin's (1993) sex hierarchy ... prostitution is regarded as bad, abnormal or unnatural, as it is promiscuous, non-procreative, casual and commercial'. In addition, this hierarchy is gendered, as the prostitute is marked by a female-gendered stigma (Pheterson, 1996), namely, 'the whore'. Pheterson (2009) describes the 'whore stigma' as women divided physically as well as ideologically into moms and whores, wherein mothers are not supposed to be sexually active and the whores (meaning any woman marked by her work, colour, class, sexual activity, age or history of abuse) are not supposed to bear children. This whore stigma is a female-gendered stigma, 'a mark of shame or disease on an unchaste female slave or criminal' (Pheterson, 1996: 65). Following the whore stigma, a sex worker is a 'bad' woman with a 'spoiled identity' (Goffman, 1963), while a customer is merely a naughty boy or a dirty old man with sleazy habits. In other words, 'she is bad for who she is and he is bad for what he does' (Pheterson, 1996: 48).

Within these discourses, it is acceptable for 'women to exchange sex for money (Salutin, 1971) as long as it is constrained to marriage and love (Safilios-Rothschild, 1977)' (Ronai and Ellis, 1989: 295). However, sex work reveals the rawness of this exchange, the unequal distribution of power and the often cold, calculating nature of the micro strategies. Here, 'sexuality is carried out in public between strangers'; 'dancers use sex as a direct currency of exchange: turn-ons for money' and there is no illusion of love (Ronai and Ellis, 1989: 296). Sex workers are therefore positioned in society as 'bad girls' who are unchaste (Kong, 2006). Within sexual politics, an important distinction is that between 'chaste' and 'unchaste' women; the prostitute is merely the prototype of the unchaste (and thus stigmatised) woman (Pheterson, 1996). The category 'unchaste', 'defined as indulging in unlawful or immoral sexual intercourse; lacking in purity, virginity, decency (of speech), restraint, and simplicity; defiled (i.e. polluted, corrupted)' (Pheterson, 1996: 65), has a disciplining effect on all women. To avoid or reject the 'whore stigma', women constantly have to convince others and themselves that they are chaste, decent, honourable and pure, and in the process their range of possible actions is constrained (Stenvoll, 2002).

Research involving sex workers often generalises 'prostitute' as representing all sex workers. For example, Sanders (2005), in her research into sex workers' strategies for capitalising on sexuality, moves through discussions using 'sex worker' as a category to contextualise her arguments, to 'prostitutes' as a category to highlight examples of the arguments and back to the category of 'sex worker', thus generalising prostitute as representative of sex workers. Penttinen's (2008) recent analysis of the sex industry which identified exotic dancers as a forgotten group of sex workers also uses 'prostitute' to categorise these dancers. However, there are differences between, and within, sex work(ers).

> Apart from the fact that a prostitute can take up different subject positions, prostitutes are stratified according to the status hierarchy in the industry (for example, call girls, escorts, massage parlour girls, brothel women, street prostitutes) as well as from within the hierarchy along the lines of ethnicity, age or physical appearance.
>
> (Kong, 2006: 429)

Our position is that not all women sex workers present themselves as prostitutes; not all exotic dancers are the same and not all sex work is alike (Weitzer, 2000). Differences exist across occupations within the sex industry and even within the same occupation across different organisations. For example, ' "many" (sex with more than one partner) and "money" (sex for money)' (Kong, 2006: 422) are defining features of a 'whore', and these defining features underpin a hierarchy of stigmatisation and status within the sex industry; 'i.e., the lowest status is the street prostitute (maybe too many men but too little money), followed by those who work in a one-woman brothel, then those who work in a massage parlour, karaoke bar or nightclub' (Kong, 2006: 422).

We accept that the sex worker epitomises the inseparability of bodily performance from the product being sold and that exotic dancers do gender as a given. Their performance, body work and presentation of sex and sexuality in a dirty work occupation provide a context to explore self-identity construction, surface identity roles and the heterogeneity between and within sex workers.

Identity construction, dirty work and exotic dancing

Sex and gender play a significant role in organisations in the production of identities (West and Austrin, 2002) and therefore sex work offers a unique opportunity to study the construction of favourable identities in an organisation where gender and sexual relations are prevalent. The concept of individualised identity is problematic and as Grandy (2008) argues, researchers challenge the notion of identity as fixed, stable and directly observable, offering a view that depicts identity as dynamic, multiple and contradictory (Kohonen, 2005; Thomas and Davies, 2005; Thomas and Linstead, 2002). For the purposes of this research our approach to identity is one which favours more situated, processual and pluralist views and emphasises social embeddedness, in that we are always in the process of becoming (Bryans and Mavin, 2003; Watson and Harris, 1999). From this view, identity is an ongoing achievement – an emergent, messy process of knowing oneself and others, retrospectively (Thomas and Davies, 2005; Watson and Harris, 1999). Identity is therefore emergent and mediated by the interactions between a person, their context and significant people around them, as we are 'continuously negotiating both co-operatively and in conflict with others to bring about "organization"' (Watson and Harris, 1999: 18). The dirty work of exotic dancers provides a unique context for the study of identity construction, as 'a person's identity within a particular context is continually the subject of the interaction between that which the person themselves wishes to be seen as, and that which significant others ascribe to the person' (Holmes, 2002: 8). As Grandy (2008: 177) argues,

> The position of exotic dancing as both sex work and dirty work, in a paid hierarchy is the ongoing result of various historical, social, cultural and political considerations – considerations which are likely to play a role in how an individual comes to understand and define herself (and other) as an exotic dancer.

As a form of dirty work (Hughes, 1958) exotic dancing is physically tainted (e.g. in contact with bodily fluids through dancers using the same stage and poles to do tricks without cleaning between sets), socially tainted (e.g. working with 'sleazy' men in dangerous areas of cities) and morally tainted (e.g. associated with bad sex, public sex, sex outside marriage, commercialisation of sex not associated with love). Occupational prestige as a composite of status, power, quality of work, education and income can depict the wide scope and variety of dirty work occupations (Ashforth and Kreiner, 1999). Therefore the position of a work sector in society as well as of the organisation itself can serve as resources of identity construction, along with the individual's choosing or struggling with various macro and meso resources she encounters as she comes to understand herself as an exotic dancer (Grandy, 2008). As a result of 'tainting', we begin with the assumption that exotic dancers manage 'spoiled identities' (Goffman, 1963), and argue that the construction and maintenance of positive, favourable identities in sex and dirty work (Hughes, 1958) occupations becomes even more problematic as individuals manage stigma attached to the work and in turn the stigma associated with them as sex (dirty) workers (Ashforth and Kreiner, 1999).

To draw together our discussions, sex work(ers) symbolise bad sex – that which occurs outside marriage and is public, promiscuous and not for reproductive purposes (Frank, 2002; Rubin, 1993). Within socially constructed hierarchies exotic dancing could be assumed to be low-status, gendered and dirty work in a low position in the sex hierarchy (Rubin, 1993). We view this social positioning of sex work(ers) as bad sex by bad girls as the context in which dancers construct self-identities. We also argue that there is a lack of heterogeneity considered in current studies of sex work(ers), and we see this as an opportunity to surface distinctions between, and within, sex work(ers) in the context of the whore stigma (Pheterson, 1996), dirty work (Hughes, 1958) and the sex-industry-status hierarchy (Kong, 2006).

Case study, methods and analysis

The research took place in a UK chain of clubs, *For Your Eyes Only* (*FYEO*), which is one of the first UK exotic dancing clubs to market itself as a gentleman's club with upscale entertainment and surroundings – 'classic entertainment for the modern gentleman' (*FYEO*, 2005). Self-employed dancers are contracted to *FYEO* under formal (e.g. hours of work, dress and drinking policies) as well as informal rules (e.g. rigid physical criteria) to which dancers must conform. We interpret these rules as *FYEO*'s efforts to manage the stigma of the industry and thus it serves as a fruitful site from which to explore how dancers who work in these clubs also manage their 'spoiled identities' (Goffman, 1963).

The research is drawn from a larger study which utilised a variety of secondary and primary data. This chapter focuses upon semi-structured interviews with dancers, where individuals were asked to talk about work to explore how identity, doing gender and differences between and within sex workers emerged through discussions. Questions enabled dancers to tell their stories in their own words (e.g. 'Tell me how you first became a dancer?', 'What happens on a typical night?' and 'How would you describe a typical dancer?'). Data and analysis were an iterative process (Mason, 2002; McCracken, 1988), with 21 dancers interviewed across a diverse range of experiences. Some dancers were interviewed only once (formal interviews) and others were interviewed on several occasions (formal and informal interviews). The dancers were aged between 19 and 31, with experience in exotic dancing from two months to six years. Their employment experience ranged from topless-only to fully nude to employment in *FYEO* only or employment in other clubs in the United Kingdom and abroad. We have used pseudonyms for all the dancers, who were interviewed during working hours (and before). The dressing-room setting for interviews was challenging due to interruptions and distractions (e.g. loud music, other conversations). The close proximity of the managers may have also imposed pressure for discretion or restricted dancers' willingness to be more open when responding to some questions. Analysis of the data took place through 'rummaging' (McCracken, 1988), reading and re-reading transcriptions to categorise content. Each interview transcript was analysed individually, using initial and focused coding, and text was sorted into broad themes. This was followed by a process of reinterpretation, focusing upon how individuals defined their work and themselves in particular ways. Finally, a process of constant comparison across themes and interview transcripts was performed.

Exotic dancers constructing positive identities: identity roles

Through our analysis we highlight how exotic dancers struggle to construct self-enhancing, favourable identities within a context of doing gender and against a number of socially constructed hierarchies: a sex-hierarchy (Rubin, 1993); the whore stigma (Pheterson, 1996); dirty work (Hughes, 1958); and a sex-industry-status hierarchy (Kong, 2006). In doing so our research reveals a number of interrelated identity roles, where exotic dancers are seen to construct positive identities and position themselves against these hierarchies. These identity roles are fluid, and individuals can enact multiple, overlapping and contradictory identity roles. To illuminate the various roles and how they emerge through the stories, we note each identity role in italics.

One contradiction we faced in our analysis is that we have acknowledged others use 'prostitute' as a term generalised to other sex workers. Further, we note that various degrees of social stigma are attached to this generalisation and that not all sex workers are prostitutes. However, we have consciously continued to draw upon this work while aiming to highlight the heterogeneity of sex work(ers).

Competing for 'freedom': the exploited, empowered and competitor identity roles

Through the stories expressed by the dancers a messy picture of contradictory motivations and emotions emerged. Most dancers indicated that their primary (but often not only) motivation for starting to dance was linked to the economic benefits they attributed to the job. In addition to the financial freedom they experienced, many of the dancers also talked about how they attributed their work to their increased confidence and sense of control as well as a greater comfort with their sexuality (*empowered*). In this way, dancing is a means through which an individual can feel empowered as a woman. This freedom is tied, however, to 'doing gender', as economic and social arrangements restrict individuality and choice. The result is feeling trapped in the industry, with few alternative opportunities that offer a comparable income (*exploited*). Moreover, achieving freedom is often a competition, where dancers compete for the finite resources of clients (*competitor*).

Freedom re-presents the opportunity to do and be otherwise, whether in a material sense, through increased earnings and additional leisure time or in an emotional or ideological sense, through developing a sense of control, self-determination or a different understanding of one's own being (*empowered*). Exotic dancing can be a means to a better lifestyle, where the money earned generates greater independence and control over one's life (*empowered*). Dancers working at *FYEO* are self-employed, which means they, at least in theory, choose the number of shifts they work, the nights they work and where they want to work (*empowered*). According to Maggie dancing provided a sense of control that other employment opportunities did not; however, she noted there were limits to this 'freedom'. 'We tell them when we want to work. It's not the other way around. So we're in charge – to a certain extent.'

The dancers also described how the work was preferable to the other employment options available to them and that they *chose* to work as dancers to afford themselves a better lifestyle (*empowered*). Nancy compared the work to that of a waitress and described how dancing (self-employment) provided more autonomy and control. At the same time, she also noted that dancers could come in and choose not to work (just sit around), but management would not approve of it (*exploited*).

When you're a waitress you're working for the company and a group of people are sat down, you've got to look after them for the whole night. You're running backwards and forwards with drinks, change, cigarettes everything. But if we're tired we can sit down, we can have a cigarette, we can drink or we can come in here for five minutes [dressing room] and just get away from the whole thing. [As a dancer, you] work only for yourself, so if you come into work and you feel I really can't be bothered tonight, you can make yourself a couple of pounds and then just sit down for the rest of the night. If you're sat around all night getting drunk they're [management] not going to like it.

Flexible working arrangements are attractive for those with other life commitments (*empowered*). Rona, for example, was completing a science degree and this meant she had little time to commit to the structure required in most jobs. 'I couldn't fit a normal job around it [university studies] so I did hostessing for a while, but I really didn't like that so I thought I might as well give dancing a try.' Dancing also serves as a means to achieve other life objectives (*empowered*). Sam indicated that dancing was used as a 'stepping stone' and as a 'a good way to earn money very quickly and you might set up your own business when you're finished or buy a property or something and you know pay your debts off' (*empowered*). Both Amy and Anna also described how dancing enabled them to travel, something they otherwise would not have been able to do (*empowered*). Dancers emphasised these aspects of the work to draw attention to the positive opportunities available to them by working as exotic dancers. In turn, this focus allowed dancers to minimise the stigmatised aspects of the work they performed and the stigma associated with their occupational identities.

Maggie illustrated how money was the main motivation for most dancers but that there were other empowering aspects of the work. Dancing made her feel confident and beautiful.

> I think money's the key reason although it makes you feel good when you go on stage and you can dance. I've danced all of my life so it comes naturally, you know when you get up and you go on stage. It's nice to dress up and come in, do your hair, do your nails and get your make-up on, nice yah.

Dancers also drew upon the exclusivity of *FYEO* as a gentlemen's club and the self-employed nature of the employment in constructing positive identities in this stigmatised occupation. While the increased income assured them the lifestyle they wanted (*empowered*), this self-employment and financial independence remained under the control of the club and management. Freedom is, in many respects, defined by the club. The house rules indicate the amount of house fees to be paid by dancers each evening and the payment procedure. The fees charged by clubs vary and some clubs can take up to one half of a dancer's earnings in an evening (*exploited*). Dancers' incomes are not uniform across workers, and there is no real mechanism in the system for dancers to challenge or contest the calculation of required house fees determined by the management (*exploited*). Sometimes dancers are unable to pay the fee at the end of the shift and the management allows them to pay it during the next shift – the only allowance given in the determination or payment of fees. The self-employed arrangements mean low labour costs for *FYEO*, but it also grants clubs the control and authority to impose a variety of rules upon the dancers (*exploited*). As a result, *FYEO* influences dancers' identity work within and even beyond organisational life.

The piecemeal nature of the work – that is, dancers get paid only when they secure dances or sit-downs from clients – creates an environment where dancers view others as competitors. This means that the freedom that dancers allude to, when they describe the positive aspects of the work, comes at a cost. They have to compete for their freedom. Dancers recognise the competitive nature of the work, but they try to distance themselves from those they view to be competitive 'bitches'. In this way, they can frame their own workplace identity more positively relative to the *competitor* (bad girls). In a discussion of how the organisation makes hiring decisions, Carrie commented that the organisation needs to do more than just have women demonstrate they can dance. She acknowledged the competitive nature of the work but distanced herself from other dancers who went too far. 'Any situation like this where there's this many girls together, in competition with each other is going to get bitchy. I'm talking about people who are absolutely lunatics.' Similarly, Lana commented that the job required them to be competitive, but those who were too competitive were 'bitches'.

When money becomes involved it's definitely competitive, whether people admit it or not. You have to [be competitive] to a certain extent. I mean you have to obviously be competitive without being a bitch. I think some girls might take it a little bit too far, they get really nasty [*competitor*].

Dancers also have to sort through the negative reactions they experience from clients and men in general, given an image of dancers as promiscuous and cheap and as objects of beauty, but without brains (*exploited*). Sam said that many customers felt dancers were different from the women they might have met on the street (*exploited*). Customers ask personal and intimate questions about dancers' personal lives. Sam's comments illustrate how dancers confront stigma from clients on a daily basis and that there are a variety of situations that a dancer has to learn how to 'manage' at work.

A lot of men think because you're doing this job they have a right to ask you things like 'do you do this for your boyfriend', 'how much money do you earn'? Personal questions that you wouldn't ask somebody else [*exploited*]. But again I expected that of a man anyway especially a man in a place like this. The typical man in here would be somebody that generally feels that girls in here aren't the sort of girls that they meet on the street, therefore they can push the line with them [*exploited*].

Emphasising temporality: the 'temp' and lifer identity roles

In constructing positive self-identities dancers used tenure in the profession to justify their work and set themselves apart from other dancers. Some dancers indicated that the strict physical requirements of the job limited their tenure in the industry, making it a temporary source of employment and in turn, they framed their short tenure as something more positive than working at the job for a long period of time. Others indicated that they saw dancing as a means to an end and not as a part of their 'real' careers. In this way, dancing was positioned as fun, less serious and less important than other 'real' career aspirations. Dancers who were dancing for a 'legitimate' reason (*temp*) were viewed more positively than those who chose to dance long-term (*lifer*).

Dancers working while finishing their studies (*temp*) constructed differences between dancers who danced full-time (full-time, permanent job; *lifer*) and those that were there temporarily (*temp*). It was acceptable only if it was for a short while and for a good reason (*temp*). Most student-dancers did express a desire to justify and draw comparisons in order to set themselves apart from other dancers. Others talked about how they intended to go back to school and that dancing was not a job for someone who wanted a 'future'. Lesley made a reference to becoming 'mature' as she considered her future in dancing.

I've just started saving. I've just started being mature I would say about my job. I want to get myself to college this year and think about the future because I've figured out like your boobs are not going to be this perfect forever you know. I mean I won't be able to swing off poles when I'm 50. So if I don't want to end up doing this job as a future [*temp*], I want to start concentrating on saving and thinking about my future.

Lesley implied that dancing was a temporary, less serious occupation with an expiration date (partly because of the physical requirements).

In this way, those who decide to stay long-term are marginalised relative to those who do it until they 'grow up' and find 'real' work. In a similar way, Alex stated that she was only dancing to support her professional dancing career (*temp, artist/e, professional*). Sheena started in the industry because she thought it would be exciting, but as a trained professional make-up artist (*artist/e, professional*), she too planned to dance only until something else that was more interesting came along (*temp*). In this way, Sheena, like Alex, did not focus upon the stigmatised nature of the job. They redirected attention to the positive aspects, thereby legitimising the dirty work in some way. Rationalising dirty work in this way neutralises or minimises the stigma attached, thereby allowing dancers to create a more favourable sense of self as an exotic dancer.

Unlike many dancers, Michelle expressed a longer-term interest in dancing (*lifer*) and acknowledged that other dancers would think this was not an acceptable path to follow. 'Most girls say "what are you thinking about?" when I say like eight years or ten years. I really do want to do it for like quite a long time.' In constructing and drawing upon the temporality of the dirty work as a means to rationalise their position in the sex-industry-status hierarchy, dancers constructed the Other – that is, lifetime dancers – the bad girls, viewed less favourably and with a lower status in the hierarchy to those dancing to meet a specific goal or for a specified period of time (*temp*). If it is a means to an end, then it is 'legitimate' work by good girls.

Acceptable levels of nudity and drinking at work: the good girl, artist/e, dirty dancer and professional identity roles

Dancers use the extent of nudity that they, or others, deem acceptable as a means through which to construct separate private and public selves and to separate themselves from others in the whore stigma, dirty work, sex and sex industry hierarchies. Some dancers also construct 'professional' standards (e.g. no drinking at work) that they expect themselves to follow and use as a comparison from which to evaluate their own behaviour and identities relative to other, less professional dancers.

Carrie had worked as a dancer in other UK establishments and in France. She described how she initially did not disclose her job details to her partner. When he did discover she was an exotic dancer, this became a source of conflict in their relationship. In managing this conflict she confirmed her sense of commitment, loyalty and fidelity to her relationship by emphasising that the dancing is topless-only (*good girl*). Therefore, her dancing did not threaten the stability of her relationship or invade her private life. The creation of these barriers allowed Carrie to manage the uncertainty involved in creating a coherent identity as an exotic dancer as well as the stigma enacted by others playing an influencing role.

> He was a bit angry at first and then after like probably about two days he was alright. He always asks me about it and stuff. But he's been here, he's had a look around. He knows it's just topless, he doesn't see anything that badly wrong with it now [*good girl*].

Carrie neutralised the moral taint (e.g. infidelity) associated with topless-only by denying impact. It was topless-only, therefore it did not jeopardise her identity as the faithful partner and *good girl*. Topless-only was re-presented as more skill-based by the dancers, who also constructed it as more professional. Fully nude by comparison got positioned as unprofessional, and the taint again shifted from topless-only to Other fully nude dancing and dancers. At the same time, neutralising the moral taint was not always easy or effective. Amy expressed that there was nothing 'wrong' with dancing, yet she appeared to struggle with competing *good girl* and *bad girl* identity roles and the consequences it had on her relationship and sense of trust with her partner. 'It makes it hard because you do to an extent feel like you're cheating, even though we're not doing anything wrong [*good girl*]. And also because we're doing this in here you wonder what they're doing outside because they think they can get away with more.'

Topless-only dancing also serves as a way for dancers to more easily align their work with creative and training-based professions (*artist/e, good girl, professional*). This creates public–private divides and also infuses their jobs with the same positive value attributed to other work recognised as skill-based, legitimate work (*artist/e, good girl, professional*). Frankie described herself as a dancer, that is a skilled dancer with extensive experience (*artist/e, good girl, professional*) in dancing beyond exotic dancing realms. She had danced topless elsewhere in Europe, prior to working at *FYEO*. She saw her time as an exotic dancer as a temporary decision (*temp*) to help pay off some bills. For her, dancing was positioned as a job requiring real physical competencies (*professional*) and skills in performing (*artist/e, good girl*). She also noted how topless-only, at least at *FYEO*, is fun but not sexual (*good girl*). By default, anything falling outside the realm of topless-only could indeed be considered sexual and cross the boundaries between that which is sexual and private and that which is public.

I've been a dancer, well I've danced all my life. All types of dancing I can do [*professional, artist/e*] ... just a few months here. But I've danced well abroad yah, but not in lap dancing clubs though, no, only table dancing clubs [*good girl*]. Stripping is more like showing [*artist/e*] *and* topless is more for fun, and music [*good girl*] and being sensual with the customer and stuff. That's it, nothing sexual though, not in here anyway [*good girl*].

The extent of nudity is also used as a criterion for determining the image of the club and its position in the sex-industry-status hierarchy. Some dancers emphasised the topless-only rule as an indicator of the upscale nature of the job and the club. 'The standard of dancers would drop', as Sam noted, if the club where she worked implemented fully nude dancing. In comparison to those who worked in fully nude establishments or who did fully nude dancing, the topless-only dancers positioned themselves more favourably and as less stigmatised (*good girl, professional*).

Finally, some dancers discussed how drinking while on the job was encouraged, but monitored by the club. Dancers were encouraged to drink so that clients would spend more at the club; however, dancers could be disciplined if they became too intoxicated. Lana described the need to act professionally at work, which was no different from the expectations associated with other jobs. To increase the legitimacy of the work she performed and her identity as a dancer, she stated that she did not drink at work. She viewed her work as a job, and in a job there is an expectation to view it seriously and act professionally.

It's all about self-control really [*professional*], isn't it? You've got to take a step back and take a look at yourself. You know at the end of the day it's a job, it's like any other job [*professional*], you've got to treat it like that. It's not a night out and I know you can sit down and have a laugh but at the same time you've got to realize there's no point ruining the rest of your life just for a few hours. It's not worth it, depends on how you look at the job really.

Doing gender

Dancers are expected to conform to certain gendered scripts in order to be successful at their jobs. Similar to other service-based occupations, dancers are expected to be interpersonal, adaptable, act professionally and adhere to a certain 'feminine' aesthetic (make-up, dress, body). All of these 'skills' are integral to the labour required for the job and are tied to more embedded social codes of 'being a woman'. The work requires dancers to act out certain gendered scripts, that is behavioural and physical expectations, constructed through social, economic and political arrangements, of being a 'woman'. 'Bodily appearance and demeanour is moulded to send out certain signals about capabilities' (Brewis, 1999: 92) and for exotic dancers this is moulded to personify doing gender – exuding sexuality, desire, sex and femininity within established gender scripts.

Anna described how she learned (as a woman) what appealed to most clients (men) and how she used this knowledge to increase her earnings (*exploited, empowered*), illustrating how she was able to distance herself and 'act out' particular feelings and roles to service the desires of clients. Anna had a routine that most clients liked and performed the same routine over and over; it required little physical or mental effort. She knew the specific facial and body movements (of women) that are required to produce the desired response in clients (men). She indicated how she could deliver this without having to engage emotionally with the tasks or with the clients, separating herself from the dirty work.

> I think it's taught me a lot more about men. Like I can, I wouldn't say manipulate them but I know how they think a lot more now [*empowered*]. Well, here it sort of teaches you, you have to be smart [*professional, artist/e*] to get a dance out of a guy. So it teaches you to think what to say to them, what appeals to them what doesn't appeal to them [*professional, artist/e*]. I've kind of picked up on different things that most guys seem to like. For every dance now, I can do it with my eyes shut, I have a routine that works [*professional, artist/e*].

It is also important to note that within gender scripts, the clubs regulate what is acceptable and appropriate. House rules provide 'guidance' on appropriate topics of conversation and behaviour to ensure an 'authentic' performance and successful transaction (*exploited*).

Physical appearance is also integral to the transformation involved in dancers' identity work. A further expectation of dancers' performance is body movement. Most dancers indicated that one of the key elements in selection decisions was how a dancer moved (*artist/e, professional*). The *Pole and Tableside Dancing School Manual* (FYEO, 2004) lists FYEO's tableside dancing's basic moves. Five categories of moves, including Breast Teasers (e.g. breast caress, nipple squeeze), Head Turners (e.g. head roll, neck exposer), Pelvic Pleasures (e.g. pelvic grind, pelvic rub),

Bump and Grind (e.g. bump, cheek slap) and Body Stroke (e.g. thigh rub, hair caress) are presented to new dancers. The technical elements (e.g. particular movements), practicalities (e.g. fill your three minutes) and illusion (e.g. make the client wonder by removing your clothes slowly) are ways to ensure a successful performance (*artist/e, professional*) without the client thinking you are simply acting out or working to a formula. In many ways, these expectations are underpinned by an assumption that heterosexual desire is uniform, at least in this context. Dancers contend clients have different interests, yet the expectations of movement noted here portray a very narrow depiction of heterosexual desire.

It can be argued that *FYEO*'s expectation that dancers will conform to gendered cultural expectations in terms of dress, body and performance is no different from that of organisations in general. Indeed, 'Kerfoot (1999), proposes, there is a tendency within organizations to view the competency of a manager in his or her ability to display the body in a manner that is culturally acceptable to their organization's bodily code in terms of dress and physical appearance' (Haynes, 2008: 335). Women's bodies are not consumed only in sex work. Women educators, for example, also face similar challenges. As Perriton (1999: 296) suggests, 'Women educators are a semiotic item that is "purchased" and "consumed" … in particular it is woman as mother, as carer and nurturer that is being consumed.' Gallop (1997: 57), on the other hand, refuses the idea of teachers as motherly and argues 'teaching and sexuality are entangled and the relationship between teacher and student is a consensual amorous relation'. This means that the teaching space is sexualised and eroticised and the woman teacher, like the exotic dancer, we the authors would argue, is the star of her own personal show (McWilliams and Jones, 1996).

The good and bad girls doing gender in dirty work

Positive identity construction in the context of exotic dancing as dirty work is complex. The dancers' struggles to construct favourable identities take place within complex gendered, sex and sex-industry status hierarchies. Within this study, exotic dancers' efforts to establish positive identities within stigmatised work have been re-presented as interrelated, often simultaneous and often contradictory identity roles. Table 6.1 summarises the identity roles, highlighting the *exploited* as the basis of others and recognising patriarchal power relations and the prevailing sexist order. Moreover, the very premise

Table 6.1 Identity roles of good girls and bad girls in dirty work

Good girls in Dirty Work

The empowered	The 'Temp'	The good girl	The professional	The artist/e	The Exploited
She is confident about herself. Makes own choices & controls own destiny. Sense of control, self-determination, self-discovery & heightened sense of power. Increased earnings, leisure time, qualifications & better lifestyle.	She is 'temporary' to fund studies, to travel, to pay debts or to start own business. Not a 'proper' exotic dancer. A means to another legitimate end.	She is guided by strong morals & values based upon respect for others & herself. Fidelity in 'outside' relationships, which are untarnished. Links self to legitimate work. Interrelated with artist/e, professional; displays physical & skill competencies. Recognises & celebrates physical beauty – dancing is 'public' fun, not sexual.	She has specific qualifications, training & competencies to engage in formalised activities. Behaviours guided by rationality & logic required for legitimate, paid employment. Interrelated with Artist/e & Good Girl to highlight sameness of exotic dancing & other forms of work.	She develops & uses creative & artistic skills, emotional intelligence & physical displays to professionally engage & entertain others in performances. Interrelated with Professional & Good Girl.	She faces unfair & unjust treatment by others in, & out of, employment. Gendered, oppressed, degraded, shown no respect, with limited career opportunities.

Bad girls *in Dirty Work*

The lifer: The other	The dirty dancer: The other	The competitive: The other
She works full-time or with a long-term commitment to dancing & with no definite plans to leave the industry – a 'proper exotic dancer'. Dancing is a potential career, not a means to an end. An 'other' that allows dancers to position themselves differently & justify their work as acceptable when it is temporary in nature to fulfil a particular legitimate objective or aspiration.	She engages in activities beyond the acceptable boundaries of exotic dancer behaviour. Activities can be seen as illegal, immoral or unprofessional. An 'other' who engages in inappropriate 'dirty' conduct at work (e.g. touching, fully nude, extra services), affiliated with clubs condoning such behaviour & other lower-status forms of sex work.	She views work as first and foremost about generating income and adopts a 'win-at-all-cost' attitude to do this (e.g. moving in on another dancer's regular customer). Success is defined by the individual's ability to demonstrate or establish superiority over others engaged in similar activities. She is viewed by others as untrustworthy or non-supportive and goes too far to secure dances from other dancers.

of dancing/gentlemen's clubs is gendered from the start, providing adult entertainment for men seeking women's performances (Price, 2008). The identity roles of the *empowered,* the *temp,* the *good girl,* the *professional* and the *artist/e* are self-enhancing, favourable identities constructed by exotic dancers as they position themselves differently to Other exotic dancers, Other sex workers and Other sex work.

We have labelled these identity roles that of the *good girls in dirty work,* as the dancers distance themselves from the stigma attached to their work and re-position themselves favourably in the sex and sex work(er) hierarchies. These identity roles align with acceptable notions of morality, fidelity and loyalty, while still providing space for 'appropriate' sexual displays, relative to other types of dancing (fully nude, contact) and sex work (prostitution). The *bad girls in dirty work* (the *dirty dancer,* the *competitor,* the *lifer*) are constructed as a comparative point to the *good girl* identity roles. They serve as an inferior Other, that is more clearly stigmatised in the gendered hierarchy they construct. Constructing positive self-identities is not always easy and separating themselves from the bad girls is often complex. As Amy indicated,

> It makes it hard because you do to an extent feel like you're cheating [*bad girl*], even though we're not doing anything wrong [*good girl*]. And also because we're doing this in here [*bad girl*] you wonder what they're doing outside because they think they can get away with more.

Similar to the dancers that Kong's (2006) research discussed, these exotic dancers' 'moral standards conform very much to those of the existing patriarchal and sexist order. They do not seem inclined to explicitly challenge male domination, heterosexual supremacy and sexual normalcy. They are not sexual slaves, nor are they sex radicals' (Kong, 2006: 423). The *FYEO* exotic dancers, when accommodating the whore stigma, do so through distancing and balancing freedom and oppression between a stigmatised working persona (the whore) and a public self of 'good girl' – partner, student, traveller, professional dancer, artist/e. This chapter extends Kong's (2006) research where the dancers accommodated 'through closeting, and manoeuvre between a stigmatised working persona (the whore) and a public self of good woman/wife/mother'. *FYEO* exotic dancers accept the whore stigma by performing for and accommodating male sexuality, while at the same time they reject it in their construction of self and identity positioning. In their Othering of other exotic dancers and Other sex workers, exotic

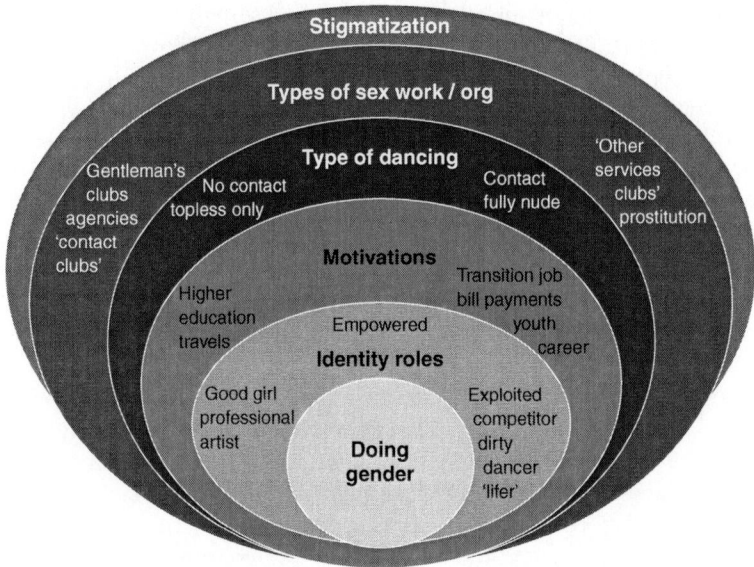

Figure within concentric ovals, from outermost to innermost:

Stigmatization

Types of sex work / org

Type of dancing

Gentleman's clubs agencies 'contact clubs' — No contact topless only — Contact fully nude — 'Other services clubs' prostitution

Motivations

Higher education travels — Empowered — Transition job bill payments youth career

Identity roles

Good girl professional artist — Exploited competitor dirty dancer 'lifer'

Doing gender

Figure 6.1   The heterogeneity of exotic dancers doing gender in dirty work

dancers reject the whore stigma and challenge the sex-industry-status hierarchy.

As a result, we the authors have been able to surface heterogeneity of sex workers doing gender. Through our analysis we have surfaced diverse pictures of exotic dancers as they do gender in dirty work. The dancers in this study recognised the stigma and taint associated with their work but did not see themselves as prostitutes, did not see themselves as bad girls and used various identity roles and strategies to distance themselves from Other sex workers and the varying degrees of taint associated with sex work(ers) hierarchies. In doing so different types of sex work have been surfaced, including perceived significant differences between topless-only and nude dancing and different types of clubs (good and bad), as well as the different motivations of dancers, used to highlight the heterogeneity of exotic dancers as they do gender. In Figure 6.1 we offer a pictorial representation of this heterogeneity to further understandings of sex and gender in organisations.

Conclusion

In our research we have acknowledged the positioning of sex work(ers) as bad sex, involving bad girls within a sex hierarchy (Rubin, 1993), the whore stigma (Pheterson, 1996), dirty work (Hughes, 1958) and sex-industry-status hierarchy (Kong, 2006). We have surfaced views of the *good girls* in dirty work and illustrated distinctions between, and within, sex work(ers). We have offered a gendered hierarchy of *good* and *bad girls* within stigmatised work and conceptualised the heterogeneity of exotic dancers doing gender in dirty work, to further understandings of women's identities, sex and gender in organisations.

Our research opens several avenues for future research. First, we recommend that future research conduct a comparative study across sex workers to further illuminate the heterogeneity of sex work(ers) and evaluate the transferability of the identity roles surfaced here. Second, comparative work across gendered dirty work occupations would also be fruitful in further developing identity-enhancing strategies across occupational categories. For example, exploring how women employed in jobs with low occupational prestige (e.g. exotic dancers, cleaners, hair dressers) and high occupational prestige (e.g. nurses, lawyers, teachers) do gender and construct enhancing identities in similar and different ways will illuminate the boundaries and opportunities for women in dirty work. Finally, we believe an investigation into how men and women do gender and identity in similar dirty work occupations (e.g. exotic dancing, nursing, construction) would reveal unique insights and further unravel the heterogeneity of doing gender.

7
Dirty Talks and Gender Cleanliness: An Account of Identity Management Practices in Phone Sex Work

Giulia Selmi

Introduction

The aim of this chapter is to explore, in the context of Italy, the ways in which identity is managed by phone sex operators. Unlike other kinds of sex workers or 'dirty workers' in general who deal with embodied tasks, phone sex operators have no physical contact with clients and face a moral rather than physical taint (Ashforth and Kreiner, 1999). Moral taint relates to work that is seen as sinful or of a dubious virtue in respect to the moral order of a given society (Drew et al., 2007). The term dirtiness therefore goes beyond physicality to define what any society symbolises as a transgression or a contradiction of its ordered relations (Dick, 2005; Douglas, 1966). As Douglas (1966) has pointed out, in all societies the concept of dirtiness counters cleanliness on a moral level: while people tend to associate cleanliness with 'goodness', dirtiness is largely associated with 'badness'.

This meaning attribution process does not affect only dirty activities or occupations, but also stigmatises the people who undertake them through the negative qualities associated with dirt (Ashforth and Kreiner, 1999). As several scholars have demonstrated in different occupational contexts (Bolton, 2005; Dick, 2005; Drew et al., 2007; Stacey 2005), individuals framed as dirty by their own society because of their work have to engage in a process of identity management in order to find strategies to *clean* themselves from the stigma and reframe both their identity and their work in positive, or at least socially acceptable, terms. In the case of phone sex, this process is extremely gender-specific, or, in other words, phone sex workers have to cope with a specific *gender dirtiness* in order to manage their subjectivity in relation to their kind of work.

The chapter is organised as follows: in the first section I present a frame to read the relationship between sex work and gender dirtiness; after explaining the context and the methodology of my research, I analyse women phone sex operators' accounts of their profession, illustrating not only how they cope with its specific gender dirtiness, but also highlighting their ability to negotiate between 'dirty talking', the different meanings they attach to the work and their sense of self both professionally and as women. Firstly, I illustrate the narratives through which they respond to the symbolic conception of commercial sex as a form of deviance or immorality of women and how they recast it in socially acceptable terms. Secondly, I illustrate the narratives through which they avoid being framed as *bad girls* not only in connection to their work, but also in relation to their private (sexual) lives and identities.

Sex work, dirty work and gender dirtiness

Phone sex, as well as every other form of sex work, is a gendered activity (Overall, 1992), in both material and symbolic terms. Even if women are beginning to enter the sex industry as customers (Kempadoo, 1999), the selling of sexual services is still mainly performed by women to men. Further, the commodification of sexuality has been historically and symbolically linked to women's 'nature' and thought to be a form of 'moral pathology' of the supposedly natural female identity of wife and mother (Bell, 1994; Canosa and Colonnello, 1989; Nead, 1988). The link between prostitution and female perversity is deeply rooted in Christian morals which consider monogamous emotional relationships as the only possibility through which women can experience their sexuality. The selling of sex represents an infringement of the moral (and gender) order based on marriage. This moral (gender) order is seen to concern only women, as men's sexuality or social status is largely unaffected by their position in the sex industry as customers. In fact, as Simmel (2004) points out, it is only women that reach 'the nadir of human dignity' in a commercial sexual intercourse by giving away 'their most intimate and most personal quality' (p. 377). By contrast, men are not judged by the fact of their buying sex – either in terms of integrity or in terms of their subjectivity – because 'the purely sexual act that is an issue in prostitution employs only a minimum of man's ego, but a maximum of the woman's' (p. 378). The moral condemnation of the sex industry is not related to the activity itself (for in this case, it would concern both women and men), rather it is related to what this activity implies in terms of gender.

Although considered by everyone as 'the world's oldest profession', the work aspect in sexual commercial exchanges has always been undervalued. Simmel's quote underlines, in fact, another crucial issue related to the peculiar gender dirtiness of sex work: the problem of identity. What is pertinent in a commercial sex exchange is not just the real activity itself (what one does), but the identity of the people doing this activity (what one is). Like other jobs considered part of one's life, practiced in a specific time and place for specific purposes such as earning money, sex work labels inerasably those people who perform it. Within this framework, sexuality becomes the place where the female 'true and inner self' is founded and therefore the selling of sex becomes the selling of one's own identity, dignity and integrity.

Radical feminist thought on prostitution enforces this argument, albeit for different reasons[1] (Barry, 1995; Hoigard and Finstad, 1992; Jeffreys 1997). According to radical feminist thought, commercialising sexuality causes the loss of women's subjectivity, because any form of prostitution implies their subordination to male wishes and power: 'it permanently, completely and literally extinguishes her as a subject' (O'Connel Davidson, 2002: 92). From this point of view, then, no woman can sell sex as work – and therefore be a sex worker – without automatically becoming a sex object (Barry, 1995).

This social narrative about sex work together with the complicated interactions between a female's identity and sexuality has been eloquently defined by the Dutch scholar Gail Pheterson as 'the whore stigma': 'a mark of shame or disease on an unchaste female slave or criminal' (Pheterson, 1996: 65), leaving women sex workers out of the acceptable idea of femininity. This stigma, in fact, separates the women into 'good girls', that is wives and mothers, and 'bad girls', that is the sex workers – taking into account the private and public use of their sexuality. Moreover, this stigma has a wider social meaning that, going beyond the narrow realm of the profession, disciplines every woman's sexual behaviour, whether they work in the sex industry or not. The risk of being considered a 'whore' is not run exclusively by those who sell sexual services for money, but is a social archetype that disciplines the sexuality of all women in terms of their sexual reputation and honour (Pheterson, 1996). For instance, being sexually available out of marriage or wearing sexy clothes are social behaviours that can make a woman fall into the *bad girl* category.

In this sense, in the sex industry the process of reframing (both the work and identity) has to cope with a specific gender dirtiness that is twofold: firstly, workers need to account for their work 'as proper work' by responding to the symbolic conception of commercial sex as a form of deviance or immorality of women and to frame it in socially accept-able terms; secondly, they need to constantly reframe their identity in positive terms in relation to gender models to avoid the risk of falling into the *bad girl* category not only as workers, but also as women in their private (sexual) lives.

Research setting and methodology

Phone sex is a type of virtual sex work (Velena, 2003) that refers to sexu-ally explicit conversations between two persons via telephone, where at least one of the participants masturbates or engages in sexual fantasies. However, customers of these services may call not only to have a sexual conversation, but also to fulfil some other need such as for nurturing, sympathy or other forms of emotional intimacy. In other words some clients call this kind of service to buy sex over the phone, while some others pay to find a sort of 'virtual girlfriend'.

Commercial phone sex services offer this sexual or emotional experi-ence over the phone through premium-rate calls during which certain services are provided and for which higher-than-normal prices are charged. Unlike a normal call, part of the premium-rate call charge is paid to the service provider, thus supplying businesses with their revenue. Sex workers do not have any economic transactions with cus-tomers but receive a salary from the phone sex company in proportion to the length of the call. However, from the Italian legal standpoint, rules on premium-rate services state that calls must end after three to five minutes (depending on the phone company) and in any case when the maximum cost has been reached. Therefore, 'minutes' play a crucial role in work organisation, both in terms of operators' income and in terms of operators' working performances. Operators seek to make the calls last as long as possible and, above all, to encourage the clients to redial after the call ends as a result of law restrictions.

Since phone sex workers have no contact with the client in either physical or monetary terms, the sexual services they sell are not legally considered forms of sex work. While they are part of the sex industry in that they inhabit the same symbolic universe, they occupy a 'border area'. Firstly, there is no selling of a 'real' body (Bell, 1994): sex is sold, but through technology and voice, without any corporeal involvement with the customer. Secondly, from a legal point of view, while in Italy phone sex work is the only part of the sex industry that is legally recognised (e.g. workers have a labour contract), women working in this sector are framed in the same symbolic imaginary and they have to cope with the same stigma as any other sex worker. In this respect, they must manage the complex relation between the *dirty* talk through which they perform their work and the need to preserve a *clean* identity outside the phone call.

The accounts presented in this chapter originate in fieldwork I carried out in two erotic call centres in Italy: one small-sized and home-based and the other medium-sized and office-based, from now on referred to respectively as 'Kappa' and 'Lambda'. Three women aged 25–45 worked in the centre called Kappa, from 8 am to 12 pm with three shifts of five or six hours each, while centre Lambda had ten employees (eight women and two men) aged 20–55, working from 8 am to 12 pm on working days and 24 hours a day during the weekend. I used a case study research strategy (Eisenhardt, 1989; Stake, 1994) which included qualitative data collection techniques and analysis. Data collection involved participant observation and interviews. Observation took the form of following the workers in their shifts of work and audio-recording their performances with the customers. Alongside the observation, I conducted several interviews in the field (Spradley, 1979) to seek further information on issues that had emerged but remained implicit during the observation.

Dirty talks and clean identities

As previously stated, phone operators must attempt to satisfy clients' desires and expectations in order to make the call last as long as possible and earn maximum revenue from each conversation. In the interactional space made possible by the telephone, operators act out sexual and gender identities to match clients' requests: Lolitas and femme fatales, dominators and slaves, Angels of the Hearth or good girlfriends and so on. What meaning do the operators give to these interactions? How do they position themselves outside of the phone calls? In the following paragraphs, I highlight how operators negotiate (and sometimes contest) the narrations they activate for the clients, by inscribing their activity in a framework different from the one within the call and by renegotiating their own position towards the clients.

The operators (the not erotic ones) and the social workers

Operators identify their callers as *clients* or *customers*, depending on the nature of the conversation requested. Clients are those men who call for an erotic and sexual conversation aimed at sexual arousal. These men usually call sporadically. They do not form a relationship with the operators and they never ask for the same operator twice. Customers are those men who call regularly. They do not necessarily seek a sexual encounter over the phone, but an emotional relationship,[2] forming bonds with the operators they talk to. These two categories are useful to define clients and can help explore the different meaning operators attribute to their work. In this respect, they not only define the interaction's modality but also the two different symbolical universes to which those interactions belong.

The term *client*, for instance, highlights the commercial aspect of the interaction and gives operators the possibility to consider the work, especially in the case of occasional erotic phone calls, as any other service encounter. In fact, while talking about their work, operators often compared themselves to other call centre operators:

> We are not that different from the Wind,[3] I mean, he pays and we supply him service. There you want a promotion, here a blow job, it is not that different, is it? They pay and they have to receive what they paid for.
>
> (Lara, Kappa Centre)

Lara focused on the economic aspect of this work, marginalising the sexual aspect. She saw no difference between offering a commercial promotion and oral sex, and the peculiarity of the work lay in the commercial typology of interaction between the client and the operator rather than in the content of the conversation. From this point of view, an erotic operator is no different from a phone company's operator, for what defines each work is not its content, but its modality and structure: a client calls a number, asks for a service, pays to get it; the operator who is supplying the service is also paid. The idea that the 'client is always right' allows the operator to see the work as a commercial exchange where the client has expectations that are to be satisfied by the seller.

Therefore, while sex plays a key role during the performance with the client, it disappears from the operator's narration which focuses instead on the commercial aspects of the exchange:

This is a service, it's a work as any other work, where you give people the information they want. The only difference is that in our case the information you are asked is about sex, but there is not such a difference, look, when I do this work I think like I am offering a service to someone who pays me, the fact that this is about sex it is their problem [the clients'] not mine.

(Susanna, Lambda Centre)

Susanna constructed the sexual nature of her work as secondary and located it within the clients' domain. For operators, the defining feature of the work is its transactional nature in the form of earnings, divorcing it from more personal considerations. Locating the work within the broader arena of services helps operators position themselves within the collective imagination of 'clean' work. Even if phone sex operators experience less stigmatisation than other sex workers – at least because of the absence of physical contact – the commercialisation of sexuality might easily transform them into *whores*, implying a judgement over their whole life.

The only people I tell about my job are my friends. For everyone else, I just work in a call centre. And it is not like this is a good job: one is paid €400 a month, what work! People here are narrow minded, they do not understand you are a phone call operator, they think you are a whore instead than thinking you have an expertise and you do your job.

(Lara, Kappa Centre)

I try to figure what people who do not know anything about this work and happen to watch the advertising in television might think about it – who you are and what you do, I mean, concerning sex. But the point is giving someone a service, we are 899 operators and we give this service, and whatever it is said during our exchange – what you would do to somebody and somebody would do to you; all this might sound wrong, but it's a service one is paying to receive, and we are paid to provide.

(Elisa, Lambda Centre)

Insisting that phone sex work is a legitimate service – *we are not whores, we are 899 operators* – saves operators from being identified with their (sexualised) performance during the phone call as well as with the image spread by the advertising, a process particularly pertinent in dealings with *clients* who seek sexual arousal. Interactions with *customers,* who are seeking an emotional relationship, can easily translate into a 'social worker' caring role, drawing on listening skills and the ability to provide comfort and support.

> Can you imagine? When I got started with this job, the money I was earning was meant to pay for my study as social worker after my graduation. My mum used to say to me, 'you have even studied, why can't you find a job related to your expertise?' As any other mum she was worried, but eventually, I did find a job related to my field [laughs], because . . . tell me, what else I am for Luigi – poor thing! – if not a social worker?
>
> (Sara, Kappa Centre)

> You see, with those usual clients is different. It's about listening, because they might not have that much people to talk to; or it's about telling them some sweet words which maybe for them is kind of a miracle, right? I mean, someone calling here because he is looking for a girlfriend doesn't feel fine, and our work is to give him some relief.
>
> (Loredana, Lambda Centre)

> Well, we help them, we listen to them, we give them the life they would like to live, we give them a bit of happiness, poor things, this is what you do when you talk with a customer.
>
> (Lara, Kappa Centre)

In the operators' narration, the ability to provide support and to perform 'care' is presented as one aspect of their professional expertise. Offering the clients 'the life they would like to live' transforms the operators into benefactresses dispensing happiness to those men unable to find it outside of the phone interaction. From this perspective, the work has little to do with sexuality but instead is presented as emotion work, where they have to take charge of the problems of people who 'are not fine'.

Being able to listen, empathise and give comfort to the person on the other side of the phone are considered abilities similar to the ones that a therapist has to make use of with his patient:

> Because at the end one thinks, let's say you think, that maybe this is a work where you just have to say some dirty words and that's it. Which is also true, of course, but you also have to get into other people's minds, you have to be a bit of a therapist because there

are people who tell you stuff that OH MY GOD!, and there are lonely people, without a wife nor friends, and then they call the 899 and on the other side of the phone, there you are .... So, yeah, it's also this, it's a work of psychology with people, a job? How are they called again? A socially useful job.

(Lisa, Lambda Centre)

In this case, discourses around psychology – the ability *to get into other people's minds* – replace those that relate to sexuality. Operators refuse the identity on offer (the work is more than just saying *some dirty words*) and instead present an image of their work as socially significant and as one which requires relational and emotional competence.

'Half males', ordinary women

As we have seen, operators redefine their work by focusing on the service and emotional elements. In addition, operators find both themselves and their clients a new space within the sphere of sexual and gender relationships. While in the course of the interaction, the client's masculinity has to be confirmed as part of satisfying his requests, outside of that context that same masculinity is often denied, and the client is positioned, for different reasons, as a 'half male':

C'mon people calling here are not male, I mean ... does it seem normal to you someone calling here to have sex? They're all perverts. I mean, on one side it's good because we make money and if they weren't here we would not have our work, but at the same time it makes it clear how many people have problems, and maybe they even have a wife or children but then they spend all their money on those things.

(Lara, Kappa Centre)

According to Lara, men calling up phone sex operators were not men (rather perverts). In fact, a 'real' man would never need to call those services to have sex. Male callers also challenge ideas of family-centred masculinity, with associated meanings of honesty, integrity and reliability. Notions of 'normal' sex underpin descriptions of client requirements and further support notions of male deficiency:

Through this work you soon realize how the most of the men are not men, they all want to take it in their ass, 99 per cent of them want to have something in their ass, I am realizing a lot of things, there

is a lot of bad shit out there, people suck...because by phone they
tell you what they want, but then maybe they are wandering with
their wife or their friend...and as soon as they see a gay man, they
criticize him while they are the real assholes. And this is not cool.

(Loredana, Lambda Centre)

Men accordingly are seen by operators to violate norms of 'appropriateness' with regards to male sexuality in the sense that their demands do
not match operators' cultural expectations of what a 'real' man should
desire. Operators also express disapproval regarding the double moral
standards displayed as men practice deceit with family and friends –
only able to share their desires (which they may critique in others) with
the phone operator. Clients are then 'half male', not just because their
sexual desires may be different but also because they practise deceit.
A moral distance is thus created between operators and their clients.

The connection between clients' desires and the idea of perversion
and non-masculinity is particularly evident in the case of sadomasochistic (S/M) requests. Here, clients require a reversal of traditional gender
roles, whereby male clients assume the submissive, subservient position:

I do not like it, I think is something out of the grace of God, this
thing of being insulted, I don't like it, even when they ask you to be
a slave, but I have to do that 'cause I'm working...But these men are
sick, they are mentally ill. I mean, do you think they are men? Is it a
man someone who call to do these kind of things? I mean, a man is a
man. A man is not someone that likes to be ordered to lie down and
lick the floor to get to come hard.

(Sara, Kappa Centre)

According to Sara, those who needed to be dominated were mentally
ill and they could not be considered as 'real men', because a 'real
man' would not need to abdicate his power within a sexual relationship to achieve arousal. Defining the customer as someone who is 'sick'
allows the operator to position herself in relation to her own sexuality,
by creating a dichotomy between 'sane' and 'healthy' sexual practices and 'insane' and 'unhealthy' ones. Defining clients as 'half males'
also enables operators to position themselves as normal and 'ordinary'
women. Indeed, locating these interactions and performances within
the context of work helps prevent the risk of any 'contamination' of
their non-work lives:

I mean, I do these things here, maybe I perform the mistress and I tell them the things they want to hear or I tell them that I like the absurd things that please them, but it's because I'm working, while they're not. Out there I am a normal woman, I am a real woman and I have real sex like normal people have, right? It seems that we are the weird ones because we work in such a place, but they are the ones having problems, it's not us!

(Lisa, Lambda Centre)

Therefore, while over the phone, which has its own rules, operators activate some specific cultural and symbolic universes of sexuality and gender, away from it they position themselves as 'ordinary women' in contrast to their 'not-normal' partners. While a customer's identity is strictly defined by their S/M sexuality or the passion for some fetishism (since operators believe that clients' requests express their 'true' desires and identity), this is not the case for the operators who locate their 'true' (sexual) self outside the frame of the call. The ongoing positioning of clients as deviant in comparison with sexual and gender norms, therefore, is useful for the operators in order to create distance from this label. As in the previous cases, the frame of work is continually invoked as guardian of this process:

They call here and they think they can ask you to make them anything because you're working, right? Maybe they also feel they can treat you bad ... I mean do they realize they are the ones who are calling this kind of services? I always wonder if they get they are so loser they need to pay to have sex over here ... and maybe they do it over the phone because they're ugly like death, right? I do not need to pay anybody, I go out on Saturday night and if I find someone I like ... that's it, I don't have to pay. So I'm normal, they aren't.

(Susanna, Lambda Centre)

The frame of work where the interaction is performed redefines the relationship between worker and client and establishes the positioning of both. Customers, in fact, are the *losers* who have to pay to have a sexual interaction, while the operators are the 'ordinary women' who do not need that form of transaction.

Despite the saying 'the customer is always right' and the operators' commitment to confirm and comply with every client's desire, the very fact of paying for sex (especially phone sex, which operators paradoxically consider something weirder than other forms of commercial sex) places the clients in the 'bad' dimension of this symbolic dichotomy and makes the operators 'good girls', despite the nature of their work. Moreover, by emphasising the working frame in which the interactions take place, the operators reinforce the good/bad dichotomy in their favour: in their understanding, customers are 'dirty' exactly because they call and pay for these kinds of services, where they reveal their 'true' sexual selves or perversions. Operators, by contrast, while 'talking dirty', do so in a work context that is removed from their non-work gender and sexual identity.

Conclusion

In this chapter I have analysed how women manage the specifically gendered 'taint' of phone sex work, the different meanings they attach to their work and the processes of identity-making as workers and as women. Firstly, I have illustrated how women respond to the symbolic conception of commercial sex as a form of female deviance or immorality by recasting it in socially acceptable terms, that is as ordinary service work and as a form of social work. Secondly, I have illustrated how through their narratives, they avoid being framed as *bad girls* not just in connection to the work they do, but also in relation to their private (sexual) lives and identities. Here, women draw clear lines of demarcation between the interactions and identities performed over and outside the phone.

This process of 'identity cleansing' is deeply gendered and can be partly located within the strategic use of, and distancing from, symbolic elements of the *whore stigma*. Here, by diluting the explicitly sexual nature and content of their conversations with clients, operators seek to dismiss the moral stigma concerning the 'misuse' of female sexuality. Further, operators mobilise traditional and acceptable femininity through discourses of care, shifting the attention away from the sexual content of their work towards feminine empathic and emotional competences. In this way, as a process of 'cleansing', they invoke the symbolic elements of dominant feminine models of *good girl*: wife and mother. Finally, to avoid the risk of being considered *dirty* not only as workers, but as women in their private lives, they make strategic use of dominant notions of 'good sex', that is as non-commercial, marital and 'normal' in terms of sexual fantasies. This is achieved by positioning clients as 'bad': they have sex outside of an emotional relationship, often practice deceit, engage in 'perverted' fantasies and 'buy' sex through commercial exchange.

Notes

1. The goal of the radical feminists in fact is not to criminalise the women who prostitute themselves, but to preach for the abolition of prostitution itself.
2. I define emotional relationships – including the sadomasochistic ones – as having the same features of 'girlfriend' conversations in terms of the emotional commitment of the clients, the duration and frequency of the calls and, last but not least, in the operators' own perception.
3. Wind is a well-known mobile phone company in Italy.

8
Embracing Dirt in Nursing Matters

Robert McMurray

Standing in the magnolia painted corridor I wait a moment to let the elderly gentleman pass-by. Stepping forward I knock on the door of the consulting room. 'Come in'. I enter to find Jo (Advanced Nurse Practitioner) aerosol in hand, wafting floral scents around the room. Smiling she greets me: 'Hello, come in, take a seat'. Pointing with her eyes to the aerosol she continues 'sorry about this, just lanced a boil. Poor pet [colloquial reference to the patient who just left]: a great big thing in his arm pit'. Opening the window as we both sit she adds 'there's something very satisfying about lancing a boil, but the smell is terrible [grinning]and I don't want the next patient thinking that smell is me!'.

(McMurray, 2006)

This chapter is concerned with dirt and dirty work, as enacted by those in the occupation of nursing. Tracing a shift from Nightingale's assertion that 'every women is a nurse' (1860, preface) and that a nurse's concern is sanitation, through to the development of Advanced Nurse Practitioners (ANPs) who claim jurisdiction as diagnosticians, the chapter considers how dirt may be used to claim preferred occupational positions. It explores how the ascription of dirty work to nursing acts as a dividing practice, affording occupational space for nurses while simultaneously rendering them as something less than professionals: feminised and subordinated adjuncts to the dominant other that is medicine. The chapter concludes by considering the status of those nurses (ANPs) who work to disrupt and transgress such neatly tended divides, so much so that they not only work *with* dirt but are themselves positioned *as* dirt: as 'matter' that is 'recognisably out of place' (Douglas, 1966: 35, 160).

In this sense dirt becomes suffused with multiplicity, danger and potentiality, and this is precisely why embracing dirt in nursing matters. Before turning to nursing specifically, it will be useful to reprise what we mean and understand by dirty work.

Much of our concern with dirty work and its affects stems from the writings of Hughes (1962, 1984) and his concern with those tasks, occupations and people engaged in cleaning up the social, moral and physical dirt that results from the functioning of societies. His concerns with dirt range from the everyday mundane to the profound. In 'Good People and Dirty Work' (1962), Hughes takes us to the extreme, demanding that we confront the horrors of torture, concentration camps and mass extermination. He reminds us of the evil that men do: the acts of 'personalities warped toward perverse punishment and cruelty' (Hughes 1962: 10). Left at this, as the 'warped' acts of others, dirty work can have little to say about us. Yet, in considering the work of the SS officer and prison guard, Hughes suggests it is our concern because we often remain silent while others manage incarceration and ultimate solutions. It is our concern because we wish not to know about certain types of work that others do. It is dirty work, Hughes reasons, precisely because those who do such work are in some respects our agents, undertaking the tasks we avoid, often in respect of 'other' people we would rather not know.

Over time the work of Hughes has been refined and extended. Greater attention has been paid to the ways in which physical, social and moral dirty work differ and overlap (Ashforth and Kreiner, 1999). Research with meat cutters, road sweepers and veterinary technicians has fleshed out what it means to work in contexts that are *physically dirty* insofar as they are associated with effluence, grime and death or working conditions that are unpleasant or deleterious (Ashforth and Kreiner, 1999; Ashforth et al., 2007; Jervis, 2001; Meara, 1974; Pullen and Rhodes, 2008; Stacey, 2005). Observations of the social worker, nursing home attendant and psychiatrist have refined our understanding of *socially dirty* work, defined as such by association with stigmatised publics or servility to others (Ashforth and Kreiner, 1999; Ashforth et al., 2007; Stannard, 1973; McMahon, 1998), while the occupations of exotic dancer, abortion clinician and debt collector have offered glimpses into *morally dirty* work insofar as concerns are raised with respect to sin, dubious virtue or deception (Ashforth and Kreiner, 1999; Ashforth et al., 2007; Chiappetta-Swanson, 2005; Grandy, 2008; McMahon, 1998).

Of course all occupations have a dirty work (Hughes, 1984) component but the proportion and affects are more significant in some than others. In the jobs listed above it is not just an aspect of the work but a defining feature of the occupation. For the prison officer, street walker, traffic warden, state executioner and refuse collector, contact with phys-ical, social or moral dirt leaves a taint (like the lingering odour of the lanced boil). It suggests an occupational stigma 'that can be transmitted through lineages and equally contaminate all members of the [occupa-tional] family' (Goffman, 1997 [1963]: 73). The affect upon the worker – on *our* agent of dirty work – is presumed to be such that 'an individual who might have been received easily in ordinary social intercourse pos-sesses a trait that can obtrude itself upon attention and turn those of us whom he meets away from him' (Goffman, 1997 [1963]: 73). In these ways we begin to conceive of the importance of dirt and dirty work in terms of characteristics that define, divide and stigmatise – dividing practices separating in-groups (clean-us) from out-groups (dirty-them) (Douglas, 1966; Hughes, 1962; Stacey, 2005).

Those who live with the stigma of occupational taint often seek to reframe, recalibrate or refocus concern with dirty aspects of their work as part of the narration of more positive identities in which desirable values or functions are stressed (Ashforth and Kreiner, 1999; Ashforth et al., 2007; Stacey, 2005). Overall though, there is a sense in which dirt and dirty work have to be endured. There is a presumption that dirty work is not something which people with career aspirations and life choices do.

In this chapter I want to argue that while dirty work is in general and by definition seen as that which is to be avoided, there are conditions under which dirt might actively be 'claimed', so much so that some occupational groupings and their members not only deal with dirt, but claim it as their prerogative and speciality. Specifically I want to consider the ways in which dirt has been employed by nursing to claim occu-pational spaces from marginal positions. Reading a history of nursing through Douglas's (1966) work on dirt, the chapter argues that occu-pations such as nursing are at times found objectionable by 'others', not because of association with stigma or taint, but because as matter out of place their existence questions and threatens preferred organisa-tional and occupational orders. This, it is argued, is precisely the threat posed by ANPs who transform themselves from handmaidens who know their place into inter-occupational workers who claim a new space. Con-ceived of thus, dirt and dirty work need not be associated solely with that which is to be avoided or brushed away, but also with the yet-to-be-organised potential of marginal peoples who challenge us to 'create a new pattern of reality' (Douglas, 1966). This process of pattern creation can be traced back to Florence Nightingale.

Nature, order and dirt

> Again, women, and the best women, are woefully deficient in sanitary
> knowledge; although it is to women that we must look, first and last,
> for its application.
>
> (Nightingale, 1860: 1373–1375)

Writing in 1860 Florence Nightingale's engagement with dirt appears as
a manifesto on disease, hygiene and sanitation. It stands as a proclamation of nursing's need and right to claim jurisdiction over dirt in all
its unorganised forms pursuant to the development and application of
sanitary knowledge. It is a strident account where the focus is not the
malaise caused by infection or disease, but rather the additional harm
caused by the failure of formal or informal nursing to tend appropriately to the needs of the sick with respect to sanitation, sustenance,
environment, administration and routine. Throughout the text there
are references to 'pestilence', 'abominable smells' and 'offensive matter'
(Nightingale, 1860: 145–166) along with the concomitant need for the
five essentials of the healthy household: pure air, pure water, efficient
drainage, cleanliness and light.

The tone of Nightingale's writing is that of the well-educated middle
class, instructing those of lesser station – or those heads of household
charged with organising those of lesser station – on their past failings
and future improvement. In often condescending tones Nightingale
questions the intelligence of women and women as nurses, berating
them for their absence of common sense and of care:

> If a patient is cold, if a patient is feverish, if a patient is faint, if he is
> sick after taking food, if he has a bed-sore, it is generally the fault not
> of the disease, but of the nursing.
>
> (Nightingale, 1860: 29)

She goes on: 'All these things require common sense and care. Yet perhaps in no single thing is so little common sense shewn, in all ranks, as
in nursing.' (Nightingale, 1860: 122)

For all its condescension, paternalism and liberal presumption, *Notes
on Nursing* served to reinforce the value of nursing as a legitimate occupation (Attwell, 1998; Holliday and Parker, 1997), requiring scientific
training, organisation, dedication and skill (Monteiro, 1985). As a treatise on the necessary management of dirt in home and hospital it sought
to raise the position and profile of the nurse as the appropriate authority

to impose order where there was mess. It spoke of an occupation worthy of recognition within the wider social system (Selanders, 1998).

It can be argued that in many ways what Nightingale did was to advance the position of women as nurses through the promotion of a new discourse on dirt: what others have labelled a 'sanitary discourse' (Abbott and Wallace, 1998). She did not simply acknowledge examples of matter out of place but began to redefine those conditions and practices that had long been accepted as normal:

> There are other ways of having filth inside a house besides having dirt in heaps. Old papered walls of years' standing, dirty carpets, uncleansed furniture, are just as ready sources of impurity … People are so unaccustomed from education and habits to consider how to make a home healthy, that they never think of it at all, and take every disease as a matter of course, to be 'resigned to' when it comes 'as from the hand of Providence'.
>
> (Nightingale, 1860: 211)

In the above extract, and throughout the wider text, Nightingale works to relocate disease and illness from the domains of providence and nature, where little can be done, to the realms of sanitation and matter out of place, where intervention and proper ordering are real possibilities. For Nightingale and her followers dirt is that which causes offence and stands in opposition to order and goodness. Dirt speaks of impurity and contamination in a physical, social and even moral sense, the latter signified by the failure of the ignorant and unscrupulous to pursue better sanitation and order (Lawler, 1991).

Through her incitement to nurses and wider society to account for dirt, including the pioneering use of statistics as a public health tool (Selanders, 1998), Nightingale promotes a discourse designed to encourage obedience and order in others. She claims for nurses a systematising role in which dirt and its ordering are employed as weapons in the organisation of hospitals, treatment regimens and relations (Holliday and Parker, 1997). It is a primary example of the ways in which the defining of dirt can be viewed as a process of social construction through which those facets of life that were once unquestioningly accepted or tolerated (e.g. dirty carpets, uncleansed furniture) are reclassified as 'matter out of place' (Douglas, 1966: 35) and, in this instance, amenable to the authority of the nurse.

In considering the work of Nightingale it might be argued that the desire for order and a firmer foundation for the occupation of nursing

preceded dirt so that, as Douglas observes (1966: 161): 'Dirt was created by the differentiating activity of the mind, it was a by-product
of the creation of order.' Read thus, Nightingale's writing stands as an
ordering of nursing's claims to dirt and with it occupational identity
and worth. In defining and then claiming dirt for nursing, Nightingale
initiates a process of occupational framing in which women as nurses
reclaim a legitimate role in the promotion of health. While Douglas
(1966) will go on to speak of the need to separate pathogenicity and
hygiene from our notion of dirt, Nightingale's project 100 years earlier
was precisely the establishment of the said link in the mind of the public, and thence the organising necessity of the nurse in managing and
banishing the harm supposed to exist in this newly identified dirt. Thus
the real significance of Nightingale's claim to dirt as nursing work lay
in the social and occupational ordering of relations that its claiming
facilitated. Some 150 years later nursing's association with such dirty
work has been maintained and extended though, as the consideration
of Chiappetta-Swanson's (2005) work below shows, not always in ways
that are positive or wanted.

The dirt of others

> Every woman, or at least almost every woman, in England has, at one
> time or another in her life, charge of the personal health of some-
> body, whether child or invalid, – in other words, every women is
> a nurse ... every women must, at some time or other of her life,
> become a nurse.
>
> (Nightingale, 1860: preface)

While the framing of nursing as an occupation rested in part on the
claiming of dirt, not all dirty work is claimed or wanted by nurses.
Sometimes the dirty work of bodies, people, emotions and taboos are
imposed at a considerable personal cost on nurses and related workers
(see Bolton, 2005; Hughes, 1951; Lawler, 1991; Wolf, 1988). This is the
unwanted dirt of others. It is the dirt of caring that other occupations are
able to eschew. It is, as considered below, the dirty work that defines relations between occupations and which would render nurses subservient
to that most significant occupational other: medicine.

Few accounts of dirty work and nursing are more powerful than
Chiappetta-Swanson's (2005) analysis of genetic termination (GT). This
at times harrowing account of being required to terminate what were
wanted pregnancies due to foetal anomaly recounts the experiences

of nurses who are required to engage with tasks 'viewed as unpleasant and undesirable, work that others would prefer even not to know about' (Chiappetta-Swanson, 2005: 93). Routinely subordinated to the hierarchical authority of hospital bureaucracy and doctor's orders, these nurses are called on to deal with induced labours, stillborn and still-live foetuses, grieving mothers, insanitary conditions, institutional neglect, societal condemnation and occupational isolation. It is dirty work not just because it is physically, socially and at times morally distressing, but because it is imposed work which is avoided by others.

While nurses prided themselves on providing quality care in difficult organisational circumstances, they were well aware that this was imposed work, relating to a largely abandoned patient group passed over by other occupations. Chiappetta-Swanson (2005: 101) recounts how nurses were 'left to manage GTs on their own. The normal division of labour that characterized patient care on the ward disappeared with GT cases'. Procedures normally deemed medical were passed on to nurses by doctors who were absent or reluctant to be called on due to the stigma and biomedical failure associated with termination.

This is an extreme example of the oft-observed tendency of medics and medicine to cast off their dirty work (Dingwall, 2008; Hughes, 1984), placing that which is mundane, undesirable and dirty in the hands of nursing. Under these circumstances it is not dirt as pathogenicity that is at play, but dirt as moral taint and social servility. Morally the work is contested because it deals with death and foetal termination. Socially it is dirty because it is work cast off by others. It speaks to a sense of occupational subservience that has long overshadowed nursing (Abbott and Wallace, 1998; Attwell, 1998; Jinks and Bradley, 2004) and is a product of a hierarchically organised division of labour, which is dominated by medicine: the significant 'other' that works to position and define nursing. Indeed, to understand how the dirty work of nursing obtains its subservient taint it is necessary to take a moment to consider the position of nursing vis-à-vis medicine in a little more depth.

Medicine's domination of the occupational division of labour in health care is predicated on a claim to be the only profession qualified to make pronouncements in matters of health (Larkin, 1981). Its practices are based on privileging scientific discourses, abstract knowledge and tightly defined and rationed interventions (Finn, 2008; Katz, 1969; Walby and Greenwell, 1994), the social, material and technological advantages of which are jealously protected (Finn, 2008; Larkin 1981; Nancarrow and Borthwick, 2005; Scott, 2008). Its claims to pre-eminence in curative matters are generally supported by the state

(Dingwall, 2008), with competitor occupations being vigorously resisted or where sanctioned, required to submit to medicine's supervision (Freidson, 2001).

In this way medicine has come to dominate the ordering of relations with other health care occupations (McMurray, 2011), passing on those tasks which it deems dull and routine (Larkin, 1981) to others. It is this dominance that has long placed nursing in the position of handmaiden (Currie et al., 2008; Finn, 2008; James, 1992; Jinks and Bradley, 2004; Katz, 1969; Kirkpatrick et al., 2005), there to tend the patient, dress the wound and dispose of the everyday detritus of medical work (Dingwall, 2008; Katz, 1969; Nancarrow and Borthwick, 2005). Considered thus, nursing as an occupation emerges as an adjunct to medicine, there to enable the latter to present itself as rational, specialised, masterful, powerful and privileged (Abbott and Wallace, 1998; Davies, 1995; Wegar, 1993).

The roots of such thinking are deep. Nightingale suggested that while the nurse draws on 'knowledge which every one ought to have', the doctor is privy to 'medical knowledge, which only a profession can have' (Nightingale, 1860: preface). Thus she appears to reinforce an exclusionary type of intellectual gendering in which masculinised notions of medical professionalism are at odds with and prioritised over more feminised constructions of caring. Never mind that Nightingale's vision was of an 'organized, practical, scientific training, the purpose of which is to produce nurses who are servants of medicine, surgery and hygiene, and not of physicians and surgeons' (Holliday and Parker, 1997: 487) for, in utilising the language of separating, bounding, abstracting, controlling, possessing, dominating and governing, she implicitly promotes a masculine logic of organising (Abbott and Meerabeau, 1998; Davies, 1995; Guy and Newman, 2004). This can be seen as at odds with a more feminine 'ethics of care' based on connectedness, intersubjectivity, relatedness, selflessness, self-sacrifice, reflection, facilitation, contextual thinking and being there (Davies, 1995; Nancarrow and Borthwick, 2005). This alternative logic struggles to find a voice in a professional medical discourse organised around rather bleak and exclusionary accounts inspired by Weberian masculinity (Jinks and Bradley, 2004), where gender often passes 'unnoticed, denied or disavowed partly because it is "done" routinely and repeatedly unknowingly' (Pullen and Knights, 2007: 505).

In defence of Nightingale there is evidence to suggest that she was all too aware of the hidden nature of the work that women do. Writing on marriage as the ultimate prison she contended:

Behind *his* destiny woman must annihilate herself, must only be his complement. A woman dedicates herself to the vocation of her husband; she fills up and performs the subordinate part in it. But if she has any destiny, any vocation of her own, she much renounce it in nine cases out of ten ... A man gains everything by marriage: he gains 'help-mate' but a women does not.

(Nightingale, 1979 [c. 1852]: 40–41, cited in Selanders, 1998: 236).

In this and in her assertion that any attempt to limit people on the basis that 'this is women's work, and that's men's' are 'assertion and nothing more' (Nightingale, 1860: 1324) can be read not a willingness to subordinate nurse/women/feminine to medicine/man/masculine, but rather an acknowledgement of the struggle to work within the strictures of social and historical context. Considered thus, the work of nursing is gendered dirty because it is (in part) presumed to be imposed and unlauded. It is rendered doubly invisible by the assumption that it is naturally *women's* work (Abbot and Wallace, 1998; Bird et al., 2004; Davies 1995; Guy and Newman, 2004; Wegar 1993).

When set against the associated ideas of possessing discrete knowledge, autonomous action and clear jurisdiction (the very essence of a profession), this leaves little room for alternative conceptions of what it might mean to be a profession. Yet, as dirty work the difficult tasks and unavoidable emotional involvement that nursing requires, and which other occupations pass on, often represents 'for many what nursing was all about, total commitment to caring for one's patient' (Chiappetta-Swanson, 2005: 110; see also Bolton, 2001). While others seek to render such work as dirty because it is unwanted, in committing to an 'ethics of care' rather than self-service, nurses work to frame an imposed and dirty position as something notable.

Here then we begin to get a feel for the multiple nature of dirt and dirty work. It can be unwanted, unbearable and undesirable from the perspective of self and other; but, where imposed and at the same time claimed, it can be the source of identity, giving and satisfaction. To be clear, it is not a case of either/or, nor a case of which perspective is selected (Moll, 2002). Rather, dirt and dirty work are marginal matter that cannot be securely contained and placed, but exist in all positions at once. Both self and other may agree it is dirty work, but differ as to the nature and value of the dirt enacted. Sanitary knowledge, genetic termination, clearing up and caring work all link dirt to the nurse through subordination and yet, all such work defines the occupation and may even suggest some sense of emancipation where considered outside the rationalising logic that prioritises the 'self' over 'other' in assessments of worth.

The self as dirt

> It is often said by men, that it is unwise to teach women anything about these laws of health, because they will take to physicking … There is nothing ever seen in any professional practice like the reckless physicking by amateur females.
>
> (Nightingale, 1860: 1288–1296)

Despite 150 years of campaigning and working it is arguably the case that the overall position of nursing is little changed. Nurses continue to find themselves in a position of material, social and political disadvantage as compared to members of the medical profession (Abbott and Wallace, 1998; Nelson and Gordon, 2004). Worse still nursing appears trapped by apparently irreconcilable binaries which recursively question whether its members belong to an occupation or a profession (Currie et al., 2008; Katz, 1969; Kirkpatrick et al., 2005; Raelin, 1985), whether they should believe in extending competencies or caring compassion (Abbott and Meerabeau, 1998; Bolton, 2001; Katz, 1969; Morgan and Ogbonna, 2008; Nelson and Gordon, 2004) or whether they must commit to holistic generalism or more divided specialism. These interminable binaries serve to keep nursing in its place as facilitative support to the orderly production of medicine (Holmes and Gastaldo, 2004).

Latterly, however, there has emerged in the United Kingdom (UK) a type of nursing that disrupts such order. In daring to diagnose, prescribe and treat in their own right, ANPs challenge the neatly ordered boundaries between care and cure, protocol and discretion and feminine versus masculine perceptions of professionalism. As explored below, these nurses not only work *with* and *through* dirt, but as transgressors of the usual occupational order they are positioned *as* dirt.

In one form or another advanced nursing has existed since the 1960s in the United States and since the 1980s in the UK, Europe and Australasia (Duffield et al., 2009; Furlong and Smith, 2005; Lewis, 2001). The roles, titles (e.g. higher-level practitioner, modern matron, consultant nurse, physician assistant), duties, position and autonomy of such nurses vary according to the country and health care sector in which they are employed. What makes the ANP working in primary care in the UK worthy of particular attention is their push to undertake many of the tasks traditionally reserved for general medical practitioners (GPs).

UK-based ANPs typically have five years of post-registration train-ing, are educated to the Masters level and possess the skills required to take histories, carry out physical examinations, make diagnoses, enact treatments (including limited prescribing) and, where they deem it nec-essary, refer patients to secondary and tertiary specialists (Daly and Carnwell, 2003; Duffield et al., 2009). They work independently as clinicians, see patients with undiagnosed health problems from undif-ferentiated populations and are answerable for their diagnostic decisions in much the same way as their GP colleagues (RCN, 2009). Such nurses see themselves working collaboratively *with* rather than for or in place of GP colleagues (Cox, 2001). However, in a further break with tradition, a few ANPs have secured ownership of primary care practices and even employ GPs on a salaried basis (Lewis, 2001; Peckham, 2007). This is highly unusual in a sector traditionally dominanted by GP contractors; indeed there are only eight such nurse-owned practices in the UK.

These are not then Nightingale's obedient and observant nurses. They are a vanguard who organise, deliver and claim responsibility for cru-cial components of cure and care. By placing themselves in positions where they are the first persons to see patients, they cross the 'boundary of diagnosis which has (officially at least) formed a part of professional lines of demarcation' between medicine and other (Tovey and Adams, 2001: 700). Through training, accreditation, state sanction and practice they assert a right to share the doctor's claim to jurisdiction in matters of cure. In working to own practices and employ doctors, they eschew sub-ordinate positions. They use medical, managerial and entrepreneurial authority to claim, and where necessary assert, superordinate positions over doctors as salaried staff, in what constitutes an *'ordinal switching* of the occupational hierarchy' (McMurray, 2011). What is more, in terms of the efficacy of their provision the available evidence suggests that they are generally as or more effective than their medical counterparts in terms of patient satisfaction, information provision, selected outcomes and treatment costs (Cox, 2001; Kinnersley et al., 2000; Salisbury et al., 2002; Venning et al., 2000; Woodroffe, 2006).

The development and success of the ANPs is not universally applauded. There is a suggestion that their expansion has more to do with shortages of doctors (Daly and Carnwell, 2003; Lewis 2001) than any inherent benefit in the occupation itself. Others characterise the development of advanced skills in terms of a regrettable medicalisation of nurses (Holmes and Gastaldo, 2004), 'driven by individual practition-ers (the so-called tall poppies)' with little observable benefit to the wider profession (Glover, 2008). Moreover, Holliday and Parker (1997: 487) question accreditation processes in which 'nurses continue to collect bits of paper which qualify them for so-called extended roles' on the basis that they only afford access to those dirty roles (e.g. vein stripping or surgeon's assistant) discarded by more senior occupations. Considered thus, they are little more than upmarket versions of the doctor's handmaiden in a 'semi-professional mini-doctor role' (Jinks and Bradley, 2004: 126).

ANPs themselves do not claim or aim to be mini-doctors (Coombes, 2008; *Nursing Times*, 2009). For them it is a matter of combining the caring skills of traditional nursing – the dirty work of boils, emotions and social problems – with knowledge and practice of curative regimes based around diagnosis, prescription and treatment in pursuit of greater holism (Daly and Carnwell, 2003; McMurray, 2011). Rather than be diagnosed by a doctor, have your blood taken or wounds cleaned by a practice nurse, and then return to another doctor for a prescription; the ANP will do it all in one session. In doing so ANPs enact a reversal of the division of labour that has seen clean and dirty work separated in health care (James, 1992). They are not just nurses who care or doctors who cure, but hybrid practitioners who straddle the boundaries of both occupations (Coombes, 2008).

Yet it is precisely this straddling of traditional boundaries that is in part problematic for, as Douglas (1966) has observed, those individuals who cross more than one system boundary are often thought of as unsafe or dangerous. Douglas goes on to observe that while those who have recognised positions within a social structure are 'credited with consciously controlled powers', those who have a less explicit (straddling) position tend to be 'credited with unconscious, uncontrollable powers. Menacing those in better defined positions' (Douglas, 1966: 101). Moreover, the latter's 'double loyalties and their ambiguous status in the structure where they are concerned make them appear as a danger to those belonging fully to it' (Douglas, 1966: 102). This is the position of the ANPs. Still workers who hold tight to their traditional values and skills in the caring and the 'dirty work' of nursing, yet also members of medical worlds engaged in diagnosis, prescribing and referring, they stand as neither wholly one nor the other. Rather they are themselves representatives of dirt: 'things recognisably out of place, a threat to good order and so regarded as objectionable and vigorously brushed away' (Douglas, 1966: 160).

Such 'brushing away' can be read in claims that ANPs represent 'the abandonment of nursing by modern nurses', are to the 'detriment of health care in this country' (Coull, 2006: 51) and are ill-equipped to provide the requisite standards of care in areas – such as diagnosis – which have long been seen as the sole preserve of doctors (Chakraborty, 2006: 51; Morgan and Ogbonna, 2008). Here we see the person of the ANP reconstituted and repositioned as dirt: condemned as an 'object or idea likely to confuse or contradict cherished classifications' (Douglas, 1966: 36). It is this repositioning that enables representatives of the dominant occupational system – medicine – to call for a restoration of order in which we 'get back to basics and have trained nurses to nurse and trained doctors to doctor' rather than having 'care assistants playing at being nurses, nurses playing at being doctors, doctors playing at being managers, and managers just playing' (Coull, 2006: 51).

ANPs are a system pollutant and health risk not because they afford a particular safety threat to patients (there is no evidence to such effect) but because they are occupationally transgressive. They subvert an occupational order that has lasted centuries in health care and threaten to 'redefine parameters for practice between nursing, medicine and related professions on the health care team' (Furlong and Smith, 2005: 1063). For those who object to such redefinition, the ANPs effectively *become* dirt, a 'by-product of a systematic ordering and classification of matter, insofar as ordering involves rejecting inappropriate elements' (Douglas: 1966: 35). These 'physicking' nurses are rejected because they are deemed to have no place in the mainstream grouping of nurses and doctors. Their very existence resists the rational masculine project of clear categorisation and ordering. Their rejection could therefore be seen as an example of 'the casting out of the feminine in organization ... the viscous and the fluid that are uncontrollable, unmanageable, and have the potential to disrupt order ... The abject must be expelled to maintain order' (Pullen and Rhodes, 2008: 251).

And yet there is a need for caution in this discourse on dirt. As we explore the position of ANPs as transgressive and anomalous, there is a danger that we frame them (once more) as subordinate and victim, positioned as dirt by others. This would miss the point. Just as ANPs choose to combine the dirty work of nursing with the interventions of medicine, so many of them choose to take up the marginal positions abandoned by others. For many the chance to flourish as practitioners rested on an active decision to serve populations and run practices that mainstream medicine had discarded as undesirable (Lewis, 2001; McMurray, 2010b, 2011). They rejected the notion that these marginal places and people were not worthy of their work, just as they rejected the falsely imposed binaries between cure and care and between doctor and nurse. Yes, marginality was partly imposed, but it was also pursued and selected.

Under such circumstances the work and existence of the ANPs stands as an active project of transgression and disruption premised on the proclamation that 'advanced nurse practitioner practice is not bound by any conventional definition of the difference between "nursing" and perceptions of "medical" practice. Such parameters are spurious ...' (RCN, 2008: 6). This is a personal professional project that threatens to pull and shape the fundamental experience of doctoring by testing the system where it is weakest: at its margins. In showing that nurses who care can also cure, they resist the 'constraints that are made, laid and held firm within the framework of interacting with others' (Douglas and Mars, 2003: 764). Moreover, in resisting those constraints ANPs effectively invite all health care occupations, including medicine, to 'turn round and confront the categories on which their whole surrounding culture has been built up and to recognise them for the fictive, man-made, arbitrary creations that they are' (Douglas, 1966: 170).

This then is a challenge to any presumption of a natural occupational order. It is a refutation of the masculine project of becoming either/or as ANPs reject the gendered binaries between female/carer/nurse on the one hand (James, 1992) and male/curer/doctor on the other. One could even go as far as to suggest that theirs is a project designed to facilitate the process of 'unsettling gendered norms of work, organisation and the academy – it is about dissolving boundaries' (Pullen and Knights, 2007: 510). Considered thus, it has the potential to be endlessly creative and pertinent dirty work.

Conclusion

> There is no such thing as absolute dirt: it exists in the eye of the beholder.
>
> (Douglas, 1966: 2)

Boils, blood and bandages; urine, grime and tears; snot, coughs and colds; abuse, smears and fevers; poor, well and worried: all are the work – the *dirty work* – of the nurse. The work is dirty because it speaks of physical, social and even moral taint (Ashforth and Kreiner, 1999). It is dirty because it deals in leaky bodies (e.g. boils, decay, rupture), others' social problems (e.g. poverty, drug misuse, subordination) and moral conundrums (e.g. HIV, termination, rationing) that threaten to taint not just those with such problems but also those who would work to care and cure (Goffman, 1997 [1963]). Yet despite this, nursing has claimed such dirt and its ordering as its jurisdiction. This has been done in part to reassert the caring role of the nurse and the possibility of payment for the purifying work rendered. It is also done in claim of an occupational identity (Attwell, 1998; Holliday and Parker, 1997). Rather than let the care that (mostly) women do (Guy and Newman, 2004) be disregarded, dismissed and pulverised until 'in the end, all identity is gone ... ', as the 'origins of the various bits and pieces is lost and they have entered into the mass of common rubbish' (Douglas, 1966: 160), we have seen that the identity of the nurse is constituted in the naming of dirt – in actively linking matter to pathogenicity, pathogenicity to sanitation, sanitation to nursing and nursing to order. The reworking of nursing's relation-ship to dirt is then a reworking of occupational positions, recognitions, rewards and opportunities.

From Nightingale in the 1860s to ANPs in the twenty-first century, embracing dirt in nursing has mattered precisely because it stakes and makes relational claims. Initially there were claims to sanitary knowl-edge that might secure modest incomes through handmaidenly subordi-nation to medicine. Latterly, in the executive-entrepreneurial authority of the ANPs (McMurray, 2011) we witness the potential for a com-plete renegotiation of inter-occupational relations, as nurses combine the dirty work of care with curative regimes in a move that threatens to 'invert the common, medically dominated culture of primary care and to radically restructure professional identity' (Lewis, 2001). Inso-far as these diagnostic nurses are rejected and resisted they move from a position in which they simply work with dirt to a place outside the acceptable ordering of health care relations, a movement that renders nurses themselves as dirt: matter which is recognisably out of place. Dirt is not then just something to be worked *with* or *on*. It is also that which may be used to define the position of self in relation to others. What it means to be and work with dirt is not a singular simple matter, but rather multiple and fluid and suffused with potentiality.

It is of course possible to object that this chapter – this very attempt to account for dirt and nursing – is itself an exercise in imposing order: that in constructing a single account I have subjected the story of nurs-ing and its relations to medicine to the violent external imposition of 'experts who propose to speak on behalf of others' (Holmes and Gastaldo, 2004: 267). In offering some sense of linearity and coher-ence with respect to the lives and dirty work of hundreds of thousands of nurses, I have succumbed to masculine notions of serious, pure, abstracted, academic writing that alienates the other it purports to describe (Höpfl, 2000). Worse still, I have offered text that makes organising and organisations 'knowable by a process of reduction that pushed out the dirt' (Pullen and Rhodes, 2008: 245) and annuls potentiality.

In most important respects such criticism is correct. The very act of writing imposes a sense of stativity, fixity and concreteness on an everchanging world (McMurray, 2010a). It gives the impression that a world characterised by continual becoming can be captured and known. Writing is necessarily a simplifying device that is all too crude in its grouping of experiences, motives and actions according to broad and objectifying occupations (e.g. nursing and medicine) resulting in and from 'a violence that makes the world, knowable, ordered and organized' (Cooper, 1986: 187, cited in Pullen and Rhodes, 2008: 247).

What then is to be said and done? Hughes (1951) suggests that the best that those who are outside of, yet observing, other occupations can hope to do is give basic pointers. While I am not 'outside' in the sense of standing beyond reality looking in with the neutral eye of the dispassionate observer (Law, 2004; Moll, 2002), neither do I belong to the occupations on which I write. As a researcher/writer I must allow for the possibility of having had affect, while acknowledging that I do not know what it is to enact/be a nurse in all its forms and meanings.

The aim of this chapter is thus more modest than that proposed by Hughes. Despite its unifying appearance, it does not seek to give pointers or answers, but instead to render visible some notion of the complexity and multiplicity of nursing in its relations to dirt. Yes, it has simplified and ordered the messy flow of life and lives as lived, but it has done so in an attempt to foreground the oft-ignored, marginal and taken-for-granted work of the nurse in relation to dirt. It has attempted to foreground the struggle of nursing, reversing its more usual position as 'a ghost – never really seen, but always a haunting presence' (Pullen and Rhodes, 2008: 247) at the ordering feast of medicine. The point has not been to claim superiority for nursing, but to actively consider developments in nursing in relation to notions of dirt and dirty work.

Accordingly, the chapter has sought to explore the various ways in which nursing rests on matter out of place, with respect to dirt in its physical, social and moral forms, where work done threatens stigma and taint; dirt as an ethics of care that prioritises others over self; dirt as a discourse that promotes occupational claims; and dirt that is positional, describing as it does the transgressive and transformative potential that exists where people refuse to be told their place. In these ways what it means to be associated with dirt is multiple yet always intimately relational. There can be no stigma without the judgement of others, no call for occupational recognition without a claim on others and no positioning as dirt except in relation to the organising and order that is continually negotiated with others. In this sense it can be argued that dirty work is always boundary work, organising work and ordering work (Douglas, 1966; McMurray and Pullen, 2008).

In ending this chapter on dirt in nursing matters the point is not to arrive at some definitive conclusion as to the current state and future direction. It is to acknowledge that writing, like life itself, is often a mode of ordering in which the phallocentric urge dominates, so that even in seeking to make space for the potentiality, multiplicity, ambiguity and nomadism that resides in dirt (Holmes and Gastaldo, 2004; Höpfl, 2000), the act of naming such matter serves to contain and restrict. Dirty work is that which is simultaneously abandoned, imposed and claimed. It is a source of taint and stigma. It speaks to a history of sub- and superordination. It is dirty because it speaks to that which others would rather not know about or do (Hughes, 1984). Yet it is also a potential source of pride, service and care that requires the prioritisation of others over self. It is a position of ascribed and claimed transition that can usefully be called upon to challenge and question the preferred order. In this sense, dirt matters because it speaks of the potentiality that exists in alternative and emerging relations.

9
Dispersing of Dirt: Inscribing Bodies and Polluting Organisation

Paul White and Alison Pullen

> As if in a magic trick, the patient vanishes, hidden behind machines and tubes, there unseen by doctors and nurses. But as in any good magic trick, the patient also reappears...
>
> (Zussman, 1992: 81)

Introduction

The opening quote summarises how ethnographies of hospital intensive care units emphasise the ways in which the bodies of patients are made visible and invisible (Place, 2000; Zussman, 1992).[1] This is especially evident during their admission and through the ways in which bodies are rendered legible via biomedical technology and organisational processes (White, 2008). In this chapter we locate our analysis of the body within the space of intensive care. Here, critically ill persons are located within a complex circuit where bodies are de-corporealised and de-subjectivised through technology. Concurrently these bodies become a prosthesis of technology, while technology functions as a prosthesis of the subject. We understand the intensive care body as a latent body (Leder, 1990) so as to consider the *corporeal absence* of the intensive care patient where 'every presence is dependent on a corresponding absence' (1990: 62). As we will develop later, bodies can be read through a 'cascade of inscriptions' (Latour, 1987), as critically ill bodies are manipulated, pierced, breached and processed into the fabric of the organisation, both physically and metaphorically (White, 2009). Critically ill patients' personhood is concealed and unconcealed at different points and for quite different purposes, through processes of admission, stabilisation, weaning[2] and discharge. More accurately, personhood is obscured as critically ill bodies are effaced through technologies of life support, notably mechanical ventilation that necessitates voicelessness to ensure adequate ventilation of the lungs.[3] In so doing, the context of supportive technologies amplifies sites of visibility (and legibility) of the critically ill body, obscuring the performance of personhood through interaction (Goffman, 1990 [1959]).

During the technological staging of the body, there is a vacillation between subject and object at these points of (un)concealing – unconcealed in the sense that nothing is purposively concealed or hidden. Rather, the body becomes an object of attention (particularly for invasive procedures) and a subject of *clinical* interest (Becker et al., 1977 [1961]), as the critically ill *body* is smoothed (Deleuze and Guattari, 1987) into the organisational processes of intensive care.[4] The body – and through extension the person – is read through medical intervention and analysis in intensive care or what we argue through physiological 'interpretations'[5] (such as blood chemistry, heart traces). In this way these interpretive readings become 'social *fact*' (Garfinkel, 1967[6]). These 'facts' are themselves read in relation to a refinement of the multiple 'stories' of the body (Berg and Bowker, 1997; White, 2009), transforming 'hard' clinical science into the world of social relations. In this chapter, we focus on the concealing and unconcealing practices of intensive care work beyond what Zussman (1992) refers to as the 'magic trick'. The aim here is to get closer to the idea that all revealing work is concealing and that all concealing work reveals, and we make this explicit in relation to the sanitising effects of organisational processes. In this sense, sterility and its *other* can be similarly seen as a trope to concealment/unconcealment as we figure dirt in relation to a supposed other.

In 'opening up' this chapter, we make explicit the ethnographic terrain of intensive care to situate bodily punctures. In doing so, we move away from conceptualisations of dirt, particularly as 'matter out of place' (Douglas, 2002 [1966]: 36), towards 'clean' – or matter *in* place to make visible allusions to sterility (or indeed sterility as illusionary) in clinical practices. Indeed, as we will make explicit, matter can be seen not only as those physical materials out of place, but things that matter in the sense of words or ideas, which are seen to matter to some, being played out in their 'proper place'; to act out of place is to risk 'being put in place', suggesting that there is a proper place to be and a proper way of thinking and behaving within spaces of organisation. This playing out situates dirt in its 'proper' place as processes of sanitation are examined to understand dirt, predicated upon an assumption that a 'proper place' is known and is necessarily knowable.[7] We stage the clean and the sterile as sites of organising, as both empirical and theoretical functions. In making this move, we emphasise that focusing on dirt limits the realm of possibility to that contained within the putative notion of dirt, much as pursuing a particular theoretical lens, ontology or subject position will reproduce assumptions that emanate from such a lens or subject position in the first instance (Gouldner, 1971; Law, 1994; Strathern, 2004). Following this claim, dirt as matter out of place can be read in relation to the means through which dirt is avoided, regulated, eradicated or sanitised rather than reproducing polluted assumptions through a dirty lens. Dirt and its other are therefore read through the tacit and explicit programmes, rules and procedures of *culture* (Geertz, 1970, 1973, 1985) that govern behaviour – the *accomplishments* (Garfinkel, 1967) of dirt and its processing. Yet the extent to which dirt can be truly disposed, or even the desirability of disposal, produces further questions concerning cultures of disposal and cultural desires for sanitation and the illusion of sterility.[8] In short, allusions of sterility are examined through processes of rendering different or othering dirt.

> ... Remembering is not the negative of forgetting. Remembering is a form of forgetting ...
>
> (Kundera, 1996: 128)

In keeping with Kundera's remembering, we show that dirt of itself is a social consequence of modes of classification (Bowker and Star, 1999) and suggest that processes of sanitation are themselves technologies for the *dispersal* of dirt.[9] To clean is to render notions of dirt visible and produce a moral demand to act, not as the negative of dirt but within a system of dispersal. Perhaps another means of understanding dirt is in relation to Derrida's word play involved in *différance* (Derrida, 1984 [1972]), where the interplay between difference and deference recognises difference, and as a result of recognising (diagnosing) such difference, a deferral is made to dominant and dominating ways of thinking or of ordering (Law, 1994).[10] In this sense, dirt and pollution are differed from a desired state, as matter out of place, which tells of the cultural significance of dirt. For Foucault (2002 [1972]), the notion of dispersal recognises that nothing (a given ordering of matter, for example) is ever truly disposed.[11] In line with Douglas, it is dispersed spatially or put out of mind and as a relation of extension to cultural materials, certain ideas (as cultural materiality) could be seen to be 'bodied forth' (Munro, 2005; Strathern, 2004), or conversely, to let go, to put out of mind, remembering as itself a form of forgetting (Kundera, 1996). As such, following Douglas's allusions to or illusions of potential pollutants, they are dispersed for a period before their eventual return, such as in relation to new organisational forms or bodies of knowledge (White, 2008).

Broader cultural preoccupations with disposal (again derived from Douglas) have been highlighted by Munro (2001), where an attempt is made to deny or re*fuse*, to rubbish or *ref*use and by association to dispose of dirt as rubbish and refuse it as risky material. Refusal and refuse within health care frequently translate in practice as translocation[12] of microbiological flora 'out of place' in terms of infection or to return to Foucault, a dispersal of 'bugs'. As a consequence we refer to ideas of difference (Hetherington and Munro, 1997; Munro, 1997), with a concomitant labouring of division where divisive practices become part of the ways in which particular agendas[13] render legitimate a certain ordering of difference, the deferring processes of that found wanting or simply not fitting current reconfigurations of the moral order (Garfinkel, 1967), which can legitimate an eventual disposal (of ideas or persons[14]). This of itself, we argue, presupposes a return of dirt as something simply dispersed, and eternally set to return (Nietzsche, 1974). The relations of dirt and sanitising processes are figured as being tied to the discursive moves[15] of difference (empirically and epistemologically) and as we will make explicit sanitising and sterility are tethered to the attendant risk of pollution.

In the opening sections of this chapter we have made visible our ethnographic position theoretically rather than empirically. In the next section we unpack the position of the critically ill body in the space of intensive care by focusing on a circuit where the body can be perceived, before moving on to discuss the space at which we are looking through our particular dirty/sanitised lens, namely the administration of intravenous drugs (injections) and the means through which such processes are conducted, the policies that guide them and the ceremonial order (Strong, 1979) in which they are situated (Clarke, 2005; Goffman, 1991 [1961], 1963, 1983).

Circuiting the body

In intensive care, for all practical purposes the body and the technologies that support life are one and the same thing, as they are tethered to form particular circuits. Indeed, Fox (1992) makes visible what he terms 'circuits of hygiene' within the operating theatre where specific

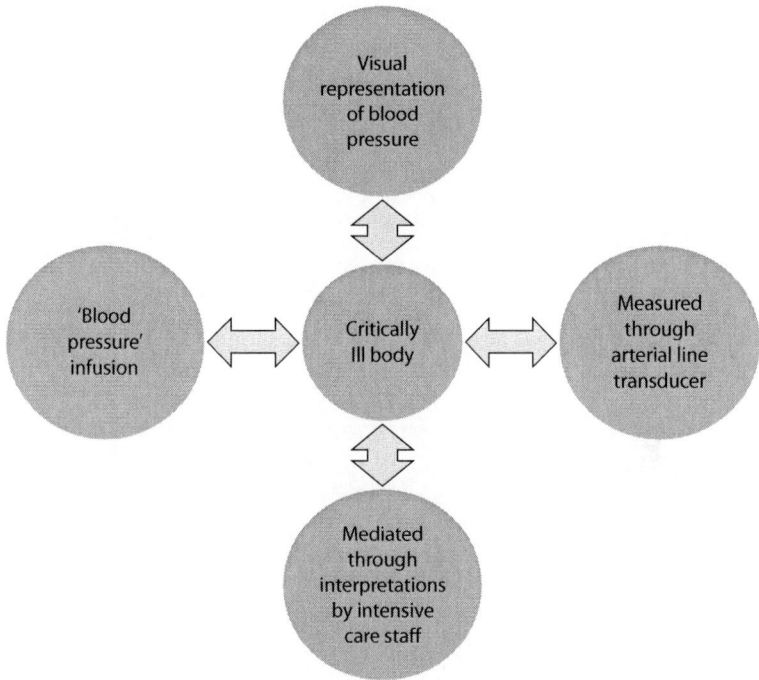

Figure 9.1 Circuiting the body

patient, staff and instrument circuits constitute a space and where the movement of bodies and things come together. Here we focus on blood pressure, specifically on how it is read in relation to and manipulated by inputs, outputs and throughputs into the body – mediated by intensive care staff, who ultimately regulate the internal environment of the body as it is made visible, knowable and controllable. Figure 9.1 assists in visualising the complex connections and interrelationships between the bodies of patients, staff, materials, technology and organisational processes that constitute a circuit of such control. Materials themselves call upon health care staff (and families to some extent) to regard materiality and the body in particular ways, much as the materials and body themselves are regarded through a particular medico-technical ontology.

The more ubiquitous continuous infusions within intensive care practice are those that control blood pressure and anaesthetic agents (such as drugs that paralyse and/or sedate). There can be numerous infusions in addition to the delivery of routine intravenous drugs (as in the

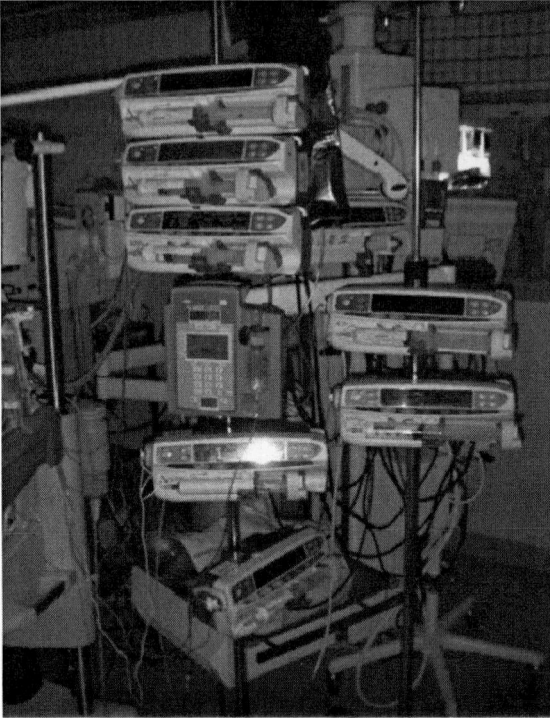

Figure 9.2 Syringe drivers

illustration of syringe drivers on the drip stand in Figure 9.2). Physiological interpretations of the body are represented on the monitor
screen (such as that in Figure 9.3). A central line (to infuse the drugs)
and an arterial line (to read blood pressure and act as a source of arterial
blood for analysis) are inserted into the large veins (in the case of central
lines, generally in the neck or in the groin) and the radial artery (in the
wrist or femoral artery in the groin) respectively. This represents part of
the ceremony of sorting out the body,[16] and more generally part of the
technology that 'smoothes' the body, rendering it amenable to organisational interpretation and manipulation to fit in with very particular
forms of organisational knowing.

Drugs that aim to maintain blood pressure are injected into the central line and adjusted to achieve a particular level, alongside the use of
blood products and fluids that aim to increase the circulating volume.
Generally, intensive care staff adjust the rate of the drugs administered

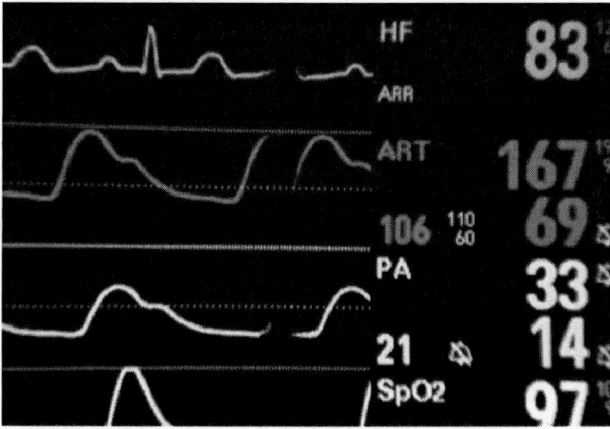

Figure 9.3   Visual representations of physiological waveforms

to maintain a particular blood pressure, which will have been set by the senior medical staff (or in consultation with them[17]). The body is transgressed through the skin at the point of insertion of the lines where drugs are delivered into the body and measurements of pressure come out from the body which are then transduced into a waveform display. In this respect the body is tethered to technologies that support the maintenance of a given blood pressure; the body and technology form a circuit of flesh, pharmaceutical agents and electronic representations of physiological 'fact'.[18] The critically ill body is punctured, interpreted, manipulated and *managed* by technology. Intensive care nurses interpret data to maintain physiological homeostasis through the intervention of human and non-human actors and materials, where the nurse becomes the control mechanism to ensure physiological 'integrity'.[19] The nurse in this way functions to maintain order and containment. The docile body of the anaesthetised subject is disciplined by technology, although the technological circuit of which the body is part disciplines intensive care staff in relation to their point of perception of the re-organisation of pathophysiology within the circuit. The focus of the body can be seen within a fabric of relations (Lyotard, 1986), where the body, the normal, the pathological, subjects and objects are read through such a fabric of relating the body materials and technologies. The integrated techno-body within such a circuit demands a particular regard, a normative gaze that becomes a normalising ontology (Foucault, 1989 [1973]). The techno-body creates the ontological world anew.

It is through this circuit as a medical space and associated ceremonial order that we apply our analysis of processes of sanitation surrounding the preparation of drugs that make up this circuit.

Drawing (up) the body

Most of the drugs used in intensive care are intravenous on account of the anesthetised state of its patients. Many drugs such as drugs to support heart contractility, anaesthetic agents or insulin will be administered as continuous infusions, while others such as antibiotics and those drugs required in the treatment of particular diseases will be administered at regular intervals. Preparation of these drugs takes place near the foot of the bed, to the left or right, on a trolley (similar to that depicted in Figure 9.4) containing the patient's drugs, emergency drugs, assorted needles, syringes, cannulae, sterile pots, bungs, tubes, bags of fluid, alcohol wipes, bandages, sterile towels and gauze. The trolley contains most of the equipment required for the preparation and administration of drugs. The stainless steel top acts as a

Figure 9.4   An example of an intensive care utility trolley

drug preparation table and is organised according to how individual nurses prefer to arrange their equipment (within reason), whereas the contents of drawers are more ordered.[20] While recognising that there is a potential for nurses to organise the trolley in a way that suits their working habits, in practice, the ordering of the trolley conforms to a particular spatial and colour-coded convention that may be followed as part of the bed-area checks undertaken at the commencement of a nurse's shift or the trolley may simply remain the way it was bequeathed to the nurse by the previous shift. However, for materials to be out of place is to risk admonishment from the shift leader on the off chance that the shift leader or nurse relieving the space at break times could require items which cannot be easily found.[21]

Needles are located in (or sometimes on) the trolley and are referred to by their colour coding that denotes needle size and consequently function; syringes are referred to by size and/or function (having no colour coding). The trolley is the space on which most drug preparation takes place and is one of the few sites where needles and syringes are used in order to mix diluents with drug powder and then introduce them to an administration solution. Consequently, a 'sharps box', a large bright yellow box (Figure 9.5) is located next to the trolley, with a contaminated waste bin located on the floor next to the trolley. This enables easy access to the sharps box where ampoules, needles, tubes, syringes, those things associated with injections, although not necessarily contaminated by

Figure 9.5   A sharps box found in each bed space

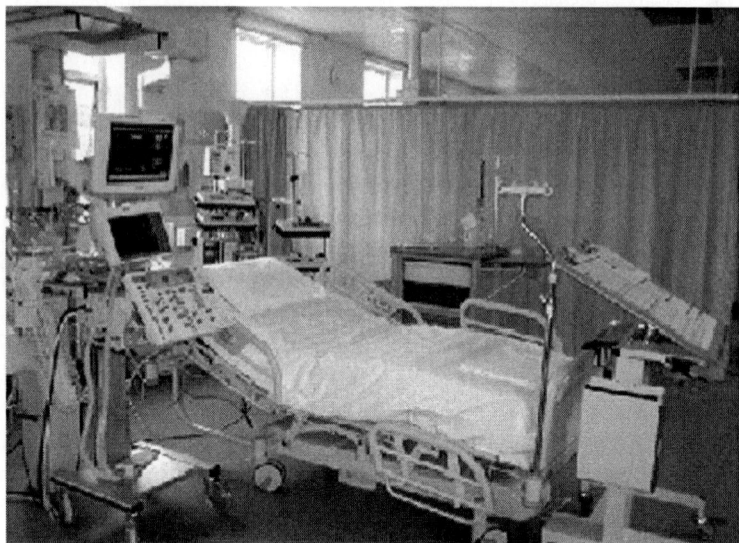

Figure 9.6   A typical intensive care bed space

bodily fluids, are disposed. The box itself contains the materials (sharps) associated with injections, not necessarily just the sharp objects that they were designed to contain safely.

In the photograph of a bed space (Figure 9.6), the trolley and sharps box are located in the position from where the photograph has been taken. Boxes, beds, trolleys and monitoring equipment hold a position in space that becomes intuitive for staff[22] – that is, the layout of the bed space should be uniform across the intensive care unit so that irrespective of the bed space, the nurses or doctors are able to reach equipment, similar to that of the utility trolley, easily. The most difficult areas to work in are those where space is limited, such as the cubicles (which are referred to colloquially as cupboards) and areas away from the main 'floor'. Partly this is on account of the non-standard equipment and layout which needs to fit the space, but also on account of the isolation from the main floor where relief and emergency support is not in sight, and as often felt by the nurses, 'out of sight is out of mind', where the ward round may forget the 'cupboards' and break relief may not be forthcoming.

Drugs are prepared (or 'drawn up') in this space by a single nurse (who has responsibility for one patient) and a second nurse is called upon to check the drug in line with unit (not hospital) policy. The extent to which drugs are checked varies in practice, from a cursory glance towards the nurse preparing the drugs, which generally occurs when the nurses are relatively senior, to a more detailed examination of volumes, calculations and preparation in the case of junior nurses. In the latter case, the preparation of drugs becomes a teaching opportunity, where questions about uses, side effects and contra-indications are posed (when staffing levels allow). In common with making the critically ill body legible, the definition of junior corresponds to length of time in a particular intensive care unit.

The education policy at the time of the fieldwork was to undertake competency-based training, where it would be unlikely that a nurse would be able to administer drugs before spending at least six months in a post and completing all of the competencies required. Pedagogically, this was seen as a means through which staff new to the intensive care unit focussed on learning how to nurse intensive care patients and become familiar with all the technical information without having to focus on drug administration. This policy applied to all staff who entered intensive care as junior staff nurses as denoted by pay grade or band, irrespective of intensive care experience or equivalent experience elsewhere in the hospital. Indeed, such junior staff felt conspicuous by the yellow stripes on their epaulettes, which were indicative of their being an undergraduate or pre-registration student. In this respect, junior nurses or those new to this intensive care unit were rendered both visible and other as a consequence of such demarcations which legitimated (occasionally) demeaning speech and action on the part of more 'experienced' staff.

Viewing Mary Douglas's classic *Purity and Danger* (2002 [1966]: *xix*) as a text concerned with risk, we read the policies and educational practices surrounding drug preparation and administration as concerned with assuaging such risks. Intensive care can be figured as an embedded form of risk management, where each facet of a patient's physiological status is known and interpretable. Much of the labour in intensive care is concerned with holding technical knowledge of the body and its relationship to life support technologies. The body is read in extension to numerous representations, such as breathing waveforms, electrocardiograph traces and arterial blood gases, among numerous other forms of knowing the body. In this sense the body is strictly ordered and regulated; deterioration in physiological condition and particularly emergency situations are relatively rare as the body is prefigured in relation to patterns.[23] For example, blood chemistry is tightly controlled and regulated to assuage abnormal heart rates and rhythms. The tight control of insulin became an aspect of intensive care work as it was associated with reduced mortality among intensive care patients. The normal patterns of physiological existence are emanated *par excellence* in intensive care, where the body as a physiological entity is acted upon in relation to any deviation from the normal 'numbers',[24] and in this sense the space could be viewed as the *'altar to modernity'*, at least in the sense of biomedical control, where a way of seeing and knowing enables a prediction or prognosis on which physiological control is situated. The danger of deviation from normal values is extremely risky as this is attributable to physiological deterioration. Spatial and organisational practices, including the spaces for the drawing up of drugs, are part of this regulation and similarly tightly controlled. The organisation itself demands visibility of physiology, waste and drug administration practices and as such visibility is associated with practices of reducing risk. As a consequence cleaning organisational processes or the cleansing of clinical practices are undertaken in the pursuit of risk minimisation.

The chapter now unfolds by introducing the polluted and polluting context of intensive care work and the means through which bodies are rendered legible. Beginning with the mundane oozes of bodies, we examine procedures associated with the administration of injections and engage in a more general examination of the ceremonial order of 'sterile procedures' before examining the sanitising effects of policy on practice. As the body's self-containment is transgressed by the 'needle', so too are the cultural categories that seek to control order, cleanliness and wholeness (Douglas, 2002 [1966]).

Un/concealing ooze, rendering bodies legible

As we have shown, intensive care bedside spaces are organised to execute effective and efficient intensive care practice. Technologies such as the mechanical ventilator, monitoring equipment, supportive technologies and syringe drivers are positioned so that they can be easily connected to the body. When the patient's body is staged it appears attached to these technologies and becomes literally and metaphorically 'plugged in' to its spatial surroundings through the insertion of prostheses,[25] including numerous cannulae (intra-arterial, intravenous and so on). The intensive care unit is not a space which deals with patients' expectations and needs, as unspoken norms emphasise the core function to survive with every other facet rendered secondary to that goal.[26] For intensive care staff, in common with other health care spaces (Charles-Jones et al., 2003; Hillman et al., 2009), the objective is for the patient to be discharged from intensive care, which is itself a space of disposal.[27] It is only within the space that the work of transforming the body from that of the sick to that of the critically ill can begin to 'sort out' the body (Place, 2000; White, 2009), that is to organise and process the critically ill body so that it can be rendered legible to intensive care. Until the critically ill body is staged in its rightful place there is little treatment which can be undertaken; once positioned in place technologies subsume the body within a complex circuit of technological and social interaction. The body needs to be physically, organisationally, metaphorically and culturally embedded in intensive care. It is only when the body has been rendered legible, meaningful and stable that treatment of the critically ill body can begin. Bodies become concealed through intensive processes, yet when worked on reappear through interaction:

> The consultant is sat behind Kevin's [the patient] head and holds his hand, supporting it so as not to disturb the infusion during the transfer. 'Blues and Twos' as the ambulance speeds onto the motorway...He talks over Kevin to Daisy [the staff nurse] who is sat in line with Kevin's right arm. He is talking about his son. There is some oozing of blood from the line in the right side of Kevin's neck, which lands on the consultant's arm, he stares at it, unable to clean it off. The patient remains motionless, with no obvious movement, strapped into a 'Rugged' stretcher, sedated and paralysed.
>
> (Retrospective notes of inter-hospital transfer)

The consultant in the above extract then changed topic from discussing his son to consider the apparent frivolity of some intensive care nurses who, in his view, laughed too much during their work. From his perspective, this defied the serious nature of intensive care. As a result a series of A4-sized posters had appeared reminding all (and most importantly intensive care nurses) that 'intensive care patients need their rest'. From this consultant's perspective, the sanitised nature of clinical work in intensive care was being undermined by the tendency of intensive care staff[28] to engage in mundane interaction. Such challenges to the organisational status quo derived from social registers defiant of a supposed demand for professionalism and the need to maintain the clean professional ethos of intensive care work. Such matter out of place (following Douglas, 2002 [1966]) could be seen as demeanour out of place, but as we shall make clear, such demeanour is a functional part of the *ceremonial ordering* of clinical work (Strong, 1979) as an ontological practice (*cf.* Good, 1993), yet arguably one that requires cleansing to fit in with a broader moral order of intensive care. That is, behaviour could be seen as polluting a supposed reverence that should permeate the space. Not respecting the seriousness of clinical and medical norms breaches the established order: humour punctures cultural and professional norms.

Sometimes it is through the more subtle aspects of intensive care work that the body makes itself visible. We are not suggesting that the unconscious body makes itself known, but rather that through leakages from the body, intensive care staff regard the body in a different way. During the process of sorting out the body, making it *hyperreal* (Baudrillard, 1994), it becomes sanitised through the ways in which it is re-presented on a digital display and in its (re)translation[29] (Callon, 1986; Latour, 1987) into colour-coded words, numbers and symbols on the 'obs chart'.[30] Through the leaking of excrement and other bodily fluids such as blood, the unsanitised, carnal, fleshy body is recognised (Crossley, 1996; Grosz, 1994; Merleau-Ponty, 1968, 1989 [1962]) and the mundane, everyday actions that are normally concealed in social (particularly public) life are unconcealed within intensive care (Goffman, 1990 [1959], 1991 [1961]). Mundane yet hidden events, such as toileting, become visible as a means of ensuring that excreta are easily identified, efficiently measurable and safely contained.[31] It is this intense working on the body that is seen by some intensive care staff as the heart of what the intensive care nurse is about, reminiscent of Florence Nightingale's notes about the body and the spatial (Nightingale, 1969). Even though the anaesthetised body is often concealed and contained, it is through the leaking of blood onto the consultant's arm that the body is made present – the blood pollutes and presents risk to the clinical environment. The consultant froze (in the extract), watching blood ooze from Kevin's drip onto his arm, but to move is to place the anaesthetised body at risk. Puncturing, or opening up the body, is not simply making internal material visible, but calling attention to the body, the line and the institution from which the body has been retrieved. However, this episode makes visible the need for a replacement of the central line, which potentially becomes a site for infection. A breach in the circuit calls for 'discourses of risk' (*cf.* Eisner, 1997), as the bodies of both consultant and patient potentially become polluted. Organisationally and professionally, such matter out of place demands clinical attention, yet leaks in the circuit promote the cultural transgression of order and organising.

The central line[32] acted as an entry point into Kevin's body and through this, if even for a moment, the body was rendered visible to the consultant who had no choice but to remain motionless. Through reading the leak from a catheter that had been passed into the internal jugular vein, the consultant recognised that a new line would probably need to be re-sited. Within health care settings, time is associated with pollution – lines need to be re-sited in order to prevent colonisation; endotracheal tubes that facilitate ventilation can only be in situ for a limited period of time; and the length of time on mechanical ventilation needs to be limited to reduce risks of infection, lung damage and muscle wastage.[33] Pollution can be read through temporal indices, where time creates risk of 'dirt', its infiltration (or transgression of corporeal boundaries) and translocation. The medical notes that followed Kevin were checked to affirm the length of time the line had been in situ as part of a broader cleaning of what was known about Kevin and what shaped Kevin's ontology, through which he could be known or more significantly, read.[34] Kevin in turn was systematised and sanitised according to temporal, spatial and material indices, as the body and its pollution are only amenable to meaningful interpretation once figured as being in the right time, space and place.

> Consultant: I want somebody to do the bloods, x-ray, and sort out all the structural stuff. I want somebody else to go through the notes and get a thorough history. I don't want you to just write down what I've been told, I want you to read back and find out...
> (From field notes following intra-hospital transfer)

What information is considered reliable and what information should not be trusted is demonstrated by the consultant's intensivist who had 'retrieved' Kevin from another hospital. Even though the intensive care consultant had discussed this patient at length with the referring intensive care consultant, the facts held were not considered to be totally reliable within the home intensive care unit context. He had given an account of the patient to the junior doctors, but his account could not be paraphrased and written up in the medical notes. He demanded a thorough history of the patient to be documented, drawing from the notes supplied by the referring hospital. This was in part a history of the person, how he came to be in intensive care in the first place and what had happened to the body within the referring intensive care unit. In telling of the body, it was a tale of the organisation and practice of the referring intensive care unit, a tale of the embedded body that had been physically linked to another organisation. The consultant expected a thorough assessment of the body, as he stated the 'structural stuff', the material that would form the foundation for any further treatment. He demanded that the body be read and interpreted in a way that made sense to the organisational idiosyncrasies of *this* intensive care. The intensive care patient's equipment and scarification produced from the previous intensive care unit required documentation, the old lines needed to be removed and replaced with *this* intensive care unit's equipment. *The patient's* critically ill body needed to become '*our*' critically ill body. This did not mean that the previous intensive care unit was an inferior intensive care unit, more that the body needed to be 'sorted out' in a very particular way so that the body could be presented as 'our new patient' on the consultant's shift's 'hand-over' ward round in a few hours' time. Indeed, the *supplement* (Derrida, 1976 [1967]) to the previous home of the body needed to be eradicated, excised and replaced as such material stuff is of itself, matter out of place. To sort out is to make legible, and such legibility sanitises bodies, institutions, ways of thinking; cleansing thus done to align bodies (physical, metaphorical, epistemological, ontological) with the organisation and to breach organisational requirements renders such matter out of place. The body, its treatment and its history require work to cleanse it into the idiosyncrasies of this space. The body is smoothed and rendered legible as a knowable object of attention to this place.

For reasons of accountability the new intensive care unit requires a 'clean slate' from which to work; foreign equipment needs to be removed and replaced with the local equipment. While the work of legibility has been done elsewhere, the body needs to be made locally legible; the 'sorting out' and documentation needs to be done in order for the body to be presented on the ensuing ward round legibly. The body is ceremonially incorporated into the organisation, physically and metaphorically, while those connections to a previous organisation need to be cleaned, sanitised and reordered to the tethering of the new institution, the cultural norms presented simply as the 'way we do things here' (Deal and Kennedy, 1982). This clinical space does not allow for any differentiation of policy or practice since sanitisation rests on the routinisation of cultural norms and these cultural norms become the symbolic altar through which medical practices are performed and celebrated in relation to the physiological integrity of the body. To introduce foreign ideas, concepts and equipment is to challenge the existing arrangement of the institution (White et al., 2012). Accountability in terms of clinical practice is the sterilisation of process, the cleaning of bodies and bodily prostheses and incorporation into a set of organisational practices and procedures. Matter out of place has no place here and as such matter out of place is smoothed into matter in place, as the body needs to be reduced in compliance (*cf.* Garfinkel, 1967; Lynch, 1991[35]) with the requirements of this particular organisational order. This ordering renders the body ordered, through its connection to medical practices and technologies. It is present by its absence as technology masks the body and reappears through rupture and disorder; bodies reappear when their fluids cannot be contained. The latent body ruptures the sterility of clinical ceremonial order when it leaks.

Discussion

This chapter explored the biological and social body in the medical context of intensive care, with all its technological scaffolding. The body as technology and the latent body in the circuit of technology was explored within the space of the *ceremonial ordering* of clinical work (Strong, 1979), an ordering that keeps the body contained, yet arguably one that requires cleansing to fit in with a broader moral order of intensive care. The body is circuited as part of a complex technological array that orders the body (White, 2008, 2009) in an open system which Fox (1992) labels 'circuits of hygiene' – circuits of the science of sanitation, cleanliness and sterility. This circuit houses medical architecture such as the space of surgery and social relations in which 'the movement of things and bodies come together' (Fox, 1992: 33). The technological circuit as hygiene surfaces the maintenance and promotion of the sterility of intensive care practice and the critically ill body. Breaching the circuit pollutes. While Fox differentiates between patient, instrument and staff circuits we the authors wish to bring these together to show the complexity and interrelatedness of the technological circuit of the patient in intensive care. This circuit 'moves the patient from a dangerous social state to a safe one, someone who is healed' (Fox, 1992: 45). Rituals in the ceremonial order enable the containment of risk and rituals that are transgressed bring forth pollution, risk and ultimately death.

The body is both an extension of technology and a technology itself; the body is both a prosthesis of technology at the same time as technology is a prosthesis of the body. It is through this circuit that bodies become transformed as techno-bodies, a transformation which suppresses the social subject through technological ordering and containment. While the body in the circuit becomes a site to be worked on and through and as such disciplined by the circuit, the body disciplines other parts of the circuit, including the bodies of others such as health care professionals. The latent body therefore requires the technological circuit for its completion but it is also the site which denies the corporeal subject. When social interactions interrupt the circuit, the latent body becomes the subject.

We have made visible how the body of the critically ill is incorporated into a broader circuit of material, social and spatial relations, of a particular ontology of corporeal purview. The circuit of inotropic drugs that increase blood pressure is physically, ontologically and organisationally tethered to a particular way of perceiving the body. Assumptions, beliefs and cultural practices are inscribed in the materials and technologies that support the body (Latour, 1987). In this sense, we the authors have envisaged a circuit between intensive care staff, the preparation of drugs and their delivery into the body and the physical breaching of integument through the central line as part of a fabric of relations (*cf.* Lyotard, 1986) that aim to control physiological functioning in relation to a singular organ system. However, such control and the 'happenings' related to this circuit make visible some of the mundane assumptions of cultural life within a very specific and heavily technologically imbued organisational form. Within this, we have illuminated the juxtaposition of dirt in relation to its other and crucially pointed to how a breach at any point of this putative circuit (or series of sociotechnical relations) amplifies dirt, a risk of pollution and more significantly the degree of sanitation in order to assuage risk. Matter is tightly controlled through numerous interpretations and ways of seeing that are embedded and embodied in broader cultural norms that form the conduct of clinical practice.

In this chapter we the authors have performed this analysis of the critically ill body to render the body visible in order to explore the relationship between dirt as an absent presence (Shilling, 2003) by focusing on the containment of dirt through sterility. Sterility and its *other* can be similarly seen as a trope to concealment/unconcealment, as dirt is figured in relation to a supposed other. The focus on the body as part of the circuit for its containment becomes the circuit for pollution: the body is both a site for pollution and a vehicle for its return. More simply, dirt is dispersed through and from the body while being returned. The body is at risk of pollution and is itself a polluting force. The dispersion of pollution prefigures a return of risk as we have seen in injecting the body and the oozing of the body. The body therefore becomes a site of vulnerable return – vulnerable without the circuit and a circuit that brings vulnerability with it. Dirt presents vulnerability; it breaches the ceremonial order of sterility, clinical practice and medical norms despite the weight of organisational (clinical) practices that aim to eradicate dirt and pollution as risk.

The chapter unfolded by considering the injection site as a site for the transgression of the body by the needle and oozing of blood and the risk entailed to the critically ill body and that of staff themselves as read through experience and the placing of receptacles for safe disposal. In both instances we the authors demonstrated how organising processes and sterile practices sanitise the body and its organisation with dirt being the absent presence, which presents itself in the management of sterility and fear of pollution. Simultaneously the body and its workings are concealed and unconcealed – the body is rendered visible and invisible in both the allusions of sterility and its othering of dirt. Dirt as matter out of place – or matter in place – has been shown by looking at how dirt is avoided, regulated, translocated and managed rather than through the exploration of dirty practices. In this vein, this is the containment of disorder, and the containment of risk represents the smoothing of clinical, individual and the ontological as:

> ...the yearning for rigidity is in us all. It is part of our human condition to long for hard lines and clear concepts...
>
> (Douglas, 2002 [1966]: 200)

Transgression of the ceremonial order contaminates; contamination presents risk. As the body's self-containment is transgressed by the needle or the leaking of blood, so too are the cultural categories that seek to control order, cleanliness and wholeness.

In closing, recognising the technology of the body and that technologies maintain the body as matter in place, the body is read through a circuit of technology, materials, ontologies and epistemologies. The body set within its circuit recognises the body as both managed and disciplined to constrain critically ill bodies but also as important to the maintenance of the social order. The disciplined body therefore is analysed as a body to be worked on for survival and also for the functioning and maintenance of the social system (*cf.* Merleau-Ponty, 1968, 1989 [1962]). The body is not only constrained by cultural determinants but it also structures its relations, even though the critically ill body is a non-moving body which survives by it technological attachments and tethering to the organisation. Even though without the body there is no space (Merleau-Ponty, 1968, 1989 [1962]), as we have shown in intensive care, the body constitutes the social space. Without the circuit of technology-relations-body, there is no intensive care as a distinct organisational and cultural practice. Within the ceremonial order of sterility, the return of dirt is always prefigured as potentiality and dispersed as a particular organisational accomplishment.

Notes

1. This chapter is based on the research fieldwork conducted by the first-named author between 2002 and 2005 and funded by the Economic and Social Research Council (PTA-030-2002-00317) through the 'open sociology' stream and the British Association of Critical Care Nurses (small research award). Full ethical approval was granted by the relevant academic and health care research ethics committees and all identifiable names have been replaced with pseudonyms.
2. Weaning has been defined as 'the process of abruptly or gradually withdrawing ventilator support' (e.g. Alía and Esteban, 2000), that is weaning from mechanical ventilation to breathing independent of 'life support'.
3. Speech that passes the vocal chords is indicative of poor ventilation, as a circuit is required between ventilation technology and the lungs. Although means exist to enable speech and mechanical ventilation, these are not always used or deemed clinically appropriate for all intensive care patients.
4. Where the patient is suspended temporally through anaesthesia.
5. Rather than physiological representations, as the indices can be highly variable, particularly when 'normal' is read in relation to the pathological (*cf.* Berg and Bowker, 1997; Canguilhem, 1989 [1966]), with abnormality resting on behavioural, social and situational factors. Unfortunately, further discussion of this issue is beyond the scope of this chapter.
6. As operational accomplishment rather than any true empirical fact (*cf.* Durkheim, 1982 [1895]).
7. Here we suggest that a proper place is seen in relation to how social actions and interactions figure in an organisational ontology.
8. We have in mind here hospital infection control policies that *in extremis* have demanded sterile spaces, which can be achieved at great expense but with little gain, lasting only for periods of hours. Human bodies (in a microbiological sense) are only 10 per cent human at the level of the cellular and to sterilise spaces simply renders a space amenable to colonisation (Gillespie, and Bamford, 2000; Playfair, 1995).
9. Following what Foucault (2002 [1972]) refers to as 'systems of dispersion', where power is dispersed within discourse and enacted through action and interaction rather than being specifically focussed. Thereby the eradication of power makes no sense; power can only ever be and only ever is dispersed. This is similarly an issue highlighted by Durkheim (1982 [1895]) in relation to crime and deviance (and indeed his corpus of the normal and the pathological), where criminal elements can never not exist, as they will always be relative and dispersed in relation to given cultural norms as a point of perception.
10. Or indeed the normative and normalising gaze of Foucault (1989 [1973]).
11. Arguably much of Foucault's work is concerned with problematising normative and normalising taxonomic structures, following Canguilhem (1989

[1966]). Systems of dispersion in particular are understood as the dispersion of power/knowledge in discourse.

12. Such translocations of microbiological flora and of dirt are the cause of infection (e.g. Gillespie and Bamford, 2000; Playfair, 1995), as translocation represents flora out of place, but with a potential for further (trans)location.
13. Or indeed a particular discursive formation (Foucault, 2002 [1972]).
14. Hillman et al. (2010) make visible some of the ways in which patients are disposed as being 'in the wrong spaces' and having this legitimated through calls to organisational process (following Weber, 1992).
15. See Latimer and Munro (2006) for discussion of moves and the concept of motility.
16. See White (2009) for a more detailed discussion of 'sorting out' the body and rendering the body legible.
17. Although in practice the nursing staff worked off a pre-printed prescription chart that reflected a generically desirable Mean Arterial Pressure.
18. At least this is how one reading of intensive care work may see it, given the caveats attached to the factitious nature of representation as interpretation (Rorty, 1979).
19. Integrity in the sense of *integer*, wholeness or completeness as well as that of integration, the incorporation of parts into wholes, where the parts of medical technology and the technology of the body become functionally indistinguishable.
20. The drawers in the trolley have a set pattern; the top drawer contains patient drugs (and a more random collection of equipment); the second drawer contains needles, cannulae, tubes, gauze and tape; the third drawer contains syringes and the bottom drawer which is deeper contains bags of intravenous fluids. Any large deviation from this can be problematic when another nurse (or doctor) comes into the bed area, particularly in emergencies where things are expected to be in their rightful place – matter out of place is not acceptable.
21. Although in the case of break relief the main concern will be that the patient would be left inappropriately, should emergency drugs be required, it is anticipated that the patient will be left with relief in a state that requires little or no intervention from others unless explicitly stated.
22. As they are embedded in the routines, procedures and practices of intensive care and are *disciplined* (in the forms of organisational norms that guide the junior nurse) and eventually embody the space in a particular way.
23. Patterns may be numerical in the case of trends and illustrations, such as arterial line traces, electrocardiograph rhythms or other patterns of corporeal or non-corporeal indices made visual.
24. 'Numbers' refer to the physiological variables that are tightly controlled by intensive care staff (see White, 2009).
25. Numerous supportive technologies such as tubes and wires breach bodily boundaries. Most prostheses extend the body into the technologies surrounding the body that support organ systems or render the body legible – a trope which is worked with from Strathern (2004).
26. Arguably this is the base application of Maslow's (1943, 1982 [1968]) hierarchy of needs *par excellence*.

27. Although as we have been pressing previously, such a disposal prefigures a dispersal from one space to another, a space of movement rather than a destructive force.
28. This consultant attributed such inappropriate behaviour of the nursing staff to a senior nurse in the ambulance. Yet observations in the field suggested that most of the intensive care staff engaged in this form of play at some time and were dependent upon the senior nurse and consultant intensivist in charge on that particular shift.
29. What we have termed here 're-translation' refers to the interpretations of physiological data, rather than the frequently assumed physiological *representation* of a physiological reality. Such a representation is often interpreted in relation to a broader array of physiological, cultural and experiential signs, symptoms and guesswork and not necessarily as clear-cut as would befit a flow diagram or textbook. The work of re-translation here refers to the layers of interpretations that hold (Latour, 1987), yet stand before (Heidegger, 1993) the cascade of inscriptions (Latour, 1987) or host of assumptions that underpin the interpretation.
30. The 'obs' or observation chart is an A3-size sheet of paper which is placed on an architect's table at the foot of the bed, where physiological and pharmaceutical parameters are recorded (at least hourly) by the nursing staff.
31. At least for a time, urine is collected over a 24-hour period for daily biochemical analysis.
32. Or central-venous catheter, as opposed to peripheral-vein cannula (which is placed in peripheral veins such as in the limbs).
33. In particular, breathing tubes have a similarly strong temporal call to risk as tubes into the mouth or nose are short-term means of facilitating ventilation; should longer-term ventilation be required, a tracheostomy is performed where the throat is punctured to prevent risk of infection and tissue damage.
34. That is patients are written (Latimer, 1993) into medical documentation (Berg and Bowker, 1997) in relation to medical (predominantly) and managerial discourses, rendering subjects legible only to such discursive frames; there is nothing beyond (or outside) of such a textual (contextual) formulation (*cf.* Derrida, 1976 [1967]).
35. We are thinking ethnomethodologically, particularly here in terms of indexicality, which is how a context is constructed in order for social action to make sense (so nonsense can make sense if the context is sufficiently furnished) and this is the normal work of everyday social action (Benson and Hughes, 1991; Garfinkel, 1967; Garfinkel and Sacks, 1970). On the other hand, the common-sense context can be constructed *a priori* and everything has to fit that given format in order to make sense; the sense in turn does not of itself represent a putative reality but is constructed in relation to a putative reality which of itself reproduces a particular assumption (Gouldner, 1971).

10
Gendering and Embodying Dirty Work: Men Managing Taint in the Context of Nursing Care

Ruth Simpson, Natasha Slutskaya and Jason Hughes

Introduction

Based on data from a recently completed project in Australia, this chapter explores the gendered nature of 'dirty work' and how male nurses perceive and manage the 'taint' associated with nursing care. From Hughes (1951) dirty work includes tasks, occupations and roles that are likely to be perceived as disgusting or degrading, while the management of taint refers to the ways in which contact with dirt, as a 'discrediting mark' (Goffman, 1963), is responded to and experienced (Drew et al., 2007). As Ashforth and Kreiner (1999) point out, dirty work has been neglected in recent organisational literature. Further, while the proportion of male nurses in the profession in Australia has risen – currently 9 per cent, reflecting the proportion in other Western contexts (AIHW, 2007) – persistent labour shortages mean that understanding the challenges men face, for reasons of retention and recruitment, is a pressing concern.

The gendered nature of dirty work is partly manifest in the way such work often conforms to traditional notions of masculinity and femininity. Service and care, for example, have strong associations with the embodied dispositions of women, while other forms of dirty work (e.g. heavy manual labour, work involving risk or danger) are traditionally the domain of men. However, with some notable exceptions (e.g. Bolton, 2005; Tracy and Scott, 2006), previous work has tended to overlook the significance of gender or has rendered gender present but implicit rather than explicit in the analysis. Moreover, as Tracy and Scott (2006) point out, work on men doing dirty work has tended to focus on 'manly' jobs associated with traditionally masculine values of strength and endurance. By focusing on a non-traditional work context, where masculinity is 'on the line' and subject to challenge, the gendered implications of work are in a general context likely to be rendered more visible (Morgan, 1992) and the gendered nature of dirty work to be revealed.

Through the research site of male nurses, this chapter accordingly seeks to explore how gender is implicated in the 'dirty' elements of nursing care, both in terms of the meanings attached to the work and, relatedly, in terms of the experience and management of taint. In doing so, the chapter not only highlights how gender is integral to understandings of such work, but also suggests that acknowledgement be given to the significance of the body and of the embodied meanings attached to the job. The study therefore extends our understanding of dirty work by incorporating both gendered and embodied dimensions.

Conceptualising dirty work

Building on Hughes's (1958) early conceptualisation, Ashforth and Kreiner (1999) from a social psychological perspective categorise dirty work under three forms of taint: physical (occupations associated with physical dirt or danger), social (occupations that involve contact with people from stigmatised groups or where the job involves servility) and moral (occupations regarded as 'immoral' or unethical). As they argue, the typology highlights the fact that 'dirtiness' is not necessarily inherent to the work itself but is perceived as such according to subjective standards of cleanliness and purity. What they share is not so much any specific attribute, task or role, but an attitude on the part of others of 'visceral repugnance' towards such work. A further body of work has explored how dirty workers manage the effects of taint. For example, from an organisational communication perspective, Meisenbach (2010) has identified several 'stigma management communication strategies', including accepting, avoiding, evading responsibility, denying and ignoring, while, influenced by social constructionism, Tracy and Scott (2006) have shown in the context of firefighting how gendered discourses can be drawn on to reframe work in preferred terms. In this respect, as Tracy and Scott (2006) argue, concepts of taint, dirt and prestige are intimately connected to powerful social categories such as gender, though these implications are rarely central to the analysis. Therefore, as they argue, gender and the significance of broader gendered discourses remain peripheral to understandings of dirty work – implicit rather than explicit in the analysis – and relatively marginal in terms of how it is seen to be experienced.

Following some recent work in the area (e.g. Dick, 2005; Drew et al., 2007; Tracy and Scott, 2006), we the authors draw on a social constructionist epistemology, which prioritises the co-construction of meanings through interaction and language (Berger and Luckmann, 1966), and which accordingly, in the current context, sees dirty work as grounded in prevailing social, cultural, discursive and linguistic practice. In short, we acknowledge that dirty work has a material, social and discursive dimension. We not only highlight how gender is integral to the meanings given to such work but also point to ways in which dirty work can be seen as embodied. This is to recognise that certain jobs may be seen as less desirable (i.e. dirtier) by some groups yet more acceptable to others, that perceptions of the 'intensity' of dirt depends partly on essential characteristics of the worker and that some skills and attributes may be devalued, depending on who practises and embodies them. Meanings attached to dirt and to dirty work are therefore connected to the gendered nature of the work, as discussed above, as well as, relatedly, to the assumed embodied dispositions of the worker.

Men, nursing and dirty work

Several themes have emerged from the growing literature on the experiences of male nurses. These relate mainly to career trajectories and challenges encountered in a caring role. In terms of the former, while some men may choose to remain close to professional practice and to reject notions of upward mobility (Simpson, 2009), others have been 'fast-tracked' into career-enhancing specialist areas or into management, benefitting from the assumption that they have better leadership and other skills and that they have a more careerist attitude towards work (Evans, 1997; Heikes, 1991; Williams, 1993). Male nurses also face challenges in a job that draws on emotional labour and requires special abilities that are culturally coded as feminine (Heikes, 1991; Hochschild, 1983). This can create problems for men whose competence and suitability are often under scrutiny, particularly if they display traditional forms of masculinity (Connell and Messerschmidt, 2005), but whose sexuality is called into question if they adopt a more feminine approach (Evans, 2002). Existing research suggests that men respond to these challenges, and to the fear of feminisation and stigmatisation, by distancing themselves from the feminine (Evans, 2002; Heikes, 1991; Lupton, 1999; Williams, 1993). Male nurses may thus aspire to management or supervisory posts (Heikes, 1991; Williams, 1993), align and identify themselves with more powerful male groups such as doctors (Evans, 2002; Simpson, 2005) and/or move into what may be seen as more 'masculine' specialisms (Simpson, 2009; Williams, 1993) such as mental health, with historic links to custodialism, or to accident and emergency, seen as more technologically oriented and 'adrenalin-charged' than standard nursing care.

As Dahle (2005) argues, these strategies comprise a 'flight from the body' on the part of male nurses. The maintaining of distance from one's own as well as others' bodies has developed as an important sign of hierarchical position (Hancock and Tyler, 2000). Thus nurses who do 'body work' involving touching are seen to be of lower status (Van Dongen and Elema, 2001), compared to nursing work involving less intimate care. In this respect, nursing work, women's work and dirty work can be seen to be inextricably linked (Bolton, 2005) through association with the intimate care of bodies (culturally defined as feminine) and with the private realm, where much of women's work and 'care' takes place (Bolton, 2005). The gendered nature of such work is exacerbated by meanings attached to basic body fluids, overloaded with ideas associated with dirt and disgust (Douglas, 1966), seen as highly polluting (Ackroyd, 2007) and of low esteem (Dahle, 2005; Isaksen, 2005).

Medicine is accordingly constructed as an occupation suitable for men only if interaction with the patient's body is limited and given to (female) nurses or care-workers. As Davies (1996) argues, within healthcare a medical division of labour exists to celebrate a masculine vision of professional expertise. Within the nursing sector itself, there are divisions of status which reflect different relations to the body such as the distinction between basic/general nursing, involving care of the physical and bodily needs of patients, and technical nursing, coded as more masculine and 'cleaner', that is tasks that are more technical and involve less touching of patients (Wolkowicz, 2003). As Jervis (2001) notes, attempts by some nurses to shed the dirty work associated with bodily waste (in the case of general nurses and care workers) has intensified the symbolic pollution of those lower down the hierarchy. Care work can thus be seen as dirty work (Isaksen, 2005) so that intimate care is difficult to combine with ideas of masculinity. This notion is supported by Bolton's (2005) study of gynaecological nursing in which female nurses see themselves as possessing distinctive qualities (of compassion and understanding) in comparison with men, perceived as too focused on the technical to fully appreciate the demands of the job.

Aims and method

Against this background, this chapter sets out to explore the gendered nature of dirty work and, relatedly, the ways in which men experience and manage taint. These aims formed part of a larger research project to look at how men perceive and perform emotional labour in nursing care. Results are based on interviews conducted in 2006 with 16 male nurses from six different hospitals in and around Sydney, New South Wales. The sample was established through personal contact and by placing advertisements, briefly explaining the purpose of the project, in professional journals and associated websites. While this sampling technique can have drawbacks, in that interviewees who self-select may have more 'issues' relating to their work context than other employees (Simpson, 2009), such techniques have been used in other research on non-traditional occupations (e.g. Murray, 1996) and therefore may be seen as acceptable, given such reservations, in this case.

Of the male nurses, four were senior managers, two were midwives and two were psychiatric nurses. The remainder were located in various specialisms (intensive care, HIV, accidents and emergencies, working in operating theatres) or were still in training and/or working in general nursing in the ward. All but two of the nurses were registered – a professional status – having completed a university-level course. The two remaining nurses were 'enrolled'. Enrolled nurses in Australia spend 12 months training at the equivalent of a further education college, followed by practical experience in hospital wards. The four senior managers had some contact with patients in their current position and all four had spent time in the wards in the past while undertaking general nursing duties. They were therefore able to reflect on their experiences in these clinical roles. The other 12 nurses in the sample had daily contact with patients that involved some form of bodily contact and bodily care. All the men interviewed were Caucasian and between the ages of 26 and 40, and the majority (12 out of 16) were born in Australia. Of the 16 interviewees, six identified themselves as homosexual. Due to its sensitive nature, issues around sexual orientation were not pursued as a specific line of inquiry and were only discussed if raised, unprompted, by interviewees. It is possible therefore that this aspect of identity and experience is under-represented in the data.

The research adopted a social constructionist approach in that it explored how men give meaning to their experiences at work and how they make sense of their reality. The goal of social constructionism is to understand the world of lived experience from the point of view of those who live it (Berger and Luckmann, 1966). This rejects positivist philosophical assumptions of an objective, stable reality and focuses on the social construction of what is taken as real (Johnson et al., 2006). The aim is to challenge previously taken-for-granted understandings and to reveal alternative meanings. This approach therefore lends itself to an exploration of meanings given to work and to work experiences.

Interviews, conducted by the first author, were semi-structured, following a set of themes that included attitudes and practices of emotional labour (what does 'caring' mean to you? what aspects of caring do you find most difficult? what challenges do you as a man face in performing a caring role?); perceptions of personal attributes and skills required (what qualities do you think you need to be a good nurse? which of these qualities do you/your female counterparts bring?); perceptions and experiences of the most difficult and challenging parts of the job (what difficulties have you encountered performing a nursing role? when has gender been an 'issue' or problem in the work that you do?); and attitudes of others to career choices (what reaction did you get from family, e.g. fathers and brothers, and from friends when you told them you wanted to be a nurse?). Interviews were conducted in the place of work and lasted between one and one-and-a-half hours. All interviews were recorded and subsequently transcribed.

Thematic data analysis was undertaken as appropriate for a social constructionist methodology (Braun and Clarke, 2006). Here, 'patterns of experiences' (Aronson, 1994), based on 'conversation topics, vocabulary, recurring activities, meanings, feelings' (Taylor and Bogdan, 1984, p.131), were identified through a process of 'abduction' (Blaikie, 2000), which involves moving between a priori concepts and emergent meanings. Thus, analysis was guided in part by existing typologies of physical, social and moral taint (Ashforth and Kreiner, 1999; Hughes, 1951) so that data was explored for instances where these constructs were surfaced in the text and for meanings attached in terms of how such taint was experienced and managed. Thus, common descriptors of physical taint were often accompanied by gender-based constructions of difference, as men presented themselves as having 'special qualities' in undertaking such work. Data was also analysed for new meanings that lay outside these constructs. For Braun and Clarke (2006), analysis involved familiarisation with the data through repeated readings, generation of initial codes across the data set and identification of themes through collating codes. For example, initial codes of 'feelings of discomfort', 'being treated differently' and 'problematic masculinity' were combined into a theme entitled 'matter out of place' to capture perceptions that men and their bodies do not 'belong' in a nursing role. Analysis was a recursive, rather than a linear, process in that there was movement back and forth between codes, data and themes. Analysis was undertaken by each author separately in the first instance with later corroboration given to emerging themes by comparing and discussing, in a reflexive manner, individual insights and interpretations.

In recognition of the researchers' implication in the production of accounts (Pullen, 2006a), interviews took the form of a dialogue. Reflexivity was sought through a shared process of exploration. Here, interviewer and interviewee discussed the meanings of recounted experiences and respondents were encouraged to consider, in the manner of reflexivity put forward by Martin (2006), their attitudes, emotions and behaviours. Concerns that the gender difference between (female) interviewer and (male) interviewee might raise epistemological issues concerning the standpoint from which an understanding of men and masculinity (Evans, 2002) can be developed as well as influence the willingness to disclose were kept in mind during the interview situation. However, as Evans (2002) notes, women's greater awareness of gender may offer a broader and more 'comprehensive' lens for examining issues of masculinity. Further, men spent a large part of their day working and communicating with women and there was an ease in terms of shared reflections and disclosures in the interview situation.

Gendered meanings of dirty work: physical, moral and social taint

Physical taint

Issues around physical taint were evident in nurses' accounts of their experiences. Here, men referred to the 'messiness' of dealing with sick bodies, drawing attention to the blood, the vomit and/or preparing bodies for the morgue:

It's a messy job – no one likes to pick up faeces or vomit – it's seen as very much a caring thing, a girly sort of job.

(midwife)

Dead bodies – it's not nice dealing with all that. At first I found it quite disturbing – repellent really. But at the end of the day, you just have to get on with it. Perhaps it's a male thing – you quite literally have to roll up your sleeves and do it.

(General nurse)

In physical terms, bodily excreta and contact with bodily fluids can be seen as dirty (Jervis, 2001), highly polluting and invoking feelings of discomfort and disgust. Gendered implications of bodily care were often drawn upon in nurses' descriptions and accounts. Thus, in the above quotes, intimate care was coded as feminine (a 'girly job'), while at the same time, the ability to deal with the physicality of death and to endure the unpleasant and repellent was conferred on men.

In terms of the latter, men commonly presented physical taint in masculine terms. As Kreiner et al. (2006) argue, the tainted aspects of dirty work are often projected onto the dirty worker – making social validation problematic. Taint can be managed through 'reframing' the work and its ideologies in positive terms (Ashforth and Kreiner, 1999). Thus, some male nurses mobilised feelings of disgust to claim special expertise and heroic qualities – qualities which were differentiated from those of women. Here, women were presented as reluctant to undertake such work and as prevaricating to avoid the day-to-day cleaning, showering and bodily care of patients:

> I'm told by my superiors that taking them to the toilet is the most rewarding thing you can do, well ten times a day it isn't... and I'm honest about that I don't want to take this Billy Bloggs to the toilet again but I'll do it – but I've found that a lot of my female colleagues will just turn off, they won't answer the bell.
>
> (General nurse)

The ability to 'stomach' the physical 'dirtiness' of the job was also a source of differentiation from other men. One nurse commented on his choice of career vis-à-vis those of his male friends:

> Some of it's [the work] upsetting, they couldn't cope with the smells, can't cope with blood, can't cope with opening bodies, with crisis and emergencies and disaster, but particularly just unwell people... so many males find it quite foreign to take on a role as a nurse.
>
> (Accident and emergency nurse)

Another recalled how, faced with his own child falling ill with breathing difficulties through a bad cold, he had used a tube and 'sucked out' the mucus from her nose – much to the disgust of his wife. As he commented nonchalantly, 'My wife gagged and went running and I said why not, I figured it would work'.

As Dahle (2005) has argued, it is hard for men to construct a credible masculine identity in nursing work, where male surgeons colonise the heroic and often ignore the qualities of bodily care work of the nursing staff. However, by presenting their abilities in 'masculine' terms and as special qualities (different from women, different from other men), men can create a distinctive space for the practice of masculinity through meanings associated with endurance and fortitude. Gender is thus drawn on in an active strategy to reframe meanings around such work.

Moral taint

The practices of touch, as Evans (1997) notes, can add a further dimension of taint that has a 'moral' nature (defined above as jobs or roles regarded as sinful or of dubious virtue). This is particularly the case when men are required to touch, often in intimate ways, the bodies of women:

> Taking vaginal packs out, that sort of thing, that's some of the most intimate things you can be doing to people. Now that has to be done and if you're the nurse on the ward and you happen to be a man who's allocated to that patient then it's something you do.
>
> (Midwife)

By drawing attention to the need for male nurses to undertake intimate care of women, gendered norms are surfaced that suggest an incongruity when such tasks are performed by men. Notions of 'deviance' (Evans, 1997; Mangan, 1994) through stigmatising labels of homosexuality or through the 'sexualisation' of men's touch (Evans, 2002) can create discomfort and suspicion on the part of patients and colleagues, impacting on nurses' own perceptions of their safety while performing intimate care. This is in contrast to women's touch which, from Evans (2002), is seen as harmless and non-threatening – a natural extension of their caring role. In this respect, the use of the terms 'people' and 'patient' rather than 'women' by the nurse in the above quote may serve to distance from the source of taint, drawing attention away from the 'femaleness' of the body in his care and so lessening the potential for negative judgements. The 'marking' of men's bodies as potentially dangerous, disruptive and problematic can accordingly have implications for how men experience and negotiate intimate care as well as for how it is managed. In the latter respect, one nurse recalled a sense of confusion over appropriate practices and procedures when he worked in a gynaecology ward:

> Dealing with or working with females on surgical wards, gynae wards, my managers went through great problems to work out whether I needed a chaperone or not to do a procedure on a female patient. I thought how stupid, I'm a nurse. It doesn't matter whether you're male or female, you've got the skills and the knowledge to do a procedure.
>
> (General nurse)

Perceptions of 'moral taint', associated with body ascriptions of danger or deviance, are thus mitigated by mobilising discourses of body integrity, captured in a language of 'agendered' and 'asexual' professional expertise. In this way, meanings attached to the masculine body that raise issues pertaining to 'moral taint' can be rendered less salient through a language that creates distance from the source of taint, through the mobilisation of asexuality by identification with a (ethically positioned) professional body and by invoking meanings around skills and proficiency.

Social taint

Elements of social taint (e.g. jobs/roles that are servile to others) also emerged from the data. In this respect, the subservient relationship with doctors was a common source of discomfort:

> I don't put up with it – the doctors can treat you like servants really, expect you to go running around after them. I've not done all this training to be handmaiden to a doctor. The women I think find it easier.
>
> (Psychiatric nurse)

All male nurses referred to a 'special' relationship with male doctors – a relationship that was based either on conflict and confrontation, as in the above quote, or on masculine bonds of fraternity. In each case the relationship was presented as special in that it was not shared by women.

> I don't do all that looking up to the doctors stuff – I'll say 'Hi Doc, how was your weekend?' and I think they like that, they like a more informal approach and they listen to me more than if I stood on one

side saying 'yes doctor, no doctor'... the women tend to do that and I don't think the doctors appreciate that.

(Theatre nurse)

Women were routinely constructed as 'deferential' in their dealings with doctors in contrast to the more informal attitude of men. As Lupton (1999) points out, the taking up of an inferiorised identity can be more difficult for men, leading to uncomfortable feelings of servility. This may be particularly the case when men are forced to confront a privileged masculinity at the workplace. Experiences of and responses to expectations of servility, captured in the concept of social taint, are accordingly coloured by gender as male nurses, through 'narratives of difference' (Ashcraft and Mumby, 2004), seek to separate from women and seek to align themselves with, or actively confront, higher-status men.

Undesirable, 'inequitable' work

One further source of taint, which fell outside the typology of dirty work presented above, emerged from the data. This related to specific tasks which were seen as undesirable, inequitably distributed and marginal to the core practices of nursing. As other studies of male nurses have found (e.g. Evans, 2002; Heikes, 1991; Simpson, 2009), men were routinely co-opted into tasks that demanded physical strength or discipline – lifting heavy patients and equipment, being given the difficult patients or being sent to 'crisis' situations as 'boundary setters'. Such work was assigned specifically to men and was often strongly resisted:

> I was looking after this difficult, obstreperous, domineering, argumentative man with a varicose ulcer on his leg... as a male nurse I get all the cruddy patients, all the difficult ones you know.
>
> (General nurse)

> I'm expected to do all the heavy lifting   forget it!
>
> (Intensive care nurse)

> I'll get a buzz from the desk to say there's a problem somewhere can you sort it out – and I'm thinking, what am I supposed to do? Just call security... I'm not here to do that, so I say I'm in the middle of something, I'll go when I've finished.
>
> (Psychiatric nurse)

As Dick (2005) has argued, all occupations are likely to contain tasks or roles that are considered undesirable or demeaning. As seen earlier, perceptions of such taint, as with other forms of dirty work, are highly subjective, dependent partly on the attitudes of those who perform it. For some men, these ancillary tasks were welcomed as an opportunity to affirm their masculinity and special contribution to nursing. They accordingly facilitated the uptake of a 'protector' role, which was presented in a traditional way as masculine chivalry and a concern for the welfare of women. For others, however, such work was 'tainted' – seen as demeaning and inappropriate. Based on stereotypical gendered expectations, and linked to masculine bodily ascriptions and meanings (e.g. authority, discipline, strength), the assignment of these tasks to men was seen by many as inequitable – adding to the workload and undermining professional status.

Matter out of place

Meanings around 'disorder', resonant with Douglas's (1966) definition of dirt as 'matter out of place', permeated much of the data and helped surface the implications of a mismatch between the masculine body and the social expectations of the job. In this respect, men were seen as unsuitable for a nursing role:

> When I was on the wards, geriatrics, it was like, what are you doing here? You're no good at all this stuff – the bed changing, the cleaning, showering, changing patients with double incontinence... It's not something you should be doing.
>
> (Senior nurse manager)

> There was this constant undercurrent that (a) you shouldn't be here, either because you're a bloke or (b) because you're too intelligent and you should be a doctor.
>
> (Midwife)

As Evans (2002) notes, there is often an expectation that men should be fast-tracked out of general nursing, which involves a higher element of physical care and is seen as disruptive and out of place, into 'cleaner', more technical specialisms or into management. As she argues, along the lines of Connell (2000), while nurturance, service and bodily care are inscribed upon the 'softer' bodies of women, meanings attached to men's bodies (e.g. of independence, cleanliness, detachment, authority, containment) are out of line with the social definitions of nursing care, which is thus seen as 'unsuitable' for men. In the following quote, which contains a strong racial element, a nurse recalled the reaction of his brothers to the news that he was taking up nursing as a profession:

> So when I told them I was going to be a nurse they said, you don't need a brain if you want to be a nurse. We can teach black women how to do that work, you know? So that is one kind of stigma I actually experienced because they thought that it was inferior, it was only good enough for black women to do.
>
> (Intensive care nurse)

Another nurse similarly reported the response of a close friend:

> He said, what do you want to be a nurse for? That's a girl's job – all those bed pans and stuff and clearing up sick, running around after the doctors. It's not a job for you. I had quite a job to convince him that it was what I wanted, that it's OK for a bloke to want to be a nurse.
>
> (General nurse)

Notions of 'suitability' based on gender (and race) can thus underpin perceptions of dirt, as 'disorder' and 'matter out of place' (Douglas, 1966). In this respect, as Douglas argued, the body serves as an image of the social system in that bodies are hierarchically arranged and inscribed with status-related meanings. White men are thus normative to notions of 'clean' rather than dirty work (Duffy, 2007). Not all male nurses, however, are perceived to be incongruent with a caring role. Homosexual men, 'othered' by their sexuality and their bodies already aligned with meanings of disorder (Churchill, 1990), could be seen to be more suitable for work involving intimate and bodily care:

> From my friends, they didn't have a problem with it. But I think it was because I'm from a marginalised community – because I'm a gay man I think it was OK, it's OK to be a nurse.
>
> (Midwife)

> My father wasn't happy at first 'cos he thought it wasn't a job for a bloke and he was I think ashamed that I was doing what he thought

was a girls' job – he thought it was just emptying bedpans and stuff [laughs]. But then when I told him later I was gay he kind of came round to it. I think he put the two together and thought it was all part of being gay.

(Psychiatric nurse)

Within the regulatory framework of heterosexual masculinity, male nurses can be subject to the judgements implied by the conventionally gendered and heterosexual gaze (Simpson, 2009). As Chung and Harman (1994) point out, links are often drawn between gay men and non-traditional careers because they both endorse unconventionality. A greater sense of 'fit' can thus be identified between the 'feminised' homosexual body and the 'feminine' nature of nursing care, mitigating the incongruity perceived when such work is performed by (heterosexual) men. Overall, this suggests that conceptualisations of taint (e.g. physical, social, moral) can only be fully understood in relation to the significance of the embodied characteristics of the worker and that some groups may be seen as more suitable for such work. Gender, as well as the significance of meanings around the (heterosexual, white) masculine body – thought to be detached, clean, rational and potentially disruptive in a caring role – have emerged as central to understanding the dynamics and experiences of such work. Drawing on Douglas's definition of dirt, some men, normative to notions of clean work, can be seen as 'matter out of place' in these roles, and perceptions of taint and disorder may accordingly intensify when this group performs them.

Discussion

This chapter set out to explore the gendered nature of dirty work and the way men manage taint in the practices of nursing care. The study addressed a neglect of dirty work within organisation studies (Ashforth and Kreiner, 1999; Kreiner et al., 2006). It has significance given the need to attract men into the profession to alleviate labour shortages (Evans, 2002) and given that labour market instability, a common feature in contemporary national contexts, is often associated with men considering 'non-traditional' careers. Occupational taint and 'stigma' can play a negative role in job commitment, performance and turnover rates (Ashforth and Kreiner, 1999) suggesting, from Meisenbach (2010), a need to understand the factors that make individuals vulnerable to such threats. We the authors addressed a tendency in the literature to adopt an 'identity-blind' approach to understandings of the meanings ascribed to dirty work – specifically, from Tracy and Scott (2006), a neglect of gender in conceptualisations of the dirty work experience. In doing so, the study surfaced, relatedly, how an understanding of dirty work must acknowledge the significance of the body in terms of the relationship between occupational discourses and meanings given to embodied dispositions of workers. Through this study, gender and the body have been implicated in several ways in conceptualisations of dirty work as well as in the way taint is managed.

Firstly, gender and meanings ascribed to the masculine body have emerged as integral to some constructions of dirty work. Thus, notions of moral taint in the context of nursing care can be founded on meanings (of deviance/danger) ascribed specifically to men's bodies and to their touch (Evans, 2002). This form of taint may accordingly – within nursing – be exclusively related to men. Equally, some tasks that are perceived as undesirable, inequitable and ancillary to the nursing role (e.g. heavy lifting, boundary setting) are assigned only to male nurses and aligned with assumptions of their essential qualities and aptitudes. The fact that not all men perceived such roles as tainted highlights Dick's (2005) claim regarding the contingent nature of meanings attached to such work in that their constructions depend in part on the attitudes of those who undertake it. In general terms, however, from our data, some tasks or roles can be perceived to be tainted partly because, through normative values and expectations, a particular (e.g. masculine) body performs them.

Secondly, gender emerges as a key discursive resource in the management of taint. Here, some men invoke masculinity, mobilising disgust to create a sense of pride in the ability to 'stomach' dirt and infusing the work with special expertise. In this way they 'reframe' (Ashforth and Kreiner, 1999) meanings around physical taint into a 'badge of honour' as they differentiate themselves from women as well as from other men. This resonates with Ackroyd and Crowdy's (1990) slaughtermen who valorise the dirtier elements of the job, drawing clear boundaries from women, as well as Tracy and Scott's (2006) firefighters who mobilise the heroic to frame the work in preferred terms. Men can accordingly reframe physical taint in positive terms by mobilising masculinity to create a special status within the nursing role.

This highlights how, from Tracy and Scott (2006), physical taint may be easier to manage than social or moral taint through traditional notions of masculinity. Our data supports this to some extent. Thus, while the effects of physical taint are partly mitigated through masculine discourses, moral taint can create particular difficulties as men struggle to manage intimations of sexual deviance. Here, meanings relating to masculinity (e.g. around sexual prowess and potency) may exacerbate, rather than mitigate, perceptions of unethical intent. Rather, men turn to professional discourses that create distance from gender and space for meanings around bodily integrity. By contrast, as with physical taint, traditional masculinity finds purchase in negotiating social taint, that is in relations of servility with higher-status men. Male nurses accordingly draw on behaviours based on a rejection of deference, culturally coded as feminine, and the construction of ties of fraternity to neutralise its effects. Taken together, this foregrounds the contingent nature of how taint is managed (e.g. how gendered discourses can help mitigate physical and social taint but exacerbate moral taint) as well as how gender as a discursive resource may be differentially available and, where appropriate, co-opted strategically to manage taint and its effects.

Thirdly, notions of male nurses as 'matter out of place' (Douglas, 1966) help further surface the significance of the body in understandings of dirty work. Particular bodies accordingly are inscribed with occupational discourses (Trethewey, 1999; Wolkowitz, 2006) in the form of gendered meanings attached to skills and work practices. Thus, in the context of the present study, meanings relating to men's bodies (e.g. of rationality, detachment, cleanliness, danger) are seen as incongruent with the demands of nursing, such as those based on bodily care and emotional support. Instead, these demands are commonly inscribed on the bodies of women (Evans, 2002), with their association with 'lower-order' behaviours (Hassard et al., 2000) such as those involving service and intimate care. Men are seen to be 'out of place' and unsuitable for the demands of such roles – a perception that may be exacerbated by cultural meanings relating to heterosexuality. In support of this, in a different context, Anderson (2000) refers to how norms of acceptability deem some dirty work (e.g. cleaning) to be appropriate for women – their bodies, marked by misogyny and carrying dirt's stigma – but not, from Glenn (1992), suitable for men. This is a move away from seeing dirty work as a specifically tainted task or role, as implied within Ashforth and Kreiner's (1999) typology. Here, while acknowledging the role of perceptions and feelings in understandings of such work, notions of taint are still largely attached to aspects of the work itself. Instead, an orientation that takes into account the meanings attached to the (gendered) body and how these intersect with work practices is suggested. Dirt and taint may therefore be less stable than the classifications of physical, social and moral taint suppose – interacting in complex ways with bodily perceptions, expectations and ascriptions. In other words, dirty work needs to be seen as an embodied activity.

Finally, following from the above, perceptions of the 'intensity' (Kreiner et al., 2006) of taint may well depend on this bodily dimension. In other words, dirty work may appear 'dirtier' when some groups undertake it, that is where bodily meanings and characteristics of the worker fail to fit the social definition of the work. Thus, in terms of social taint, women are expected to be deferential in service work (Forseth, 2005) and, with regard to physical taint, (male) meat cutters are expected to get blood on their hands (Ackroyd and Crowdy, 1990). However, in contexts where incongruity exists between the social construction of the work and the embodied disposition of the worker, servile roles may appear to have more servility (e.g. when men perform them) and dangerous jobs may seem more hazardous (e.g. when women undertake them). In the close relationship that exists between the body social and the body physical (Jervis, 2001), and drawing on Douglas's (1966) notion of dirt, a 'doubling of the disorder' may accordingly emerge when (heterosexual) men, already seen to be out of place in a general nursing role, deal with the physicality and 'dirtiness' as well as the intimacy of bodily care. Conceptualisation of the 'intensity' of dirty work can therefore be seen to be 'embodied' in that it takes into account the level of suitability that exists between the meanings around dirty work and those that are ascribed to the bodies of the dirty worker. This further destabilises and complicates categories of taint to include implications of bodily dimensions.

In this chapter we the authors have 'brought gender in' to a study of dirty work and in so doing have highlighted how the dirtiness of dirty work is not necessarily intrinsic to the work itself, but partly socially constructed through differential gendered and embodied meanings that are attached to both the work and the worker. This does not rule out, however, the significance of other categories of difference (e.g. race, sexuality, nationality) that are likely to be implicated in these meanings. Following Duffy's (2007) recommendation and given that norms of acceptability with regard to dirty work are strongly influenced by categories such as race (Stacey, 2005), their inclusion can form the basis for future research on the dynamics of such work.

11
Cleaning Up? Transnational Corporate Femininity and Dirty Work in Magazine Culture

Elaine Swan

Introduction

In this chapter I analyse the textual construction of femininity through the representation of the figure of the contemporary career woman in an edition of *Bazaar at Work*, a supplement to the UK edition of *Harpers and Bazaar*, a 'high-end' glossy women's monthly magazine. Drawing on the notion of 'transnational corporate masculinity' (Connell, 2005), I argue that the idealised white glamorous femininity being imagined in the magazine could be understood as 'transnational corporate femininity' (Swan, 2010). Inspired by Brigid Anderson's (2000) argument that white middle-class women draw on paid domestic labourers as a form of cultural capital, I explore the place of cleanliness and whiteness in the cultural production of this version of white middle-class femininity. Of course, cleanliness can refer to various objects: bodies, clothes, dwellings, morality and attitudes, but as Elizabeth Shove has written, 'notions of cleanliness are...laden...with symbolic and moral import' (2003: 79). I examine this symbolic and moral import in relation to class, race and femininity.

As the introduction to this book suggests, there is an emergent literature on 'dirty work'. Drawing on studies of the political economy, labour studies, sociology and migrant studies, this research has highlighted the extent of violence, discrimination and abuse of domestic workers in a range of contexts, global and local. Some of this literature has, importantly, emphasised the resistance and survival tactics of dirty workers. For example, Blake Ashforth and Glen Kreiner (1999) suggest that dirty workers can recast their dirty work in positive terms to deal with the stigmatised nature of this work.

More specifically then, the term dirty work is being deployed to describe the changing nature and social organisation of certain kinds of labour. Some of this is clearly literally 'dirty' in the sense of being work, such as cleaning and caring, that involves 'dirt'. As the editors of this volume have written, drawing on Ashforth and Kreiner (1999), it is also about tasks, occupations and roles that are likely to be perceived as 'disgusting or degrading'. Dirty work takes place in institutions such as hospitals, care homes and older people's homes. But as Anderson (2000) and others have argued, the middle-class home is where women, and some men, are employed to do domestic work. The adjective 'dirty' then attempts to highlight the material qualities and cultural values associated with this labour as bodily, unseemly and uncivilised. But the term also is used in the literature to question the morality of being complicit with oppressive practices. Thus, many middle-class people are part of the dirty business of dirty work (Anderson, 2000; Gregson and Lowe, 1994).

Building on this literature, this chapter draws on a broader empirical project which examines cultural representations of the transnational corporate elite and pedagogies of the good life in magazine culture (Swan and Wray-Bliss, 2010). This elite has been somewhat underrepresented and underresearched in recent literature on the area of dirty work. Hence in this chapter I focus on the representations of the figure of the career woman and explore how cleanliness and whiteness operate as cultural codes for a certain classed and racialised form of femininity.

In focusing on the cultural, I am also working with a different form of data than is usual in the field. My aim is to analyse how symbolic femininity is produced through imagery and texts, and not, therefore, how individual middle-class women employ and relate to domestic labourers or vice versa. Of course, the cultural does shape the contours of these relations. The cultural representation of dirty work is important because as Anderson underlines, it is important to make domestic work more 'visible' (2000: 1). My approach shows how it is made visible in visual culture and, in particular, in 'magazine culture'.

In the field of adult education, magazines and other forms of popular culture are understood to be an important form of what is called public pedagogy: 'lessons offered in mass media, advertisements and consumption' (Flowers and Swan, 2011; Luke, 1996). Thus, feminist educationalist Carmen Luke (1996) argues that the media can be understood as forms of pedagogy which teach us about the doing of ideal genders. In a similar vein, Kelley Massuni suggests that women's magazines can be understood as 'gender primers' (2004: 51). They teach us about vocations and occupations and the 'occupational world' (ibid.: 62). She goes on to posit that 'magazines overtly suggest, through content and pictures, how women should look, dress, and act; they more subtly suggest, through exclusion of pictures and content, what women should not do, be, or think' (ibid.: 49). Other writers suggest that femininity is more variegated and contested than this; thus, magazines can be understood as cultural spaces 'where versions of femininity are legitimated and negotiated, or contested and rejected' (Andrews and Talbot, 2000: 1; Radner, 1995). Or as Lisa Blackman writes, the 'textual construction of femininity is complicated, contradictory and ambiguous' (2004: 221).

In cultural analysis, the politics of dirty work is still central. Thus, cultural discourses are significant in the constitution of class (Skeggs, 2004). In examining cultural representations of the career woman and symbolic femininity, it is possible to start to understand how notions of cleanliness and whiteness produce the figure of the middle-class career woman in ways that result in symbolic violence and privilege (Skeggs, 2004). Rosemary Crompton (2008) argues that cultural structures and processes are important along with economic ones in enabling middle-class women to draw on assets, resources, capital and structures of privilege to perform femininity. Thus, women's magazines can provide femininity resources and reproduce privilege through femininity.

The chapter is structured as follows: the next section outlines how the figure of the career woman and her politics have been seen in recent literature on dirty work. In particular, I examine the historical links between the Victorian ideology of separate spheres, ideas of cleanliness and the middle-class house manager and cultural tropes of whiteness and class in women's magazines. Following this is an overview of how academics of feminist and cultural studies have viewed representations of career women in magazines. This provides conceptual and analytic resources for the analysis of the supplement I am discussing. Using a number of different themes on femininity, I suggest that it is possible to see the emergence of a pedagogy of transnational corporate femininity.

Career women and their dirty work

Career women are at the centre of gender in management studies literature. Conceptualisations of 'glass ceilings', 'board representation', so-called 'velvet ghettoes', 'concrete ceilings' and 'gendered performativities' are the backbone of analyses and research. In sociology and cultural studies, the career woman is rarely discussed, unless as a cipher for a critique of liberal feminism for which she is seen to stand (Swan, 2010). More recently, however, there have been important studies on career women and power-dressing working women (Entwistle, 2000). There has also been discussion on how neoliberalism promotes young middle-class women and their careers as the future of capitalism (McRobbie, 2004; Walkerdine, 2003). The argument in this literature is that neoliberal governmentality aligns with tenets from feminism to suggest that young women, or women on their way up, 'can have it all'.

In contrast, Diana Negra (2009) argues that women who have 'made it' are presented as a problem in cultural postfeminism, in a range of films and other cultural texts. She writes, 'postfeminism distrusts the working woman, particularly if she is an executive' (ibid.: 6). Women executives are seen as too powerful, dangerous, unfeminine and unnatural.

Taking the definition of postfeminism further, Ros Gill (2007) sees it as a 'sensibility'. The ingredients for Gill are the idea that femininity is a bodily property, including a focus on individualism, choice and empowerment; the dominance of the makeover paradigm and an emphasis on self-surveillance and self-discipline (ibid.: 1). Postfeminism for many writers involves a recognition and a repudiation of feminism: hence, for Gill, women are seen as active desiring subjects, but at the same time they are subject to a 'level of scrutiny and hostile surveillance that has no historical precedent' (ibid.).

In relation to the literature on dirty work, several writers have pointed to the material relations of exploitation between middle-class career women and domestic workers. A dominant argument is that career women exploit working-class and minoritised women. For example, Anderson (2000) argues quite vehemently that paid domestic labour enables middle-class women and men to avoid conflicts in the gendered division of labour at home. This represents a challenge for feminist politics. Anderson argues that 'paid domestic labour poses real challenges on both a philosophical and a practical level to feminism and political theory, as well as to community groups and women's organisations' (2000: 1). She goes on to suggest that career women have their 'movement between the public and private facilitated by the domestic worker: she is their bridge between the domains' and one of the ways through which middle-class career women can adopt 'masculinised employment patterns' (ibid.: 5). Thus, she sums it up: female employers exploit and oppress. Men and capitalism benefit (ibid.: 7). In this way, dirty work and its deployment are understood to be 'generative of divisions between women' (Gregson and Lowe, 1994: 5). This represents a problem for feminists: 'a classical political impasse' meaning 'liberation for some at the cost of oppression of others' (Ramazanoglu, 1989, cited in Gregson and Lowe, 1994: 235).

A well-developed argument in this vein comes from Joan Tronto's discussion on the morality of middle-class women employing nannies. She argues that that this form of childcare is unjust in that it reproduces inequalities. As she writes, 'when the wealthiest members of society use domestic servants to meet their child care needs, the result is unjust for individuals and for society as a whole' (Tronto, 2002: 35). She goes on to argue that 'the use of nannies allows upper middle class women and men to benefit from feminist changes without having to surrender the privilege of the traditional patriarchal family' (ibid.: 47). Her overall argument is that paid domestic labour represents feminism's 'unfinished business'.

A second form of exploitation crucial for this chapter is cultural exploitation. Anderson (2000) suggests that domestic labour is crucial to the cultural production of the middle-class identity. She suggests that as well as doing dirty work, 'the domestic worker is fulfilling a role, and crucial to that role is her reproduction of the female employer's status (middle-class, non-labourer, clean) in contrast to herself (worker, degraded, dirty)' (Anderson, 2000: 108). In this view, paid domestic work produces people. In doing so, it perpetuates modes of social reproduction and relations of class, gender and race (ibid.: 13). In addition, domestic work is not crucial for survival but reproduces lifestyle and status. Middle-class women who employ paid domestic labour can be domestic without being dirty (ibid.: 18). In this way, middle-class women can 'feign alienation from their bodies', while other working-class and racially minoritised women are seen to be trapped in theirs. In other words, the mental labour of middle-class women is being supported by the manual labour of other women (Gregg, 2010).

The notion of cleanliness as a cultural resource for middle-class women has a long history (Gatrell and Swan, 2008; Hamilton, 2010). Domestic work was central to the construction of classed femininities in Victorian Britain. Thus, historian Leonore Davidoff (1973) writes of the Victorian ideal of separate spheres, the division between the masculine public and feminine private spheres based on a gendered and classed ideology. Middle-class women were seen as household managers (ibid.). They could employ domestic servants so that they could maintain a division between cleanliness and dirtiness in the home, enabling them to hold onto the order of 'cleanliness and spirituality of feminine virtue' (Anderson, 2000: 18). Davidoff writes that middle-class women in the home were seen as guardians of social mores, whereas the home, for working-class women, represented hard labour.

Women were thus divided into the pure and the dirty along class lines. This enabled an idealisation of white middle-class women as the pure, pious, moral and virtuous centre of the household (Davidoff, 1973). It created clear boundaries between the classes and their femininities and protected the middle classes from 'defiling contact with the sordid or disordered parts of life' (ibid.: 73). Emphasising the point that domestic workers reproduce people and social relations, Anderson writes of Victorian England:

> The employment of a paid domestic worker therefore facilitates status reproduction, not only by maintaining status objects, enabling the silver to be polished, or the clothes to be ironed, but also by serving as a foil to the lady of the house (35).

Her overarching point is that this facilitates the negotiation of tensions around different expectations of femininity.

It can be seen from this how the construction of cleanliness involves the 'entanglement' of historical, social, cultural, medical and scientific ideas (Shove, 2003: 80). An important dimension of this is the racialised histories of colonialism and the entwinement of notions of cleanliness and being civilised (McClintock, 1995). The inculcation of 'disciplines and routines of personal hygiene' were defined as key parts of the 'civilising' project of British imperialism through the 'empire' (Shove, 2003). Part of this was achieved through the consumption and production of soap, cleaning agents, cosmetics and associated advertising (ibid.). The promotion of cleanliness then was tied to notions of manners and civilisation and promulgated through advertising and commodities.

In sum, cleanliness and dirt have a long history of representing and reproducing classed, gendered and racialised differentiation. Thus, the working classes have long been referred to as the 'great unwashed' in Britain (Shove, 2003). As Beverly Skeggs writes, in the nineteenth century the bourgeoisie distanced themselves from the working classes as 'dirt and waste, sexuality and contagion, danger and disorder, degeneracy and pathology, became the moral evaluations by which the working class were coded and became known' (2004: 4). And importantly, she emphasises, these moral evaluations 'are still reproduced today' (ibid.: 4).

The development of Western manners was a mechanism for the 'civilising of the middle classes' in Europe over several hundred years (Shove, 2003). In this way, cleanliness became associated with purity, love, distinction and discipline – the refinement of self and discipline (Ger and Yenicioglu, 2004: 1). Being clean represented being free from moral corruption, obscenities, error or blemish (ibid.). Dirt became associated with the vulgar, corrupt, not pure and the morally unclean (ibid.). Of the North American context, Suellen Hoy (1995) argues that the obsession with cleanliness in the United States is aligned with the assimilation process of immigrants and was critical to the development of the American middle class. Important for my discussion on magazines as public pedagogy, it can be seen historically how pedagogies have been central to the teaching and regulation of cleanliness, in particular, through etiquette, conduct and how-to-do books aimed at women.

As Mary Douglas writes, dirt represents disorder (1984). In her view, cleaning is about reproducing the symbolic reproduction of order. Cleanliness then represents the outcome of classification and boundary management. It is not as Shove (2003) and Skeggs (1997) underline, a neutral classification system. As Shove writes, 'the tools and technologies of cleanliness inform definitions and classifications of dirt. In addition, they ... structure the moral landscape in which actions have meaning ... cleaning technologies are enmeshed in a landscape of moral and social distinction' (ibid.: 83). In sum then, cleanliness and dirtiness have been central to the 'setting up, obliterating and shifting boundaries between the saved and the civilised, the peasant or bourgeois, and the lower and the upper classes in the Western world during the civilisation process' (Ger and Yenicioglu, 2004: 1).

This project still goes on, of course, as I shall discuss. Before this, I want to finish this section by linking cleanliness to notions of whiteness as the ideal cultural norm. In a fascinating study of kitchen design, domestic appliances, race, gender and whiteness in South Africa, Kathleen Connellan wants to show 'how Christian ideologies of white as symbolic of illumination and epiphany connect with colonial and modernist views of white as clean and moral' (2007: 248). In relation to white goods in the kitchen, she argues this represents 'design whiteness' (ibid.: 251). In particular, she suggests there is an isomorphism between the clean white surfaces and the maintenance of the whiteness of the white middle-class woman. She writes that:

> The pervasive whiteness that exists in the skin of the 'madam' in South African homes, the sheen of the white ducoed appliances, the

brightness of the white wall, the bleach of the linen, all signify the sterility of a world primarily concerned with surfaces.

(Ibid.: 250)

As she argues, whiteness shows the dirt. It needs an unnatural force to maintain it (ibid.: 257). In sum, 'clean' white surfaces were maintained by black skins.

Dirt and cleanliness are hugely significant, then, in maintaining gender, class and racial social and cultural boundaries. Pierre Bourdieu has written that class boundaries are like a 'flame whose edges are in constant movement, oscillating around a line or surface' (1987: 100). In this chapter, I suggest that one place in which these flickering flames can be seen is women's magazines. It is to a brief history of the construction of the career woman in these magazines that I now turn.

Magazine culture and pedagogies of career women femininities

There is an in-depth history of analysing women's magazines in feminism. For some, North American Betty Friedan, the second-wave author of *The Feminine Mystique* in 1963, did one of the first textual analyses of women's magazines (Massuni, 2004). Interestingly in relation to this chapter, in her analysis of women's magazines from the 1950s and 1960s, she argued that 'happy housewife heroines' had replaced the 'spirited career girls' of the 1930s and 1940s (ibid.: 50). Since her book, feminist literature from the UK, USA and Australia has shown the contradictory nature of how women are presented across women's magazines, particularly in relation to the workplace. For example, an article from 1992 entitled 'The Representation of Women's Roles in Women's Magazines over the Past 30 Years from 1954 to 1982 in America' shows that while there was a decline in representations of women as mothers and wives and an increase in themes of women at work and in politics, middle-class women in traditional occupations were still seen as 'powerless and less competent than men' (Demarest and Garner, 1992: 367). Typically the portrayal was not progressive, so the workplace was seen as a place to dress up for (van Zoonen 1994). Women were rarely portrayed as working.

In an analysis of the cultural representation of motherhood in women's magazines, Deirdre Johnston and Debra Swanson (2003) emphasise that magazines are not representing reality but reproducing it. Citing Murphy (1994), they suggest there are four constant refrains to be found in general-interest women's magazines. These are firstly, that the normal world is white and middle-class to upper middle-class; secondly, that women are domestic; thirdly, that women are expected to be beautiful; and finally, that consumerism is a focus for women's lives. As Murphy writes, 'It may now be acceptable to be independent, politically involved, sexually active, committed to a career: even to be over forty. But it's only acceptable if you look right and have the necessary accoutrements' (1994, cited in Johnston and Swanson, 2003: 23).

My own research with Ed Wray-Bliss examines the cultural representation of white transnational corporate masculinity. One fascinating analysis that relates to this is Ann Rippin's (2007) discussion of the British upper middle-class business-focused paper, *The Financial Times*, and in particular, its glossy supplement for the super rich, *How to Spend It*. Although she does not use the term public pedagogy, Rippin argues that the supplement is a 'guidebook and style manual for the rich and powerful' (ibid.: 116). It has a performative quality, she suggests, in that 'the cultural and economic project' is about creating and maintaining an elite. This arrival at and maintenance of elite status is based on 'discernment, connoisseurship and exclusivity, display and excess' (ibid.: 123). In order to belong to the elite then, the individual needs to 'display excessive capital, both economic and cultural' (ibid.: 124). Time is viewed as a commodity that is 'precious and tradeable' (ibid.: 123) and so tracking down and acquiring the trappings of the elite requires 'help'. In fact, social capital 'is enhanced if one has the economic power to have someone else do the legwork' (ibid.: 123). The supplement offers an 'aspirational fantasy world', promising economic, cultural and psychological well-being. As is common in magazine culture, however, this idea of well-being is cannibalised by its simultaneous reproduction of anxiety in that it represents impossible standards.

In conclusion, then, magazine culture can be seen to be teaching about the world of work and leisure. Melissa Gregg, in her analysis of advertisements of career women and information and communications technology (ICT), suggests that a style of work and stylisation of work, what she terms 'workstyle', is being produced through images of mobility, aestheticised technology and 'effortless beauty and immaculately clean house' (2010: 291). It can be seen how this workstyle in magazines offers ideals of what counts as symbolic capital (Skeggs, 2004) and therefore as symbolic profit (Crompton, 2008) in classed and gendered terms, reproducing privileges and inequalities. This literature helps us to see how the boundaries between home and work, the domestic and public, cleanliness and dirty work are demarcated. What is under-analysed is how magazines draw on racialised codes of whiteness in reproducing these new femininities.

Method

As I write the above, the 'archive' for my analysis of dirty work is unusual in the literature. I am using the 2007 supplement of one high-end monthly British magazine, *Harper's Bazaar*, which dates back to 1867 in USA and was launched in the UK in 1929. In 1970, *Harper's Bazaar* took over *Queen* and became *Harper's and Queen* until 2006, when it reverted to the old name, by which it was known everywhere else in the world. In the words of one marketing website www.fashionmodeldirectory. com/magazines/harpers-bazaar-australia/, '*Harper's Bazaar* has covered fashion and "good taste", since it began in 1867 as America's first fashion magazine'. The website continues:

> The magazine targets sophisticated women with an interest in fashion who aim to be first to buy premium brands, ranging from casual to couture. *Bazaar* focuses on the luxury market with style, authority and insider insight and covers what's new to what's next.

My analysis draws on the work of David Machin and Theo van Leeuwen (2003, 2005), who have undertaken an in-depth analysis of *Cosmopolitan* magazine. They focus on styles of writing, image making, graphic design, advertising, different discourses of expertise – such as those of the psychologist, fashion expert and dietician – and constructions of female identity and lifestyle. Women's magazines comprise a range of text types, an important one of which is the feature article. Features include a range of text types from 'how to' life skills writing and inspirational stories to think pieces and service pieces where women are shown products, services and fashion tips (Delin, 2000). In particular, I have applied Machin and van Leeuwen's idea of what they call the 'problem–solution discourse' schema. This schema sets up a problem for women in the magazine and then offers solutions to this problem. They argue, for example, that in *Cosmopolitan*, this schema constructs life as a struggle for survival in a world of risky and unstable relationships. I was also interested in mapping visual codings of whiteness and cleanliness, using Richard Dyer's (2004) work on film, whiteness and light.

Bazaar at Work

The supplement entitled *Bazaar at Work* was published in October 2007 and published, as it says on the cover, 'in association with Aquascutum and *The Times*'. The latter two are quintessential middle-class UK brands with connotations of conservative luxury. The supplement announces itself then as aiming at middle-class executive career women. It does this through a number of textual and visual means, through headlines, features, sponsorship and photographs. For example, the supplement features the fifth *Harper's Bazaar*/Aquascutum-Businesswoman-of-the-year awards.

The supplement is 64 pages long, of usual glossy magazine size and includes a mix of fashion spreads, editorial, advertorials, adverts, glossy photos and feature articles. The front cover features a full-length glossy photo of a model in a £495 Aquascutum 'blazer' and a £325 'pencil skirt', with her hands on her hips. She has long, tidy, slightly waved, glossy hair, bright red lips and thick eyebrows. Her white face is accentuated through lighting, her golden brown hair in particular is lit up, and she has very white hands, reflected by the white lapels of her jacket. She looks nothing like a working woman – she is far too young, well-groomed and glamorous. A headline which takes up 25 per cent of the cover and partially overlaps the photo, says in italicised capitals: *Look the Business*. The other headlines in smaller typefaces but again in capitals are Working Fashion: New-Season Suits, Skirts, Heels and Bags; Power Hour: Fix your Life over Lunch; and finally, How to Work Less and Be a Success.

The cover then reproduces certain emblematic themes of 'post feminism' (Gill, 2007; McRobbie, 2004; Negra, 2009). Hence the continued importance of appearance and dress, women making it so long as they are made over and the problems of 'work/life balance' can be seen (Negra, 2009). As Diana Negra (2009) argues, postfeminism seems obsessed with notions of temporality, including reductive, individualised notions of managing work and home life as exemplified by these headlines.

The supplement contains typical women's magazine genres, but shot through a lens of luxury and class. These are reinforced by the use of certain fashion discourses, classed vocabularies, glamour imagery, brands and price points. In sum, the supplement draws on a number of highly recognisable women's magazine discursive 'styles' of fashion, advertising, expertise and a problem–solution schema (Machin and van Leeuwen, 2003, 2005). The big problem outlined in the magazine is how women can uphold their middle-class career, their appearance and their lifestyle when there is no time. The solution, like in Rippin's analysis in *How to Spend It*, is what the magazine calls in managerial discourse, 'outsourcing'.

Good times?

There is an overarching theme of women experiencing 'hectic demands' and very little time across the supplement. Careers are challenging. Family life is demanding. There is the burden of home. Jobs have high pressures. Life is stressful. How can you 'stop feeling overwhelmed by those small tasks that demand your attention?' asks one headline. 'How can you find order and reclaim peace of mind?' An advertisement for *The Times* 'exclusive' business podcasts intones, 'Don't get left behind, get London Business School's Global Leadership Summit Timesonline'. Several full-page adverts for expensive watches underline this theme.

The problem of 'managing time' is given full vent across a number of genres. The editor's letter, a text in most women's magazines, is entitled 'Balancing Acts', an all-too-familiar refrain. 'Is it possible to reach the top of your profession and work flexibly?' asks the letter as its opening gambit. The editor and deputy editor continue, 'That was a question at our recent breakfast hosted by *Bazaar* and Aquascutum. A new report by Lehmann brothers suggests that large numbers of women – and indeed men – in senior positions are getting to grips with the work/life balance'. The problem can be solved, the magazine is suggesting.

There is a think-piece feature article entitled 'Time on Your Side' written by journalist Viv Groskop, who reports on the findings of recent research. The article begins, 'Can you chair a meeting and bath the kids? Can you negotiate deals and be available for a trip to the park?', reproducing in almost haiku style the strange see-saw between the domestic space and the workplace.

As Negra (2009) argues, in postfeminism, 'women are depicted as particularly beset by temporal problems' (2009: 48). In her analysis of popular culture, she suggests that the solution is imagined as 'a minimization of their ambition and reversion to a more essential femininity' (ibid.: 48). This reversion is expressed through an anti-ageing regime of diet, exercise, Botox and other products and services aimed at forestalling or disguising the ageing process for the affluent minority (ibid.). While the supplement does draw on some of this discourse, it also offers images of success – career women who have succeeded in managing their work/life balance.

But the supplement does not offer a smooth, unconflicted or uncontested model of career femininity. I suggest there are three different versions in the magazine, two of which represent the successful or ideal model of transnational corporate femininity and one which represents the failing version in need of 'cleaning up'. The solution is to use services of other women and men. The three femininities I discuss below are 'Women who have made it', 'Made-up femininity' and 'Women on the verge of a makeover'.

Women who have made it

There are several representations of women throughout the magazine who are presented as the proverbial 'successes'. As Angela McRobbie writes, there is much interest in the media in 'female success', as opposed to 'feminist success' (2004: 257).

Thus, the article on 'the panel' exemplifies this. 'The panel' takes up page 7. Underneath the headline of 'The Panel', it says, 'For this issue, we brought together six big names from the business world for a working breakfast to discuss issues facing women at work today'. The 'six big names' are:

- Petra Arends, 'Collection Executive of the UBS art collection';
- Linda Bennett, 'Founder and Chief Executive of LK Bennett';
- Liz Earle, 'Co-founder and Director of Liz Earle Skincare';
- Natalie Massenet, 'Founder and chairman (sic) Net-a-Porter.com';
- Charlotte Thomas, 'Global Communications Director of Aquascutum';
- Johanna Waterous, 'Director of McKinsey and Co'.

Brief profiles are given for each of the women, together with a small head and shoulder photo shot of each individual and a sentence on their 'first job' and 'career high'. The 'occupational world' (Massuni, 2004) of the supplement is clearly that of middle-class private-sector professional career women and entrepreneurs. These are women executives. This is a highly feminised occupational world too, featuring traditional women's occupational sectors such as fashion and retailing; typical female commodities such as make-up, clothes and shoes; and traditional feminised roles such as director of marketing and the terrible neologism mompreneur!

In spite of heralding 'issues facing women today', the 'top of the agenda' issue presented is the somewhat parochial 'the internet and how it is revolutionising the work of retail'. The article continues:

> Liz Earle, director of Liz Earle Naturally Active Skincare, underlined the importance of making her staff feel cared for. 'There is that old saying', she said, 'that you can't feel happy with sore feet'. So employees who spend all day on their feet are provided with chiropody and reflexology.

The women being profiled are employers of staff. They have made it. They reproduce their distinction through being bosses and also through the way that the staff are presented in infantilised ways and their working conditions and labouring bodies also ameliorated through the postfeminist aesthetic regimes and services (Negra, 2009).

'Having made it' is also annotated with reference to the 'global' and to global travel. Gregg calls this the 'cosmopolitan lifestyle of frequent flyers' (2010). For example, a service feature on 'shop must haves' features Aquascutum's 'global communications director', Charlotte Thomas, who explains: 'Whether I am at a press conference in Milan, developing our Asian market in Tokyo, or meeting with our New York Stockist, I know I have to dress in a certain way.' A London-based architect says: 'A normal week can include anything from meetings with the company's architects to a trip to the States'. In a separate article, Liz Earle is described as taking her skincare brand 'global'. She has a 'hectic schedule', 'travelling internationally more than ever'. With a whiff of the worried white woman coloniser (Hunter, 2010), she says, somewhat incredulously, 'you can't just go into a country and buy all its sage!'

The advertorials highlight this hyper-travel with reference to a watch aimed at 'frequent flyers'. The watch, costing £9,000, thankfully can 'tell the time in 24 international cities' and has 'a mother of pearl face with 52 diamonds'. There is also a face cream by Elemis, costing £85, offering no ordinary beauty, but 'first class beauty'. An article in the beauty and health section is entitled 'Check In, Tone Up': 'It's tough for business travellers to stick with a fitness regime, so Katy Young got a top trainer to create a work-out purely for hotel-hoppers' to cope with 'hectic schedules jet-lag'.

These are constructions of women who are deemed to be successes at 'global trotting'. They can move in and out of global spaces, 'global hopping', as James Ferguson (2006) puts it; they are well-heeled people avoiding trouble spots and inconveniences, parachuting into elite enclaves and out again.

But even for those who have made it, time and managing the domestic sphere are held up as problematic. Thus, the final paragraph outlining 'how to balance their challenging careers with the demands of family life' was discussed by the panel:

> At the pinnacle of their professions, our panel all shared the same problem of how to balance their challenging careers with the demands of their family life; the general consensus was that women will always have to carry the burden at home. The solution was to 'outsource as many chores as possible' – and after, breakfast, phone numbers for caterers and personal shoppers were enthusiastically exchanged.

There is then some emphasis on the women's link to the domestic sphere. But their achievement, and therefore, their representation as 'successes' is framed in terms of their domestic responsibilities and the balance between the two. (These are not simply women who have fled the domestic for autonomy and freedom, but are positioned as managing the problem of the domestic–work 'balance'. This precarious balance is facilitated through the service economy and the labour of other women. The word 'chore' is an interesting one. At the beginning of the twentieth century, performing a chore meant filling a responsible role. In contrast, a chore is now seen as a routine household task, an unpleasant but necessary task but also as an irksome invasion of freedom (Lohman, 1964). The women are shown as managers of the domestic – a clear echo of the Victorian middle-class house manager discussed above. They represent new forms of femininity for middle-class women in which the workplace rather than the home is foregrounded (Gregson and Lowe, 1994) and in which the conspicuous buying of 'help' produces time and class distinction (Rippin, 2007).

Made-up femininity

The second successful transnational corporate femininity I want to examine is that exemplified by models in fashion images and adverts. In particular, I argue that glamour is being visually culturally coded through whiteness and class. Richard Dyer (2004) has shown how an idealised whiteness has been visually represented in films, advertisements and images, in particular through technologies of light. Thus, whiteness is produced through the lighting and lightening of white skin and blonde hair. This produces a 'glow' through which skin appears milky and a 'halo' shines behind white actors' heads. These work to connote purity, cleanliness, lightness and beauty.

In a related discussion on films, Anne Massey (2000) suggests that this image of glowing whiteness is central to traditional Hollywood glamour. Importantly for my discussion here, glamour is about 'the look of style being the source of envy, aspiration and desire is a 20th century word' (ibid.: 36). Women are being presented in the supplement as ideals, successes. She goes on, 'the white glow of the Caucasian female film star is a central part of Hollywood glamour' (ibid.). In Hollywood films, light was key to creating glamour, and augmented by the use of reflective materials and flawless make-up. As Jacobowitz and Lippe write, glamour 'speaks of confidence, empowerment and depending on its use, articulates all that is not domestic, confined, suppressed. Glamour, above all, is not mundane' (1992: 3). White glamour then is an aspiration away from the home.

This kind of imagery dominates the advertisements and fashion shots. Thus, the two main models in the supplement are consistently coded white. Their hair is blonde and golden brown, depending on the light and worn long and loose. It is glossy, shiny and clean. Of course, there are different shades of blonde, all of which denote class. The hair in these images is a soft blonde associated with middle-class whiteness. Dyer writes that 'blondeness … is the ultimate sign of whiteness' and that 'it is racially unambiguous. It keeps the white women distinct from the black, brown or yellow' (2004: 40).

The model's skin is lit up to accentuate whiteness. In the Aquascutum adverts, Gisele Bundschen, a mixed-race German Brazilian model, well-known for her blonde hair and light skin colour wears Aquascutum suits which are described as the 'perfect combination of chic, glamour and sultry sexuality', 'vintage Aquascutum'. She wears white blouses and her hands are lit so they appear unblemished and unlabouring. Her hair is lit from behind, producing a white halo effect. Interspersed through the shot is an advert for Mont Blanc jewellery, profiling a blonde model with white skin lit up modelling the 'La Dame Blanche' range of white diamonds!

There is also a constellation of images of hair, clothes and handbags as shiny, white and clean. Clothes are white and cream. A white woman doing yoga in a hotel room is wearing a soft, creamy cashmere track suit. A white trouser suit is recommended for a working mother in a makeover! Watches have mother-of-pearl faces. Black bags and heels are polished, glossy and shiny (Connellan, 2007). Like the reflective materials (Massey, 2005) used in Hollywood films, these clothes and accessories underline a glamorous white world outside of dirt and disorder. Women who are held up as living in this world are distanced from the dross of the domestic. The women who labour to make these clothes and keep them clean are of course absent.

The body, as Beverley Skeggs argues, is the materialisation of classed taste. It is the site on which class tensions are played out. Beauty, cleanliness and taste are markers that inscribe value onto bodies (Skeggs 2004: 13). There is a classed litany of adjectives to describe the clothes: luxury, luxe, glamour, stylish and the most repeated word, chic. This is not the excess discussed by Rippin of the *Financial Times*, nor the 'cool' clothing of the ICT professional of which Greggs writes. This is a more muted, conservative, classed femininity related to control, restraint and discipline. As Jo Entwistle (2000) suggests, the suited 'code of dress' for career women is related to the importance of body management and individualism, both of which align with neoliberal values of self-discipline and control. This is not just about 'access to and control of symbolic resources, but also on knowing how to display one's subjectivity properly' (Skeggs, 2005: 973). The female successes shown throughout the magazine do not need to be taught how to dress. The pedagogy is aimed at the readers and anticipates the final group of women I discuss: women on the verge of a makeover.

Women on the verge of a makeover

The third mode of femininity I want to discuss is the problematic one: women who have made it but are beginning to lose it or who are on the cusp of making it, if they can get a grip. These are career women whose bodies, shopping and outsourcing are in need of more discipline. One big advertorial sponsored by the face cream Nivea presents three career women in need of a makeover so extreme that it is called a 'lifeover'! These women are offered the services of a nutritionist, a life coach and a personal shopper. The text continues, 'all three enjoy their challenging jobs but wanted to improve how they felt, physically, as well as mentally...they all wanted to look young and healthier'.

As Skeggs (2005) argues, a woman who looks like she lacks the care of herself is seen as irresponsible. This loss of control of the body is often the catalyst for many makeovers on television and in magazines (Lunt and Lewis, 2008). Gill (2007) argues that the makeover and its associated forms of discipline and self-regulation are a paradigmatic postfeminist theme. Here they can be seen as public pedagogy. These women are subject to pedagogies of the body and mind and through their efforts, others too can learn to improve themselves. As the article highlights, it is not just these three women who may be failing at their disciplines: 'most working women experience firsthand the difficulties of maintaining a healthy work/life balance while trying to keep ahead of the challenges thrown at them'.

Femininity in this feature is not seen as pleasure but as provoking anxiety. Shopping in particular is presented as full of angst. Advice on how to consume services and products is provided to busy career women across a number of texts in the magazine. Thus, in an article on time management, wardrobe management is suggested, in which clothes can be repaired and dry-cleaned. Of such a service, 'Clara Furse, chief executive of the London Stock exchange, says "I've been relying on Julia for years" '. There are personal chefs: 'ring Absolute Taste, which has teamed up with Gordon Ramsay to serve up your signature dishes – your guests will be thrilled you did. From £700 for 10 guests'. There are suggestions for 'night nannies', trainers and a yoga class. The last article is on buying corporate gifts – raising classed anxieties again: 'Choosing the perfect corporate gift is a delicate matter – diplomatic options such as fresh oysters, lobster and langoustine, flowers, fresh baked brownies, fine leather notebooks from Smythson.'

Unlike the cool, controlled glamorous career woman, this is an anxious femininity. In 1995, Hilary Radner discussed the replacement of the child wife by 'the power wife' and 'new glamour queen working woman' in women's magazines. The glamour queen is still presented but alongside the anxious career woman. As Entwistle writes, women's dress for work is fraught with difficulties, because of the classed connotations (2000: 225). Professional women need to be 'visible, recognizable as professionals', not clerical or secretarial (ibid.: 232). If these women let themselves go, their class distinction, career advantage and lifestyles are in jeopardy. Failure trails behind successful women, dragging at their heels.

Conclusion

In this chapter, I have shown how classed and racialised codes of glamour and whiteness are reproduced to produce a middle-class femininity. In doing so, I have suggested that tropes of cleanliness can help us think about dirty work. There are three main points I would like to emphasise to conclude my discussion. First, I am arguing that the contours of a particular version of new femininity are being sketched through the imagery and magazine pedagogy I analysed. I coin the term 'transnational corporate femininity' to start to pin this version down. In doing so, I am associating it with Connell's (2005) definition of transnational corporate masculinity which involves a globetrotting, self-conscious management of bodies and emotions as well as money and a detachment from older loyalties to nation, business organisation, family and marital partners (Beasley, 2008). Crudely summarising, it represents a competitive disposition which distances itself from social or personal commitments.

We can track certain elements of this form of masculinity in the transnational corporate femininity outlined through my analysis of the supplement. The self is presented as globetrotting and as with many versions of femininity, self-conscious about the body. There is a particular inflection to this self-consciousness: an image of a body associated with a particular lifestyle and occupational class. This is a glamorous, disciplined femininity, without excess. There is no excess of sexuality or display of money. This is the femininity of whiteness and the middle class. As Skeggs argues, the body enacts 'classification systems based on visibility' (2004: 162) and produces distinction and distantiation (ibid.: 97). Unlike in *Cosmopolitan* magazine, in Machin and van Leeuwen's (2003, 2005) analysis, there is no 'pan femininity' across all women. Boundaries are clearly drawn between these women, their staff and the service class and the hierarchical relations between femininities.

Critical to this class-making is that the labour involved in producing the femininity is 'outsourced': it is not concealed, as Skeggs argues, with other forms of middle-class femininity. This is where 'femininity is the outcome of a work of which a major element is selecting and purchasing the right commodities' (2003: 495). So-called feminine skills of shopping, design and networking become marketable commodities, bringing together 'the enterprising subject and the feminine subject' (ibid.: 503). As Rippin underlines, it is the consumption of service labour to do domestic labour which makes the feminine social capital.

There is a specificity to this version of new femininity that marks it out from other workplace femininities. These career women do have domestic responsibilities and dependencies. But unlike other representations of femininity, the home is not a place to 'retreat' to (Negra, 2009). The domestic and the home are something to distance oneself from, as in transnational corporate masculinity. Key to transnational corporate femininity is the centrality of the domestic service class and the imagery of whiteness and cleanliness. This echoes Davidoff's history of middle-class women as house managers – in Anderson's words, 'domestic without being dirty', but also we might add, 'gloss without the dross'.

The second point I want to emphasise is the importance of the operation of the notions of successful women and failing women. This notion of ideals and failures could be added to Machin and van Leeuwen's (2003, 2005) problem–solution schema. Not only does the magazine set up a problem of 'work/life balance' and offer solutions through 'outsourcing', it also sets up idealised women and those who are lagging behind, including the readers. There is no single smooth representation of transnational corporate femininity. There is the ideal clean, white, pure, disciplined version and then the femininity 'on the skids'. As Hilary Radner has argued, women's magazines work on multiple levels in relation to identifying with ideals of femininity, working to create, deny, question and negotiate them (1995: 177). Femininity is seen as complex, conflicted and sometimes impossible to achieve. In relation to transnational corporate femininity, we see the representation of an anxious consumer, not knowing how to buy the services which will discipline her disordered body and work/life balance. Failing haunts many contemporary constructions of middle-class femininity (Walkerdine, 2003). It takes the labour of other bodies to civilise women and the deployment of other women's labour to keep transnational corporate femininity in a first class of its own.

Finally, it is often argued that women in relation to the workplace are 'invisibilised'. However, in magazines such as these, it is men who are rendered invisible. As Gregg (2010) points out in representations of career women, men are absent from any suggestion that they should contribute to unpaid labour in the home to help with 'work/life balance'. They are not represented or referenced in relation to domestic services. They are not shown as benefiting from the so-called outsourcing. This suggests a need to acknowledge how transnational corporate femininity – and its associations of whiteness, cleanliness and class – is also holding up transnational corporate masculinity. As Tronto (2002) reminds us, the organisation of the domestic and other forms of care and dirty work is feminism's unfinished business. For many minoritised and working-class women and men, of course, this labour is unfinished every day.

Acknowledgements

I would like to thank the participants and convenors of the stream 'Dirty work' at the Gender, Work and Organisation Conference, June 2010 for their comments, UTS for the research development grant on the global elite and Elaine Lally and Ruth Simpson for such helpful feedback on the chapter.

12
Managing 'Dirty' Migrant Identities: Migrant Labour and the Neutralisation of Dirty Work through 'Moral' Group Identity

Geraldine Lee-Treweek

Introduction

In many European countries the utilisation of 'cheaper' forms of migrant labour has become the cornerstone of the management of labour market fluctuations (MacKenzie and Forde, 2009). However, despite its apparent utility in filling labour 'gaps', migration causes controversy and concerns about its impact upon job substitution patterns, effect on wages and wider social and 'community' cohesion. The vast majority of economic migrants to the European Union do not arrive in their new countries to take up highly paid, professional jobs. On the contrary, many enter knowing that they will be working at the bottom of the labour market, in monotonous, repetitive, physically dirty and socially rejected occupations, within the 'secondary labour market' (this concept encompasses non-desirable work that many people will not undertake). This situation is not new. The work of Everett Hughes (1946, 1962), writing about low-status labour in the United States in the 1950s and 1960s, recognised the link between migrant communities and dirty work. Hughes identified that the workforce for unwanted labour is usually made up of new migrants. This long-established theme provides the background for this chapter, which examines the way migrants adapt to dirty labour and to 'dirty identities'.

There is a long heritage within work and organisational literature of examining dirty work in terms of how workers refuse negative meanings of their labour and retain a sense of control. Through changing meanings, the difficult, mundane and/or unacceptable task becomes easier through its transmogrification into valuable and essential labour, usually linked to aspects of identity. Such work might become a source of honour, a demonstration of skills, a fundamental illustration of 'real work', an exhibition (or performance) of masculinity/femininity or of community spirit and therefore make acceptable one's identity as a worker undertaking unacceptable tasks. This chapter takes this notion of the transformation of meanings around work deeper into the realms of the ties between jobs, identity and value of work. It demonstrates how the work group may sometimes focus upon its own boundaries, morality and ways of being as resistance to negative meanings of work. Such resistance is therefore not aimed at the employer, the organisation or managers, but reframes negative meanings around work through the control of group identity. It is this neutral position towards employers and organisations that has puzzled many who study migrant labour. In particular, often migrants are not unionised, they tend not to complain and appear compliant. However, settings with high numbers of migrants are not conflict-free; on the contrary, they are replete with daily disputes over 'appropriate' worker behaviour *within* migrant groups. For individual migrant workers there are drawbacks to a focus upon control within the work group, as that can replace concerns about how one is treated at work in relation to such issues as racism, poor pay and conditions. Therefore, the existence of a work culture that focuses inwards on managing 'dirty' meanings has benefits for employers.

The chapter examines the issues of migration and dirty work through qualitative interviews with and ethnographic data gathered regarding Polish migrant workers within 'Northton',[1] a predominately white, working-class town in the north of England. It will begin with a discussion of the literature on dirty work and on migrants at work, followed by an exposition of the ways in which dirty work is transformed through traditionally noted strategies, such as finding pride in dirty tasks. The chapter will then move on to present empirical data, predominately from female migrants, which demonstrates a response to dirty work firmly based on identity and, in particular, on creating and maintaining a 'good Polish woman' identity at the workplace. The chapter argues that migrants have very few resources from which to carve a sense of meaning and purpose to their work. Whereas many accounts of dirty work involve some redeeming feature(s) that can be used to reframe the labour, for workers who undertake the most monotonous, unskilled and least-valued work in society, there is little left from which to create self-worth, esteem and value (Skeggs, 2004). In this chapter, data from migrant labour in industrial settings demonstrates the loci of control to be the self, the group and managing boundaries. Organisational approaches to dirty work need to be aware of the potential negative consequences of groups being defined through the low value of their dirty work, without having other positive ways of framing what they do.

Dirty work: what are the traditional concerns?

The Chicago School of Sociology refers to sociologists working at the University of Chicago, who were pivotal in leading sociological interest in the growing urban cities of the United States from the 1900s to the 1960s. Everett Cherrington Hughes arose as a key figure within the Chicago School; arguably, his most enduring works are *Good People and Dirty Work* (Hughes, 1962) and his essays on race and work in which he examines the ways that workers undertake socially or morally unacceptable labour (Hughes, 1946). However, it is rarely mentioned in discussions of his work that Hughes had first-hand experience of working with migrants. According to Lewis R. Coser's (1994) biographical account of Hughes's academic life, after graduating and prior to his doctoral work, Hughes spent five years teaching English to new migrants to the United States, the majority of whom were concurrently undertaking low-status, dirty jobs. Hughes also chose to live amongst excluded migrant communities and saw sociology as having a duty to create social change through fieldwork and the production of empirical evidence. Hughes was influenced by his time and there are weaknesses in his work, not least the lack of discussion of gender. However, despite its flaws, Hughes's work continues to inform current understandings of workplaces and dirty labour. His theoretical concerns are more relevant than ever in a globalised world where migration is commonplace.

From the 1970s onwards, the general study of dirty work and low social-class occupations emerged in work and organisational literature as popular areas of inquiry. Meara's (1974) study of American meatcutters and Turkish butchers demonstrated the way physically dirty meat preparation was made into a meaningful activity by workers focusing upon 'traditional skills', such as using knives and sharp implements. While the work remained socially unacceptable as it was dirty, cold and potentially dangerous, these meanings were reframed through notions of what 'real' work and masculine labour entailed. Masculinity also features strongly in Thompson's (1983) account of working on a slaughter assembly line and Haas's (1977) ethnographic account of high-steel ironwork. In Haas's (1977) research, high-steel ironwork, rejected by most for being dirty and dangerous, is reconstructed by the men doing it as 'men's work' and as a demonstration of masculinity. Honour, courage and an emphasis on the performance of toughness often feature in the trans- formation of dirty work in male-oriented workplaces. However, studies of 'traditional' women's work find similar processes that transform dirty work. Lawler's (1991) discussion of the nature of nursing and care work clearly identifies ways in which caregivers reconstruct the work as nec- essary, often invoking notions of dirty caring as similar to care of kin. Similarly, Twigg (2000: 393) discussing paid care workers notes:

> In describing their work they tended to play down the aspect of body-
> work, and to emphasise 'care' instead. Though it is the body element
> that marks personal care off from mere domestic cleaning...they
> emphasise the emotional and interpersonal aspects, and the skills
> required to negotiate and maintain these.

Despite the difficulties inherent in the dirty work of dealing with bod- ies, carers are able to mobilise a sense of value that arises from caring as a morally good form of work – these are sentiments found in other accounts of nursing labour (Lawton, 1998). Other commentators deal- ing with dirty aspects of care demonstrate how working-class women care workers can choose to respond to dirty tasks through 'tough' behaviour (Lee-Treweek, 1997). Although there are different views on how dirty work in care and nursing are transformed in various con- texts, it is clear that most demonstrate women's abilities to find pride in such jobs. Other studies have found similar processes in other forms of women's labour, as shown in the various papers within Hochchild and Ehrenreich's (2003) edited text *Global Women*, which, for instance, discusses migrant women as maids, nannies, sex workers and overseas brides.

Ashforth and Kreiner (1999) note the irony that undertaking dirty work represents a potentially stigmatising situation for the worker, which one might assume would make creating a valued social identity problematic. However, in reviewing the academic literature, they found the opposite, that is numerous studies report that workers do success- fully find creative means of positively reconstructing their work. Like many commentators, Ashforth and Kreiner (1999) note the importance of dirty workers creating a close and supportive subculture that enables them to construct their work as necessary, important, skilful and so on; they do not note any negatives that might follow from transforming work in this way. But tight-knit work subcultures could create problems, such as work cultures becoming monocultural and homogenous and identities becoming inflexible. This leads us to the issue of identities at work and how they take shape in and around working environments.

The problem of identity in low-status denigrated work

Paul Du Gay (1996) notes that traditional sources and resources of identity are often no longer available to individuals in contemporary society. Stable sources of identity are often unobtainable as notions of social class, gender, place, affiliation and so forth have become uncertain. Identities at work have not been exempt from the wider destabilising of identity in contemporary society. Du Gay (1996: 25) notes that 'real work' is traditionally understood to be about manufacturing and the industrial sector, but most work now takes place in the service sector and 'soft' jobs (speaking to people, working with IT systems and so forth) which have attracted more women. Socio-economic changes have revealed the uncertainty of identities bound up with 'traditional' industrial labour; these have often been white, working-class male identities, based upon the male as the breadwinner and on gendered social relationships. For Du Gay (1996) the destabilising of such identities is not necessarily negative as new work identities emerge in relation to these uncertainties. For instance, the changing composition of workforces may positively transform organisations, making them more social.

Skeggs (2004) concurs with Du Gay that identity is particularly problematic in relation to 'traditional' working-class work but also more generally in relation to the tasks that are 'typical' of what this type of work entails. For Skeggs, a key problem lies in the notion of value, and specifically, in the high value placed on some workers' roles and not on others in UK society. She argues that many aspects of working-class culture have faced being downgraded as unimportant and non-status-bearing. The demise of social-class-based identities has gone hand in hand with the construction of such identities as fixed and archaic. Working-class identities and work roles have faced considerable denigration in UK culture more broadly – often with the association of the white, working class with 'chav'[2] culture (Skeggs, 2004: 102). This creates problems in terms of 'resourcing the self' (Skeggs, 2004: 139) or finding the means to create a valuable self at the workplace and in society. The key question is: where does the unvalued worker find a sense of identity? There is little left to draw upon in constructing a meaningful sense of self at work when the resources are few culturally.

Migrants entering the lowest forms of working-class jobs and the secondary labour force of undesirable jobs and tasks also find themselves under the influence of similar identity negating processes. Like their indigenous working-class counterparts, they suffer from a lack of 'value' and from their association with highly denigrated work (Holgate, 2005). Some forms of work in the secondary labour market such as slaughterhouse labour and cleaning up rubbish are dirty work in the traditional literature. However, in economies such as the United Kingdom, other jobs have become so undesirable that few but migrants do them. These jobs are 'unwanted' because they are the most menial, low-skilled and low-paid, and as such are socially tainting. As Skeggs (2004: 51) notes, such jobs almost sit below notions of classed work – the workers receive low wages that hardly differentiate their economic position from people on state benefits. If any jobs represent 'modern' dirty work, it is these dead-end occupations. Work agencies have stepped in to manage and populate such work; these are the same agencies that directly appeal and recruit from migrant populations (MacKenzie and Forde, 2009).

Research commissioned by the Trades Union Council (TUC) in the United Kingdom has found migrants working in poor conditions, often together (rarely mixing with non-migrant workers), undertaking labour with the lowest prospects, lowest social worth and poorest wages and at the same time often experiencing racism and discrimination (Anderson et al., 2007). Moreover, often labelled as 'temporary' through their association with work agencies or with the assumption that they will want to 'go home' at some point (MacKenzie and Forde, 2009), migrants risk a double stigma in doing dirty work *and* being seen as transient. Without work, migrants often face racism, hate crimes and difficulties in accessing public services. Similar to work experiences, many migrants live in areas with high numbers of other migrants and so mixing with other communities and participating in UK society can be extremely hard. Moreover, the 2008–9 recession raised public and political debates about entitlement to jobs, residency and social support for migrants. These factors negatively influence the working lives and self-esteem of migrants.

Understanding employment and lifestyles in Poland

It is pertinent to outline the nature of Polish society, work and work practices as a point of comparison to Northton's industrial workplaces. Work in Poland tends not to be stable, with jobs often being short-term and part-time, especially for young people. Pay is also low, which is prohibitive in terms of living independently from family and aspiring to set up a home. Gender issues are prominent in literature about Polish labour market experiences. For instance, Pollert (2003) has noted that there remain difficulties for women as workers in post-communist Poland.

Women tend to leave school with better qualifications but they generally obtain lower-status jobs and experience blocks in terms of career development. Men have lower qualifications than women but are more likely to succeed in the labour market. The role of women as homemakers is still at the core of female identity in Poland and for men, the pressure to earn as breadwinners is as strong. The other influencing feature of people's lives is the dominance of the Roman Catholic Church, which, linked with discourses of 'conventional' married family life, provides a potent configuration of traditional roles that men and women are still expected to attain (Graham and Regulska, 1997). Migration appears to offer opportunities to challenge the dynamics of traditional gender roles and lifestyles.

It is unsurprising that transmigration is not just 'economic' but often (as thought by migrants to) offers the possibility of a new lifestyle, with new values (Lee-Treweek and Gorna, 2008). In terms of the particular cohorts of Polish migrants in Northton, a significant percentage of migrants hailed from areas with the highest rates of unemployment before the EU accession. Data from the Polish government shows that these areas also have some of the lowest indicators of quality of life in the country: low health and well-being; higher-than-usual crime and lower standards of living. Many studies of migrants indicate that they do hope for a better life and often see low-status jobs as transitional. Likewise in Northton, both male and female migrants hoped not to stay in dirty low-status jobs for very long (Lee-Treweek and Gorna, 2008).

Participatory action research methods

The semi-structured interview data presented here was gathered as part of an ongoing tranche of migration-related research projects carried out in Northton since 2006. Northton is a small town of about 47,000 which, in the past, relied upon the railway industry for most employment. Today Northton is surrounded by industrial estates. Serviced well by road and rail links, the town functions as a centre for light industry and logistics. The projects carried out in Northton all used participatory action research (PAR) and aimed to study and help change negative aspects of social life. PAR prioritises the participants as co-creators of knowledge. It was created by social psychologist Kurt Lewin (1946) as a direct response to methodological approaches that separate social research from 'real world problems' and solutions. While the methodology has developed and expanded its remit and forms of application, PAR still continues to focus upon three types of relationships that were of concern to Lewin. The first type of relationships of interest to PAR researchers are those visible between individuals that operate *within* communities and groups. Second, there is a concern with relationships *between* different communities and groups, and finally the interaction between individuals/groups and physical environments. Group relationships and dynamics are therefore pivotal to the way that PAR approaches social issues and problems (McIntyre, 2007).

It is also the case that PAR continues a traditional Lewinian focus by attempting to ensure research participants are not excluded from the processes involved in the production of knowledge. A move towards equity in the relationships between researcher and researched demands that the boundaries between the two be more permeable, up for discussion and always include 'the researched'. PAR as a methodology is about influencing social change with those studied as a discursive and incremental process (McIntyre, 2007). The current focus in the United Kingdom upon research impact and engagement makes PAR approaches to fieldwork more attractive; including participants, user groups and communities is at the core of PAR practice. This also means including migrants in the development of research ideas, in setting up and carrying out interviews, in acting as interpreters/translators (where necessary), in recruiting other participants, in disseminating findings and in helping generate change from findings.

The methods of the project built on ethnographic fieldwork, which has been continually in process with economic migrants in the Northton area since 2006. The main data gathering took place over the course of 2009–10. The data presented here is from 25 semi-structured qualitative interviews with migrants working in light industrial settings in the Northton area – most of these being with women but sometimes involving male migrants also in the same households. The interviewees were aged between 22 and 32, reflecting the general age demographic of new Polish migrants arriving in the United Kingdom after European Union accession. The interviews took place, usually, within domestic homes and with a generally informal ambience. While many interviews took one hour because of stopping and starting for childcare, other 'homely' duties and visitors arriving and temporarily stopping the interview (or sometimes joining in), it was not uncommon for them to take up to three hours. After these initial interviews, further visits were made to homes to discuss findings and engage participants in discussing findings. While some areas were more challenging to feedback (specifically the findings around racism), there were other areas that participants appeared to enjoy re-engaging with. In accordance with the approach of PAR, the processes of discussion and analysis are seen as important and interrelated, feeding back into each other and informing where the research progresses next.

Reconstruction and transformation of the work: from dirty to doable

The chapter now turns to examine responses to dirty work by Polish migrants in the light industrial sector within Northton. It demonstrates the way that some of the traditional themes of the dirty work literature are visible in the accounts given by the migrants. Similar to workers in other settings, the reframing of dirty work as an instrumental means to a wage and attaining a positive sense of being a worker were important factors.

> *ANKA* Of course, this is not what I want to do to put in box mobile phones all day but this is something at this point until better job.
> *MARIUS* This is heavy job, sometimes hot sometimes cold … not a good job but money for the family.
> *ZLOTA* Your job is to stand in line one person by another and put the topping on the pizza … I have finance degree but this is pay for flat, for food and some little left over.

The nastier aspects of the job were transformed by rationalisations of the work – it was money and it was necessary. Pride arose from doing a dirty job well and reframing meanings around the work that made the demeaning aspects of the work personally meaningful and their own. In the case of industrial food production, the manner of making the food would appear to be the antithesis of home cooking – working with large-scale industrial ovens, ingredient mixing machines and production lines. The kinds of tasks involved in industrial food production were transformed successfully through worker reconstructions.

> *EDYTA* When I makes the yogurt I am happy, I think is make this myself, like home make.
> *MICHEL* This is very good cheese that we make … we are eat for lunch … sometimes I just eat cheese … this is a very good like from a farm.
> *JOZEFA* I go to shop at X [supermarket name] and I think this is our baking here, we have made in a factory and I feel pleased at this.

By establishing a sense of ownership and pride over the production of food, workers gained a sense of involvement with their work. To see the finished product as a commodity was reported to be empowering. Similarly, migrants who did not work in food production argued that they had pride in what they did.

> *PAVEL* What phone is this you have? [takes researcher's phone] Oh, this is good phone...I see many phones in the warehouse, we are put them together to work before they go out to shops...there is nothing I don't know about phones now, I am King of phones [laughs].
>
> *KASIA* I can work very fast, faster than others...and I can do any task with the PCs and other equipment, very fast, very accurate.

There was pride in having expertise in your 'field', even if this area might be regarded by others as trivial and demeaning.

Migrant workers also have an added aspect to their sense of pride in the work and their social and workplace construction as 'good workers' in relation to non-Poles or, at the very least, to non-migrants. MacKenzie and Forde (2009) argue that Eastern European workers are often considered by UK employers as good workers. With the workers interviewed in Northton, it was clear that the identity of the 'good migrant worker' also permeated migrants' ideas of themselves and the group.

> *LUIZA* The managers are think of us as good workers...it would be wrong to just sit on the line, how will they think of us then?
>
> *MARZENA* I have not take one day with sick, even when I am very ill...my manager is very nice, very kind to workers...it is good to have manager like this and I do my best at work.
>
> *PIOTR* I am not surprised that managers like hire Polish...some of these English, especially young lads are lazy bastards...they just sit on they backsides...by the time they have finished the tea break we have finished the job.

Participants placed emphasis upon not letting their English managers (and by implication their employers) down. To be competent and hardworking, even in a generally socially unacceptable work setting, such as working on a garlic bread line, was constructed as positive, and being a worker was valued above what you actually did.

Gender-related strategies in workplaces: women migrants' creation of moral order

In this section, the discussion moves to examine the position of migrant women within industrial-sector low-status labour. These women, in the main, had migrated as single and childless; they were part of an increasing migratory trend that sees women moving for their own reasons (Boyd, 1989). While these women might have had high hopes and aspirations for working in the United Kingdom, they often found that the expected traditional gendered patterns of behaviour were difficult to escape in Northton. Indeed, notions of the 'good woman', which were related to those of the 'good worker', seemed to create links back to expected identities in Poland – identities and ways of doing things they no longer wanted. All the participants were working in virtually all-Polish migrant work settings.

> *ANKA* you come here to get away from bloody Poland, to make a life and then it's like being back in Poland!.... each day is work with Polish and so it's like little Poland...what can you do about this?
> *PAULINA* There are so many rules, who you speak to, who you don't speak to...even how to look and if you don't do all this then you are bad, they are talk about you.

Workplaces provided environments that were replete with informal subcultural rules about behaviour that had to be adhered to. It was noted by participants that new women workers had to go through a process of adapting to other workers' expectations.

> *ZLOTA* If you are going to have a problem its always woman...woman criticise you, 'I see you talking to manager', then they tell everyone...this is what happens to all women...some are too weak and leave but you must get tough skin and do things that won't make a problem.
> *SYLWIA* It's important that you realise what people want of you but that's not always easy to do as it's not about the work but about who you are...without really trying you are become outside person.

Morally charged relationships within the work settings focused attention upon a worker's own behaviour, the other women around and being seen to fit in. Dirtiness was seen to situated not in the work (although all identified the work as unpleasant and generally unwanted), but in individual women workers' behaviour and attitudes. Adapting to informal subcultural rules about how 'good Polish women' behaved was crucial if one was to be accepted. Many of these rules appeared to appeal to a notion of 'traditional' Polishness and feminine behaviour.

Controlling relationships with men

One key component of good Polish womanhood was the maintenance of 'appropriate' boundaries with men within the workplace. 'Dirty bitches' were reported to be women who were epitomised by an inadequate management of their relationships with males – both migrants and indigenous workers. For many women a spoiled identity was the consequence of other women perceiving that they had real or imagined friendships (or sexual relationships) with males from work. Gossip, hearsay and blame appeared to be important in migrant women's decisions about other migrant women. Rules about abstaining from contact with males were applied to both single women and those in heterosexual couples.[3] Women in couples were very aware of the need to take action to demonstrate that any rumours were not true.

> LUIZA I know what they are say because I sit with this Polish man at lunchtime, but you are work for ten hours and how can this be bad if it makes it a little better for me and for him to have conversation in small break? When I hear they say I am dirty bitch I was shocked, I just speak to him!... I say to them I am married woman but they keep saying this and won't talk to me until I ignore him.
>
> KASIA I am have this say to me that I sleep with managers... but I don't do this and it takes weeks and weeks to get them listen and before then I am sit on my own, eat my sandwiches on my own.
>
> PAOLINA Anka is a married woman but I have seen her speaking to English and Polish men in X's cheeses [factory]... She is work on the line and it's not important to talk to men but she chooses to do this... I have never behave like this and my friends they don't. We have tell her you keep doing this and someone may tell your husband and she will not like this [laughs].

It was interesting that all the women could identify that other migrant Polish women were involved in defining them in negative ways. However, many gave accounts that outlined their own experience of personal distress caused by being negatively defined, but then went on to note that women often did behave immorally with men and so such evaluations were necessary. Karolina's account provides a typical illustration of this.

> *KAROLINA* I have been called slapper and its like it goes around the factory [mimics], 'I saw her talking with him' and then they tell the next person and the next person and before you know down the bottom of the [assembly] line they say, 'she has sleep with this man'...so story changes along the way...[ten minutes later into the interview] But there are women who are sleep with a man at work and you see them with their cakes and why are they bringing cakes into work and the give some to the manager?
>
> *GLT* I don't know ...?
>
> *KAROLINA* Because they are sleep with him! You can know [mimics] 'here have a nice cake, I have make', and then make suddenly they work on better part of the line.

It is clear that for some participants there was often incongruity between their feelings of injustice at being the focus of negative accusations and their part in accusing other women of the same activities. The imperative to find 'dirtiness' in individuals' behaviours and to ensure that it was controlled, through the imposition of notions of moral behaviour, appeared to go unchallenged. A sense of suspicion and lack of trust in one another seemed a central part of daily life on the lines, in the factories and in the warehouses. This was combined with what has been termed by other scholars of gender at work as everyday 'bitchiness' (Sotirin and Gottfried, 1999) in the treatment and definition of 'rule-breakers'.

Good family values, the 'community' and the Roman Catholic Church

According to the 2002 Polish census, 90 per cent of the population are of the Roman Catholic denomination, with 75 per cent practising. It is perhaps unsurprising then that references to religion within the interviews were very common, with most women noting some form of attendance and affiliation with the Polish Roman Catholic Church in Northton. Most participants spoke about church engagement as being part of a 'decent' way of life. The consequences of not being involved with this facet of 'Polish culture' were made clear.

> *MARZENA* You can tell she is bad woman because she is not going to church and she is also single and it is obvious what is happen to a woman like this... We don't speak to her now because she is turn her back on the Church and so she is turn her back onto us.

While for many there were issues of church attendance being about spiritual guidance and belief, there was also an aspect of demonstrating commitment to the Polish community. Church attendance was a key way of doing this; those who did not go to church or show some allegiance were perceived to be rejecting the norms of Polish life.

> *SYLWIA* I'm not a religious person... but I am going to the Church because this is what you should do. The Church is how it is for Polish, to not go is showing a lack of respect to everyone... how will you bring your children up properly if you don't have the Church? It's not a matter of believing.

Attendance at Mass implied something about you as a 'good Polish woman'. Lack of attendance indicated the possibility of misbehaviour, of not being properly Polish and of having the wrong attitude. It was reported that negative assumptions were often drawn from non-attendance, which then influenced relationships at work and evaluations of one's 'good worker' status.

Many of the participants were unmarried and lived with male partners. One would have thought that this could have been a cause for exclusion of workers in relation to religious norms, but it appeared that, as long as one still attended Church, heterosexual relationships in which couples lived together were tolerated. However, being in a relationship appeared to make scrutiny of one's behaviour much more intense.

> *HALINA* When I first come here I am meet my boyfriend and we move in together. You cannot do this in Poland, my parents would not be happy... this is a freedom here but then you face all the talking and now you had better behave yourself now you have a man.

'Having a man' was a controlling factor for women migrants in the sense that the expectation was that they would attend church and 'behave' like married women. The women who suffered the most long-standing negative definition as 'potentially' dirty by other women at work were those who had children out of wedlock and then suffered relationship break-ups, leaving them as single mothers. The scrutiny of these women's positions and the consequences in relation to their treatment in the factories and warehouses were intense, as can be seen in the case of Magda.

> *KONSTANZIA* Marriage is the proper place for the children, Magda is just have baby with anyone, not husband, now she is surprised he is leave her with bastard. I don't wish to mix with such a woman.

Konstanzia was not aware that Magda also participated in the study as an interviewee; her experience, as with those recounted by many women 'without men', was disturbing.

> *MAGDA* I am work at X where I am packer.... this is good job and I am excellent at this... when my boyfriend leave me I am single mother... I have to earn to pay for child care but I want to work... the women start at work... it's like whispers and then they ignore me... one woman is leading this and she says I am dirty woman and that the baby would be better dead... I have to work in her section... one day I don't get my bonus and my manager say I am not doing proper work... he showed me the figures from the computer [the workers enter their output on the computer as they work] ... this woman gone on the computer and wiped off most my work... I go from best worker to lazy.

Magda was made redundant five months after this, something she put down to being seen as a lazy worker after months of having her work record deleted by another migrant worker. According to Magda, other women supported this person's behaviour, giving her alibis for when she could have accessed the computer and ostracising Magda. Single mothers were 'singled out' in other ways at work; for instance, they faced negative construction as bad women, while at the same time they were seen as bad mothers as they left their children at home to work. However, migrant spouses often both worked and so it was hard to see how single women were worse mothers for being alone.

Dirtiness, race and 'othering' of host and migrant groups

As well as policing each other in terms of work behaviour, there were 'others' at work who most of the women defined as dirty. The majority of women discussed during their interviews notions of negative differences between them and other non-Polish migrants; in most of these cases, ideas of dirtiness were overtly voiced. Male English workers were, in general, seen as morally bad. Zlota worked on a line with an English team leader, Derrick, who functioned as line manager. She was scathing in her discussion of him as a 'typical English pig'.

> *ZLOTA* He is a disgusting pig because he belches and he eats badly and he lies at work...he is most lazy person you ever meet and hardly does the work...you would not want to eat anything that he touches because he just does not wash himself.
> *GLT* How do you know this? Does he tell you or something?
> *ZLOTA* You can just see it he is filthy man and he has bad behaviour at work.

For Zlota, Derrick's dirtiness was judged through her interpretation of his workplace behaviour as morally wrong. The 'filth' that Derrick represented was conceptualised as physical dirt, although no evidence was provided that he was actually physically unclean, dirty or smelly. Similarly, other migrants were noted to exhibit and/or represent dirtiness ranging from being morally dirty to being physically dirty.

> *SYLWIA* There is a problem with work with East Timorese [migrants], they are always causing problems, saying 'join this union' or 'complain about that'...it is best to avoid them...they are always whining...they cannot control themselves and they are basically lazy and no good.
> *EDYTA* They say migrants is all the same, but is not true because working with the blacks is bring difficulties...they are most racist people around...will lie to get you lose the job...they are just bad people.

Luiza, who was a teacher in Poland prior to migrating and worked in Northton in a warehouse, was quite clear what the problem was with working with other migrants.

> *LUIZA* We do not work with many migrants other than Polish because the agency sends workers from Poland...but sometimes there are some black people from England or from some other place and they are a nightmare...they are not used to work and will sit about...this is why employers want Polish...

Perhaps unsurprisingly, by association with non-Polish migrants, women could find themselves marginalised and regarded as lesser within the work group.

> JOZEFA It is not only man she is with, it is black man...We have a few girls going with men, going with East Timor [migrant] men and they have stop when they see how other women think of this.

This comment returns us to the idea of what constituted the 'good Polish worker', the 'good Polish woman' and the issue of maintaining acceptable boundaries between groups. It would be easy to construct the women's ideas as competitiveness at work, wrapped up in ideas of moral and physical dirt. However, the identification of others as the real 'dirty' workers could also be said to have diverted the women from assessment of their work as dirty and demeaning. Racist attitudes were framed by the structural constraints of the women's lives – the enforced ethnic separations often reported about the workplaces, the lack of understanding of diversity and the paucity of cultural resources that the women could draw upon to fashion their worker identities. This is not to condone such attitudes but merely to view them in a broader framework of work and community in which racist ideas were rarely challenged.

Discussion

The data discussed in this chapter raises some difficult questions about migrant women at work and their behaviour in general. It would be easy to form the view that the women were belligerent to each other, racist about other groups, controlling and bullying in their ways of working and so forth. However, the analysis of the lives of these women has to go beyond the superficial to think sociologically about the everyday work experiences of migrants in general, the conditions they work in, the wider socio-community relationships around them and their sense of place in the British workforce. The environments that they work in are tough, and they undertake mundane, socially degrading, repetitive, boring and often physically dirty labour. Unlike earlier studies of 'dirty work', which were carried out (usually) with men and in physically challenging environments, the work of migrants in this study who were involved in low-skilled industrial labour did not have many aspects that could be imbued with other, more positive, meanings. While there was some evidence that producing food, such as yogurt and cheese, could give some pride, in general this was short-lived. In terms of creating identity and sustaining a sense of self that could, in effect, compensate for 'doing dirty work', the women did not have access to cultural resources to easily reconstruct negative meanings.

Literature on dirty work has demonstrated the necessity of such resources for a positive reconstruction of unacceptable tasks at work. For instance, in Meara's (1974) discussion of the Turkish meatcutters and Ackroyd and Crowdy's (1993) examination of slaughterhouse workers, certain aspects of the work could be turned from 'dirty' to skilful, in particular the use of knives and heavy equipment and dangerous processes. These were resources at work, which were deployed to 'cleanse' the dirty worker identity. Moreover, Ackroyd and Crowdy (1993) were able to show how aspects of working-class masculinity resourced the slaughterhousemen's transformation of work. In one compelling section of this seminal paper, they discussed the pride shown by the men in being seen outside the processing plant in blood-soaked overalls. Far from rejection of the dirty, there was an elevation of the importance of providing meat for society – few could cope with such tasks and this enabled a sense of being different and special. It is not only men that appear able to directly challenge the dirty nature of their work; this can also be seen in literature about women. In Lee-Treweek's (1997) discussion of women at Bracken Court nursing home, the dirty work of nursing care for older people was transformed through promoting 'toughness' to being a skill and a feature of the 'good worker'. In this case, the resources used to transform meanings were the older people themselves and the workers' relationships with them. In comparison, putting toppings on pizza or sealing boxes are jobs that have little about them that is valued at all. For Skeggs (2004), this is a problem for the UK working class in general, as the dirty work that people now have to undertake is so mundane and valueless as to be impossible to transform positively.

Identity for the migrant women in this study came from within the group. It was generated internally to counteract the poverty of external sources of identity. In this case, the generation of a sense of self came from drawing on pre-migration identities and installing those as part of the everyday means of generating a sense of worth and of group membership. While from the outside the work groups might appear to have integrity and one could even say that the women did have access to a sense of group belonging, the cost of this to individuals was high. In particular, migrants found themselves monitored and policed by the group in ways that mimicked the controls placed upon them in Poland. For many, one of the positives of migrating was (the hope of) replacing cultural values and gendered restrictions that had constrained them. Coming to a new country represented the opportunity to live new lifestyles as well as to succeed at the workplace. However, as Skeggs (2004: 50) notes, the ability to access identity change in one's life is not equally distributed in late modern society:

> It [identity politics] is used to 'name origins' so that some people are considered to be located and others mobile. Identity politics is used to attribute locatedness to others in order to generate a means of fixing in place. This mechanism of trying to fix other is well known in racist discourse, e.g. 'where do you come from?'

Ironically, migrants are physically mobile but the relationship between their past origin and identity can appear to freeze in time, as if they are to be defined through that as their main status indicator. Both the working class and migrants can find themselves 'stuck' in notions of who, what and where they are. Denied access to means to positively 'make the self' or perhaps (given the possibilities opened up by migration) to 'remake the self' at the workplace, the migrants discussed here seemed forced back into reusing older values and ideas.

In relation to the racist comments of many of the interviewees and their attempts to separate themselves from other groups, the source of their attitudes can be seen in a variety of ways. There could be issues of competition for work, but there is no evidence of groups' competition for low-status jobs in Northton. To understand racism within migrant groups and between migrant groups, it is necessary to grasp the context in which they work and their daily experience of low status. Migrants do not just work, they also have to live in their new communities and many experience racism (Anderson et al., 2007). Some racism is what Essed (2002) labels as 'everyday'. This term encapsulates the continual grind of experiences of low-level discrimination and abuse. However, it is the persistence and consistence of these experiences that has such a devastating effect; being ignored in shops, being 'spoken down' to by officials and being turned down for house rentals and so forth have a negative impact. More extreme forms of racism, such as violent attacks or racist verbal abuse in the street, may have the effect of underscoring the experience of everyday racism. In work settings, the failure to gain employment commensurate with one's skills and education is an obvious indicator of a lack of status or equivalence to indigenous workers. Finally, finding oneself working with other migrants and few local people presents the migrant with a graphic representation of their low worth in relation to the labour market. It is unsurprising that one response to this can be overemphasis on 'my' group; a creation of boundaries based on spurious divisions but one that provides a sense of control over difficult circumstances.

Organisations that utilise migrant labour have a responsibility to think about the dirty work that these groups have to undertake and the lack of value attached to workers who do such essential but underrated work in society. The organisation and structures of work that often divide migrant and non-migrant labour tend towards reinforcing hierarchies of worker value. In the same way, society in general has to examine the issues around the denigration of some forms of labour as worthless and the lack of positive work identity available to certain sectors of society. The dirty work of the secondary labour force is essential but as more reject this labour, leaving it for those who cannot refuse it, those who do dirty work continue to search for whatever means possible to make sense of their working lives.

Acknowledgements

I would like to acknowledge the help of the participants in the study and also the support of Dr Natasha Slutskaya and Mark Simmonds in writing this chapter.

Notes

1. Northton is a pseudonym as are all worker names. Other identifying features/detail have been changed where they might compromise anonymity.
2. CHAV is a term used to label a subject of working class people, usually younger people who are often represented as below working class (an 'underclass'). The term has social associations with poor taste in clothes and a benefits lifestyle.
3. I use the term heterosexual because none of the participants discussed gay relationships within this data set.

13
Post-Feminism and Entrepreneurship: Interpreting Disgust in a Female Entrepreneurial Narrative

Patricia Lewis

Introduction

This chapter derives from an interview study conducted over a one-year period 2006–7, which sought to explore the identity-construction labours undertaken by a group of women business owners, as a means of 'fitting in' to the world of entrepreneurship. Explorations of the interview data revealed quite early on in the fieldwork the negative views and attitudes some respondents had towards women who were perceived to be inappropriately feminine within a business context. What stood out was the level of animosity towards those who were 'marked' as being excessively feminine and the effort made by individuals to distinguish and distance themselves from 'overly feminine' women. Those who were deemed to be too feminine were variously described as looking 'too maternal', labelled as 'ladies who lunch' or said to be running 'girly businesses'. What was striking about this hostility was the level of disgust attached to it, and the focus of this chapter is to consider how these expressions of disgust should be understood.

The chapter begins by outlining the positioning of femininity within entrepreneurship, along with a consideration of the notion of disgust. Following this the connection between femininity and disgust is illustrated through an analysis of one woman's entrepreneurial narrative based around the struggles she experienced when setting up a business with her husband. There are two parts to this entrepreneurial narrative. The first part highlights how abiding by the culturally prescribed role of homemaker acts as a barrier to her achieving full participation and recognition of her competence within the business she set up with her husband. The second part of the narrative focuses on business experiences outside the home, where she seeks to demonstrate her right to belong within the world of entrepreneurship. This is achieved by distinguishing herself from women she deems as displaying the wrong amount and the wrong kind of femininity (Lawler, 2002), by rendering them 'disgusting'. The chapter concludes by suggesting that expressions of disgust and their use as a means of establishing distance from particular types of women are connected to what Gill (2007) refers to as a post-feminist sensibility and broader socio-cultural trends of individualisation.

Entrepreneurship, femininity and disgust

Research which has sought to explore the relationship between gender and entrepreneurship has highlighted the masculinity inherent in this economic activity (Ahl, 2006; Bruni et al., 2004a; Lewis, 2006; Marlow, 2002). What is emphasised is that the masculinity of entrepreneurship is not simply something which is biological, material or essential, but something complex, historical and cultural in form (Dillabough, 2004; Ogbor, 2000). It can however be experienced in bodily terms, with appropriately masculinised individuals possessing physically embodied capacities which enable them to respond correctly to what is being produced by others and to create themselves in ways that others recognise as suitable in the world of entrepreneurship (Calhoun, 2003). Femininity has a specific role to play here with women business owners being 'encouraged' to sublimate their femininity so that they look like they belong in the world of business. However, as McNay (1999: 103) points out, the attenuation of conventional notions of femininity can be problematic because of 'deep-seated often unconscious investments in conventional images of masculinity and femininity which cannot easily be reshaped'. This means that the sublimation of femininity among women who embark on independent business ownership will be variable.

The existence of this variability has been recognised in the research literature, with the suggestion that there is a coexistence of a masculine and a feminine approach to doing business (Bird and Brush, 2002). The suggestion is that women can choose to either sublimate their femininity by going through a process of masculinisation (Godwin et al., 2006; Lewis, 2006) or reinforce their femininity by adhering to a process referred to as 'femalization' by Bruni et al. (2004b). Nevertheless it is important to point out that there is a hierarchical relationship between these two orientations, with the feminine attributes some women draw on not being ascribed the same value as conventional masculine characteristics. Though a feminine approach may challenge the dominant masculine ethic characteristic of entrepreneurship, it has not overthrown the masculine embodiments associated with entrepreneurship or established itself on an equal footing. Within this context the danger for women who reinforce rather than reduce their femininity is that they will not be taken seriously or are less likely to be perceived as competent or credible within the entrepreneurial realm. How then does a woman business owner who does not sublimate her femininity deal with the potentially negative consequences attached to this within an entrepreneurial context? The suggestion here is that one means by which a female business owner can nullify the impact of femininity on perceptions of her is by expressions of disgust targeted at those women who are perceived as representing the 'wrong' kind of femininity.

Too close for comfort

While much research attention has been directed at the issue of dirt in terms of cultural definitions, the intense feelings of disgust associated with dirt have not received the same attention (Isaksen, 2002). Disgust is an emotion the consequences of which have not been fully researched, particularly with regard to 'classed' disgust (Lawler, 2005). Similarly it can be argued that not enough attention has been directed at expressions of disgust manifest around representations of femininity within the world of work in general and entrepreneurship in particular. The lack of attention is surprising given what Ngai (2005: 336) refers to as the strange 'sociability' of disgust. As an emotion it demands that others share the affective relation to the object of disgust and 'seeks to include or draw others *into* its exclusion of its object'. As a group women are characterised as 'the site of the disgusting', with the male body being seen as symbolically cleaner than the female body because of women's perceived association with animality and mortality through experiences such as birth and menstruation, which render them as 'something that is too physical' (Nussbaum, 1999: 30). Disgust is an extremely visceral emotion which is characterised by strong physical reactions to people or things that have marked bodily features, with certain kinds of clothing, adornment and general bodily appearance being interpreted as signalling a deeper, underlying pathology (Lawler, 2005). Research has indicated that a major source of disgust is contact with people who are disliked or viewed as unsavoury (Nussbaum, 1999).

Central to the notion of disgust is the idea of contamination of the self, with expressions of disgust being used as a means of rejecting a possible contaminant. To feel 'disgusted' is to be 'physically conscious of being within the realm of uneasy categories ... (some) people are just too close for comfort' (Skeggs, 2005: 970). Being near 'uneasy categories' creates the fear that any kind of association means that people or things that have been in contact with each other will continue ever after to impact on one another (Nussbaum, 1999). From this perspective for a woman business owner, there are potential difficulties in trying to individually 'masculinise' herself and her entrepreneurial activities as a means of separating herself from other female business owners so as to avoid the 'contamination' of femininity. For those women who do not sublimate their femininity, the difficulties involved in avoiding 'contamination' from overly or inappropriately feminised women can be even greater.

Manifestations of disgust are one means of repelling femininity and as an emotion disgust is a powerful way to exclude groups and people to enable the establishment of 'the boundary line between the truly human and the basely animal' (Nussbaum, 1999: 29). In this sense disgust is a formidable marker of the interface between the personal and the social. The emotion of disgust is socially engineered, invoking collective sentiments relying on the affirmation that we are not on our own in our relation to the disgusting object (Lawler, 2005). It is involved in the establishment of and maintenance of difference through the drawing of boundaries, with those who fall on the 'wrong' side of these boundaries being negatively defined and excluded (Miller, 1997). As Skeggs (2005: 970) so succinctly put it:

> Expressions of disgust enable one to repel because they rely on public acknowledgement, on public recognition. In other words when something or someone is designated as excessive, immoral, disgusting, and so on, it provides collectives reassurance that we are not alone in our judgement of the disgusting object.

Thus those who 'appreciate' the inappropriateness of certain displays of femininity within the entrepreneurial realm can therefore legitimately claim a place within this arena as properly entrepreneurial. In contrast those who are unable to display the (masculine or at least subdued feminine) entrepreneurial bodily dispositions which they ought to exhibit are rendered disgusting. As the expression of disgust hinges on proximity (Lawler, 2005), representing some feminised business owners as 'disgusting' demonstrates the degree to which they must be 'pushed away'.

Disgusted entrepreneur

The interview, from which the personal narrative referred to in this chapter is derived, took place with a woman called Sarah (a pseudonym), lasted two hours and produced 36 pages of single-spaced transcript. The focus on the personal narrative of one individual follows the practice of previous studies which also concentrate on the narratives and social texts of a small number of respondents. Examples include Dick (2008) whose analysis of resistance to the notion that women experience career disadvantage within the police force is built around the accounts of two policewomen; Pitt (1998) who examines the narrative explanations of two entrepreneurs, focusing on the issue of how they developed their firms; and Anderson and Smith (2007) who delve into the morality associated with entrepreneurship through two case stories. Clearly, with a focus on one narrative, there is no claim that the analysis presented here can be generalised. However, it can be argued that it is suggestive and indicative of some of the ways in which an emotion such as disgust is used to draw distinctions. As Miller (1997: 50) states:

> Disgust, along with contempt, as well as other emotions in various settings, recognizes and maintains difference. Disgust helps define boundaries between us and them, me and you. It helps prevent *our* way from being subsumed into *their* way.

Contact with Sarah was made through attendance at an event run by a women's business network in the south-east of England. Just over two years prior to the interview Sarah had been a stay-at-home mum with a young daughter, but as she was attending school Sarah decided to go back to work. At the same time, both she and her husband were unhappy that he worked away quite a lot of the time, only getting home about once a fortnight. Their personal situation prompted them to start looking for a business to buy and they purchased their confectionery firm from a couple who wanted to retire. At the time of the interview she and her husband had been running the business for 18 months.

In the interview Sarah provided a detailed account of the experience of taking over and running the confectionery business, giving rise to a range of narratives within the transcript. However, for the purposes of this chapter the focus is on a two-part narrative of belonging in the sphere of entrepreneurship. The first part concentrates on Sarah's position within the internal context of the business and the difficulty she had placing herself at the centre of its activity and having her contribution and competence recognised. The second part has an external focus and relates to Sarah's attempt to demonstrate that she belongs in the world of business expressed through her claim to possess embodied cultural capital. What is interesting about this two-part narrative is that in the first part she places an emphasis on her femininity as a mother, recognising how this impacts on her position in the business. Nevertheless despite this emphasis, in the second part of the narrative she explicitly differentiates herself from other women through expressions of disgust which she uses to establish distance from those women whom she perceives as not displaying an 'automatic knowing' of how to behave and present themselves within the context of the world of business (De Clercq and Voronov, 2009: 400).

What follows can be understood as a type of case-centred study which seeks to explore the intersection of biography, history and society. Narratives can be understood in terms of C. Wright Mills' notion of 'personal troubles' which 'are located in particular times and places, and individuals' narratives about their troubles are works of history as much as they are about individuals, the social spaces they inhabit and the societies they live in' (Riessmann, 2001: 697). Narratives may be expressed and felt as if they are highly personal but should be understood as culturally situated, the success of which is dependent on culturally shared principles surrounding language, 'tellability' and the hearing of stories (Sparkes and Smith, 2008).

Sarah's (lack of) belonging narrative

In taking on the confectionary firm with her husband, Sarah hoped that they would build the business together. In the early stages of their ownership Sarah stated that she 'wasn't able to get involved right from the word go on a 24-hour 7 day a week basis' because of childcare responsibilities. As a consequence of this, her husband Alex 'learned a lot more about the business straight off … getting involved with the manufacturers, the packaging, the computer work and all the paperwork', while she was doing what she referred to as 'the fluffy side of it', for example preparing for shows and getting orders together. This made her feel like 'a spare part' in the firm and that she was 'not up to speed with the business like Alex' and that she 'still [has] got a hell of a lot to learn'. Though she categorically stated that 'I still want to know what's going on with the business but I will not let the business take over my looking after Louise [her daughter]', she recognised that her dual role 'holds me back with the business'.

> It is hard because I want to work down at the unit and put as much as I can in there but then there's still the house to run and there's still Louise and she is number one ... Yes I want to be involved with both but I can't physically do that and I'm not going to put Louise into a childminder ... just so I can carry on working at the business. I'm not palming my child off for anyone. So that is it, to me I've got two sides, with my life it's 50/50 ... Alex's is probably 80/20.

This is what Somers (1994) refers to as an ontological narrative which is a story an individual draws on to make sense of and to act in her life. Here Sarah tried to make sense of the difficulties she was having achieving a sense of belonging in the business in the same way as her husband. She understood her difficulties in terms of her position as 'mother' and 'homemaker', which meant she had to spend more time focusing on home rather than on business issues, unlike her husband. One strategy she implemented to deal with this situation was to ask her husband to bring some of the work home:

> I don't do any cooking or stuff like that but if there's bags that need labelling, the ribbons need cutting for size you know I can do some weighing out of stuff if it's like the boiled sweets and sealing. I can do loads of that at home and still be around for Louise and we think well it also saves us on petrol because it's costing over £100 a week in petrol just for my car alone, so for us to keep taking two vehicles down for me to only be there for a number of hours and have to get back to pick Louise up from school, it's not worth it so it saves us money.

Nevertheless despite her own recognition that it was her family responsibilities which were preventing her from fully participating in the business and the rationalisation of convenience and saving money by working at home, this did not stop her feeling angry about being undervalued and left to do these essential but underrated tasks. This emerged in Sarah's retelling of a situation where a big order of 700 bags of sweets had to go out the following day and despite Alex's working all day to complete the job, he ended up bringing it home and the 'hallway [was] stacked with crates of all the packets of sweets', which all had 'to be rib-boned ... hand-tied with precise little bows ... all the edges cut and they [had] to be done by 6 o'clock the next morning'. Despite the urgency of the situation, Sarah found that she was left to do the work on her own:

> I'm thinking I'm the one still sitting down here tonight and it's now 12 o'clock at night and I've only got half of them done and you've read your paper and you've done your crossword and you've done your Sudoku and you've had your bath and now you're watching football! You're thinking I've been working all day as well so that is when you get like a little niggly thing and you're thinking oh this isn't what I wanted it to be like.

Sarah's lament that working on her own through the night to finish an order was not how she envisioned running the business with her husband signalled her unhappiness with the situation. While Sarah would clearly have liked to be sharing the running of the business with her husband on a more equal basis, their business relationship was more like that of the solo entrepreneur, with Sarah being the supportive spouse (Hamilton, 2006). In addition to this, both her husband and other relatives in her family actively sought to construct his entrepreneurial identity, while she struggled to achieve some recognition for her position in the business. The fact that she was not recognised as a central figure in the firm in the same way as her husband emerged (painfully for her) in an account she gave of a newspaper article about the business:

> I got mentioned once in the very last sentence ... It's a centre page spread about our business, I'm not mentioned until the very last paragraph ... I was fuming ... I'm thinking a one syllable word could be turned into a little bit bigger, just one word ... 'we' – 'I' to 'we' [laughs] makes a big difference ... But 'we' that's the word I use, he uses 'I', he's singular, I'm plural. A lot of people will talk about the business as Alex, even my family, my mum will say 'Oh Sarah's husband Alex, he makes all the products and he does this and that and the other'.

Sarah's belonging (or lack of) narrative is one which highlights the impact her feminine roles of homemaker and mother had on her ability to develop the same knowledge of the business as her husband. It also prevented her from being recognised as possessing the same ability to do similar business tasks as him, even if she was not involved in the business all the time. In this sense her femininity was blocking her access to the entrepreneurial realm and leaving a question mark over her credibility as a business person:

> I want Alex to recognise that…I am still capable of doing a lot of things and that has been one of Alex's faults where I'll do this and I'll say 'No I'm quite capable', [he'll say] 'No, no I'll do that, you don't want to do it', I say 'I am capable, I am big enough, strong enough and ugly enough to look after myself, I did it before you came along and I will do it while you're here so don't wrap me up in cotton wool'. I am capable of giving that deliveryman a right mouthful because he's two days late rather than 'stand back, I'll sort this out'. I'm like 'no you stand back, I'll sort it'. I'm quite capable, I might not get it right but I don't want to be dismissed.

The plot in the first part of this narrative was a domestic one, where Sarah's role in the home blocked her entrepreneurial aspirations while at the same time the competence she did have was invisible and undervalued, impacting on her sense of belonging in the business. Sarah's experience concurs with previous research (e.g. Bachrach Ehlers and Main, 1998; Brush et al., 2009; Marlow, 2002; Williams, 2004), which highlights how women's inability to distance themselves from childcare and domestic responsibilities negatively impacts on their entrepreneurial capabilities and aspirations. Though Sarah's domestic responsibilities did not damage the business per se as her husband was there to manage it, there was an impact on her credibility and her ability to build up knowledge of the firm. What might have appeared to be the obvious answer to this situation was that she secure childminding services, which would free her up to work in the business in the same way as her husband. However, she was very clear that she was 'not stopping my motherly role to take on a career role'. This is not just female complicity and a passive act of identification with a conventional image of femininity. Rather she was also trying to work through the disappointments and tensions which were connected to her attempt to negotiate the competing roles of mother and businesswoman, and this strain must be understood in the context of deeply entrenched gender norms (McNay, 1999). In other words no matter how much Sarah may have wanted to fully participate in the business, her commitment to motherhood prevented this, as did her husband's adherence to traditional masculine norms.

Sarah's belonging narrative

While the identity Sarah constructed above is one of thwarted/ignored entrepreneur that derives from a (lack of) belonging narrative which has a domestic plot of motherhood and home at its centre, a plot which is well-recognised in the entrepreneurship literature, this is not the whole story. There is another element to Sarah's belonging narrative which is based on her certainty that she had the ability to 'fit in' to the entrepreneurial world of business. Sarah was very sure that she had the embodied cultural capital and 'instinctive knowing' of how to behave and present herself in a business context. She tried to demonstrate this through her critique of the behaviour of other women she had observed in three different business settings: a networking event, a business awards ceremony and a health and safety course. Sarah's assessment of her own right to belong in the world of business started with her criticism of other businesswomen who attended a network meeting wearing jeans. She was very critical of this, stating that 'it's atrocious that women turn up wearing jeans and trainers and they've just rushed in and they don't make any effort'. When asked why she felt like this she responded:

> I don't feel that it's portraying an image of seriousness...I don't mean to be rude to anybody...the very first meeting I went to I was appalled and disgusted that some people weren't bothering to listen. I think that is so rude...I noticed that there were two women in particular who were talking who were quite close to me when I was doing my talk and I could actually hear them talking about *Coronation Street* and I think that is just so rude.... But I did feel some of these women were very rude in not paying attention and just turning up scruffy, willy-nilly, sitting down and not ready to participate, talking about television, but you don't get that with men.

In retelling this experience, Sarah was very clearly trying to demonstrate that she had the appropriate cultural capital, that is, she knew how to behave, which enabled her to 'fit in' (De Clercq and Voronov, 2009) to the world of entrepreneurship and business. In particular she focused on what Bourdieu (1986) refers to as embodied cultural capital, that is type of dress, favoured ways of speaking and preferred forms of behaviour. Sarah was clearly suggesting that with regard to dress, behaviour and conversation, these women were showing that they did not possess the appropriate 'system of dispositions' which would allow them to 'fit in' to the world of entrepreneurship and business. By highlighting their shortcomings, Sarah was seeking to demonstrate that she did possess the culturally favoured behaviour and attitudes which distinguished individuals from each other. In contrast to the (lack of) belonging narrative, she appeared to distance herself from what she determined was an inappropriate expression of femininity demonstrated by conversations about soap operas, associating herself instead with men when she stated 'you don't get that with men' as a means of establishing her position in the field of entrepreneurship. She again asserted this right to belong in an account she gave of observations she had made at the presentation of a prize which their business had been nominated for.

> We actually got nominated for the 'Best _____ Product' for the Produced in _____ competition and we went along to the Awards Ceremony and there were no more than probably ten women in the room and it was full up with men in suits... But then there was a couple of women there who actually had made no effort at all in my opinion with their dress. I'm thinking where are they sitting, they're on a table for two over in the corner at the back of the room, why haven't they got a table for two in the middle? Because they didn't fit the role, to me they didn't portray themselves, nobody was networking with them so then they made no effort to network either and like I actually said to Alex 'My God, I can't believe, look at the state of them' and they were two people who turned up wearing jeans and jumpers.

Commenting on the behaviour of these two women, Sarah suggested that their personal deportment within such an entrepreneurial context demonstrated that they did not possess the 'cultural commonalities' (Adams, 2006: 514) required of those who operated in the entrepreneurial arena. Because of this, from Sarah's perspective, the event was not a success for these women because nobody networked with them, because they did not behave in an appropriate way in such a business setting. Sarah's comment to her husband about their dress and behaviour can be interpreted as an attempt by her to demonstrate to him that she did know how to behave in such a setting and that she was a capable, credible business person. Her account of her experience at a health and safety course was similarly critical of women as follows:

> As another experience we had, we attended a health and safety course last year at the beginning of the year... and we had people from various different businesses in there, we had chefs and bakers and bits

and pieces, people from all over the food industry, we all got together and we were completing this course and there was a couple of women sat there. I said to Alex 'Gosh even coming to do like a course...' and we sat an exam, they haven't even...I know you can have a flat tyre and I know you can get caught in traffic but to me I think well you're an hour and a half late and you've got no excuse and you sit back on your chair and you put your foot on the table and you're...This is disgusting behaviour, would you go to that person and do business? It doesn't ooze confidence...and you know we just think you can't believe that some people have actually got businesses, could they sit there and call themselves an entrepreneur because I really don't think they have a right to [laughs].

What does Sarah's retelling of these different experiences highlight? As said above it can be suggested that Sarah was seeking to differentiate herself from other women as a means of demonstrating her credibility and legitimacy within the entrepreneurial arena. While she did highlight her own characteristics and traits by emphasising that she had 'certain standards, I like things to be neat and tidy, I don't like a chaotic mess', she also placed an emphasis on repelling other women whom she designated as having behaved in an unseemly and unfitting manner in a business setting. While it would appear that Sarah could not (and would not) escape 'the feminine' at home, outside she tried to distance herself from other women by rendering their behaviour and their dress as not just unacceptable but disgusting. This display of disgust often led to the use of strong language, such as in the reference below to women as 'pigs':

Q: 'So you have a very strong understanding in yourself of how to run a business and how you should behave in business?

A: Yes I think I do, there is like an unsaid code of how you should behave...Alex is very much like that as well and you can see that women who come up to the stall, he'll just say they're just pigs, they're rude and ill-mannered because they take handfuls of samples and just walk off, they've got no interest, they don't even look at your produce.

For both Sarah and her husband, these women were just 'too material', were lacking 'proper' femininity and were rendered disgusting by their perceived greed and excess, which was for them completely out of place and improper in a business setting (Lawler, 2005). Sarah's expression of disgust and her account of her and her husband's reaction to women they deemed 'disgusting' was used as a means of demonstrating her entrepreneurial competence and her sense of belonging within the world of entrepreneurship. From her perspective she was competent because she was different from them – she believed she had an instinctive 'knowing' of how to act and behave in a business context, as demonstrated by the way she dressed and behaved in business situations, allowing her to lay claim to the possession of entrepreneurial competence. Her expressions of disgust allowed her to associate herself with the conventional masculinity of entrepreneurship, as represented by her husband, and to establish a boundary between her and other women so as to avoid being considered as 'one of them'.

Sarah's violent rejection of what she perceived to be inappropriate femininity in the form of an extreme critique of other women, as a means of asserting her own entrepreneurial competence, can be connected to the uncertainties surrounding gender in contemporary times. While the dominant image of femininity in the form of mother and homemaker has been loosened, the impact of this on women is uncertain because of deep-rooted, ingrained gender norms. According to McNay (1999), the assumption has been that with social changes such as the increase in the number of women entering the labour force, destabilisation of traditional gender norms will automatically follow. However, this eliding of symbolic transformation with social transformation overestimates the possibilities and opportunities available to women (and men) while also underestimating the difficulties faced when trying to negotiate contradictory roles such as those of mother and businesswoman (McNay, 1999). Sarah's struggles within the internal confines of the business did not lead her to be more understanding of other women. Rather the tension she experienced in the negotiation of her conflicting roles led to an extreme rejection of women she deemed as being inappropriately feminine in their conversation, behaviour and dress within a business setting.

Discussion and conclusion

In the brief analysis above we have considered some of the themes and issues associated with the ambiguities surrounding gender in contemporary times. While it is recognised that the relationship between men and women has become much more multifaceted in the twenty-first century, the extreme rejection of other women, manifest in expressions of disgust in Sarah's entrepreneurial narrative, also signals how the relationship between women is equally complicated. How should we understand these expressions of disgust? Are they simply Sarah's harsh opinion of other women or do they represent a broader social phenomenon? I would like to suggest that these articulations of disgust are more than an individual opinion, rather they are a manifestation of what Gill (2007) refers to as a post-feminist sensibility with two aspects of this being particularly pertinent here, that is individualisation and the scrutiny and criticism of women's bodies in terms of how they dress and behave.

Individualisation refers to the contemporary notion that a person's destiny is in their own hands. From this perspective an individual can create their own biography within a context where the power of traditional structures such as class, gender and family has diminished significantly. In other words individuals now have a choice biography as opposed to a standard biography, that is, individual lives are less predictable than was the case in the past (Beck and Beck-Gernsheim, 2002). Given this, the highly individualist orientation of contemporary actors means that there is a suppression 'of tracking down the links connecting individual fate to the ways and means by which society as a whole operates' (Bauman, 2001: 9). Attached to this is the notion that a responsible, autonomous person will deal with opportunities or barriers individually, without drawing on the support or resources of collective entities such as trade unions or other representative bodies. Thus from Sarah's narrative above we can clearly see the pain she was experiencing from her unequal position within the business, but she understood this situation in personal terms as connected to the choice she had made to care for her daughter. The notion that all activities and practices are freely chosen is at the heart of post-feminist discourses in which women are presented as autonomous, independent agents who are not constrained by inequalities and power imbalances (Gill, 2007). Her role as mother and homemaker was presented as something which was a personal choice as opposed to being imposed on her and in this sense she is representative of the post-feminist entrepreneur (Lewis, 2010).

The second element of Sarah's narrative, that is the expression of disgust at other women, is also a part of a post-feminist sensibility. Connected to the notion of personal choice is a contemporary emphasis on self-surveillance, self-monitoring and self-discipline with regard to grooming, clothing, posture, elocution and manners. In addition, attention and vigilance must also be directed at the self in a variety of ways, including at the kind of relationships an individual has – that is, is a person a good mother, a good friend, a good wife and a good daughter?; what kind of personal demeanour does an individual have?; or is a person approachable, a good communicator and sensitive to others' emotions (Gill, 2007)? In Sarah's narrative her ongoing surveillance and expressions of disgust at other women in terms of their dress, conversation and behaviour were highly individualised. She blamed other women for what she perceived to be their shortcomings and did not associate their behaviour with their minority presence in the ranks of entrepreneurs and the consequences that attached to this. Sarah's expression of disgust at other women also meant that she did not have to question her own situation, reinforcing the individualist stance she took with regard to her position in the business she owned with her husband. What Sarah did not appear (or want) to recognise was that her subordinate position within the business she had set up with her husband and the pain and unhappiness she experienced from this was a product of broader gender inequalities. Her revulsion at the women she had encountered in the course of her business activity precluded understanding of the structural restrictions she lived within, making it difficult for her to think or talk about this aspect of her life. Thus the disgust manifest in Sarah's narrative not only worked as a means of distancing her from women who represented the 'wrong' kind of femininity, it also prevented her from considering the structural and cultural constraints which acted on her in particular and on women in general.

A final issue to consider is what a focus on the issue of disgust can tell us about contemporary work experience, both in an employed and a self-employed context. I would like to suggest that expressions of disgust as outlined here contribute to the general pathologisation of particular types of femininity within the world of work and the disregard of those women who appear to represent them. Though an increasing number of studies are drawing attention to the emergence of a feminised form of leadership, management and entrepreneurship, this chapter signals that despite claims that these challenge the traditional masculinity inherent in the public sphere of work, conventional maleness appears to remain dominant. Following Lawler (1999) it can be suggested that one way in which gendered work is made 'real' is through the cultural mechanisms of inclusion and exclusion. Despite the acknowledgement of a feminine approach to business in both large and small organisations, embedded in this is a notion of 'proper' femininity, that is being female enough to be seen to benefit business but not excessively feminine – something which women are required to guard against. Being perceived as inappropriately feminine is cause for continued exclusion, particularly by those women who are anxious to 'fit in' the business world. It is precisely because gender is configured in cultural and symbolic terms that entry into the world of work and business can be so difficult. What needs to be recognised is that it is this cultural configuration of gender which can enable both men and women to despise and to ridicule the efforts of some women (Lawler, 1999), in effect turning them into 'dirty workers'.

Acknowledgement

The interview data presented in this chapter is derived from a project on female entrepreneurs, sponsored by the British Academy (grant reference SG-40762).

References

Abbott, P. and Meerabeau, L. (1998) Professionals, Professionalization and the Caring Professions. In Abbott, P. and Meerabeau, L. (eds) *The Sociology of the Caring Professions*. London: UCL Press.

Abbott, P. and Wallace, C. (1998) Health Visiting, Social Work, Nursing and Midwifery: A History. In Abbott, P. and Wallace, C. (eds) *The Sociology of the Caring Professions*. London: UCL Press.

Acker, J. (1990) Hierarchies, Jobs, Bodies: A Theory of Gendered Organizations. *Gender and Society* 4: 139–158.

Acker, J. (1992) Gendering Organizational Theory. In Mills, A. J. and Tancred, P. (eds) *Gendering Organizational Analysis*. Newbury Park: Sage Publications Ltd, pp. 248–260.

Ackroyd, S. (2007) Dirt, Work and Dignity. In Bolton, S. (ed.) *Dimensions of Dignity at Work*. Amsterdam: Elsevier.

Ackroyd, S. and Crowdy, P. (1990) Can Culture Be Managed? Working with Raw Material: The Case of the English Slaughterhouse Workers. *Personnel Review* 19(5): 3–14.

Adams, M. (2006) Hybridizing Habitus and Reflexivity. *Sociology* 40(3): 511–528.

Adkins, L. (1995) *Gendered Work: Sexuality, Family and the Labour Market*. Buckingham: Open University Press.

Ahl, H. (2006) Why Research on Women Entrepreneurs Needs New Directions. *Entrepreneurship, Theory and Practice* 30(5): 595–621.

Ainsworth, S. and Hardy, C. (2004) Critical Discourse Analysis and Identity: Why Bother? *Critical Discourse Studies* 1(2): 225–259.

Alía, I. and Esteban, A. (2000) Weaning from Mechanical Ventilation. *Critical Care* 4(2): 72–80.

Anderson, A. R. and Smith, R. (2007) The Moral Space in Entrepreneurship: An Exploration of Ethical Imperatives and the Moral Legitimacy of Being Enterprising. *Entrepreneurship and Regional Development* 19(6): 479–497.

Anderson, B. (2000) *Doing the Dirty Work: The Global Politics of Domestic Labour*. London: Zed Books.

Anderson, B., Clark, N. and Parutis, V. (2007) *New EU Members? Migrant Workers' Challenges and Opportunities to UK Trades Unions: A Polish and Lithuanian Case Study*. London: TUC.

Andersson, J. (2007) Hygiene Aesthetics in London's Gay Scene: The Stigma of AIDS. In Campkin, B. and Cox, R. (eds) *Dirt: New Geographies of Cleanliness and Contamination*. London: I. B. Tauris.

Andrews, M. and Talbot, M. (2000) Introduction: Women in Consumer Culture. In Andrews, M. and Talbot, M. (eds) *All the World and Her Husband: Women in Twentieth-Century Consumer Culture*. London: Cassell.

Arluke, A. (1991) Going into the Closet with Science: Information Control among Animal Experimenters. *Journal of Contemporary Ethnography* 20(3): 306–330.

Arnold, K. A. and Barling, J. (2003) Prostitution: An Illustration of Occupational Stress in 'Dirty Work'. In Dollard, M., Winefield, H. R. and Winefield, A. H. (eds) *Occupational Stress in the Service Professions*. London: Taylor and Francis.

Aronson, J. (1994) A Pragmatic View of Thematic Analysis. *Qualitative Report* 2(1), Spring, available at: http://www.nova.edu/ssss/QR/BackIssues/QR2-1/aronson. html (accessed 1 April 2010).

Ashcraft, K. L. and Mumby, D. K. (2004) *Reworking Gender: A Feminist Communicology of Organization*. Thousand Oak, CA: Sage.

Ashforth, B. and Kreiner, G. (1999) How Can You Do It?: Dirty Work and the Challenge of Constructing a Positive Identity. *Academy of Management Review* 24(3): 413–434.

Ashforth, B. and Kreiner, G. (2002) Normalizing Emotion in Organizations: Making the Extraordinary Appear Ordinary. *Human Resource Management Review* 12: 215–235.

Ashforth, B., Kreiner, G., Clark, M. and Fugate, M. (2007a) Normalizing Dirty Work: Managerial Tactics for Countering Occupational Taint. *Academy of Management Journal* 50(1): 149–174.

Attwell, A. (1998) Florence Nightingale's Relevance to Nurses. *Journal of Holistic Nursing* 16(2): 281–291.

Attwood, F. (2005) Fashion and Passion: Marketing Sex to Women. *Sexualities* 8(4): 392–406.

Australian Institute of Health and Welfare (2007) *Nursing and Midwifery Labour Force*, Labour Force Series No. 39, Canberra: AIHW.

Bachrach Ehlers, T. and Main, K. (1998) Women and the False Promise of Microenterprise. *Gender and Society* 12(4): 424–440.

Barry, K. (1995) *The Prostitution of Sexuality*. New York: New York University Press.

Baudrillard, J. (1994) *Simulacra and Simulation*. Michigan: University of Michigan Press.

Bauman, Z. (2001) *The Individualized Society*. Cambridge: Polity Press.

Beasley, C. (2008) Rethinking Hegemonic Masculinity in a Globalizing World. *Men and Masculinities* 11(1): 86–103.

Beck, U. and Beck-Gernsheim, E. (2002) *Individualization*. London: Sage.

Becker, H. S., Geer, B., Hughes, E. C. and Strauss, A. L. (1977 [1961]) Students and Patients. In Becker, H. S. (ed.) *Boys in White: Student Culture in Medical School*. New Brunswick: Transaction.

Bell, S. (1994) *Reading, Writing and Rewriting the Prostitute Body*. Bloomington: Indiana University Press.

Benhabib, S. (1995) Feminism and Postmodernism. In Benhabib, S., Butler, J., Cornell, D. and Fraser, N. (eds) *Feminist Contentions – A Philosophical Exchange*. London: Routledge.

Benson, D. and Hughes, J. A. (1991) Method: Evidence and Inference – Evidence and Inference for Ethnomethodology. In Button, G. (ed.) *Ethnomethodology and the Human Sciences*. Cambridge: Cambridge University Press.

Berg, M. and Bowker, G. (1997) The Multiple Bodies of the Medical Record: Toward a Sociology of an Artifact. *Sociological Quarterly* 38(3): 513–537.

Berger, P. L. and Luckmann, T. (1966) *The Social Construction of Reality*. New York: Irvington Publishers, Inc.

Berkowitz, D. (2006) Consuming Eroticism: Gender Performances and Presentations in Pornographic Establishments. *Journal of Contemporary Ethnography* 35(5): 583–606.

Billig, M. (1991) *Ideologies and Beliefs.* London: Sage.

Billig, M. (1996) *Arguing and Thinking.* Cambridge: Cambridge University Press.

Binnie, J. and Skeggs, B. (2004) Cosmopolitan Knowledge and the Production and Consumption of Sexualized Space: Manchester's Gay Village. *Sociological Review* 52(1): 39–61.

Bird, B. and Brush, C. (2002) A Gendered Perspective on Organizational Creation. *Entrepreneurship, Theory and Practice* 26(3): 41–66.

Bird, S., Litt, J. and Ande Wang, Y. (2004) Creating Status of Women Reports: Institutional Housekeeping as 'Women's Work'. *National Women's Studies Association Journal* 16(1): 194–206.

Blackman, L. (2004) Self-Help, Media Cultures and the Production of Female Psychopathology. *European Journal of Cultural Studies* 7(2): 219–236.

Blackman, L. (2007) Psychiatric Culture and Bodies of Resistance. *Body and Society* 13(2): 1–23.

Blaikie, N. (2000) *Designing Social Research.* Cambridge: Polity.

Bogard, W. (2000) Smoothing Machines and the Constitution of Society. *Cultural Studies* 14: 269–294.

Bolton, S. (2001) Changing Faces: Nurses as Emotional Jugglers. *Sociology of Health and Illness* 23(1): 85–100.

Bolton, S. (2005) Women's Work, Dirty Work: The Gynaecology Nurse as 'Other'. *Gender, Work and Organization* 12(2): 169–186.

Bolton, S. (ed.) (2007) *Dimensions of Dignity at Work.* Amsterdam: Elsevier.

Bolton, S.C. and Houlihan, M. (2009) *Work Matters: Critical Reflections on Contemporary Work.* Basingstoke, Hampshire: Palgrave Macmillan.

Borgerson, J. (2005) Judith Butler: On Organizing Subjectivities. *Sociological Review* 53: 63–79.

Borgerson, J. (2007) Why Feminist Ethics? In Jones, C. and Ten Bos, R. (eds) *Philosophy and Organization.* London: Routledge.

Bourdieu, P. (1986) The Forms of Capital. In Richardson, J. G. (ed.) *Handbook of Theory and Research for the Sociology of Education.* New York: Greenwood Press.

Bourdieu, P. (1987) What Makes a Social Class? On the Theoretical and Practical Existence of Groups. *Berkeley Journal of Sociology* 32: 1–17.

Bowker, G. C. and Star, S. L. (1999) *Sorting Things Out: Classification and Its Consequences.* Massachusetts: Massachusetts Institute of Technology Press.

Boyd, M. (1989) Family and Personal Networks in International Migration: Recent Developments and New Agendas. *International Migration Review* 23(3): 638–670.

Braun, V. and Clarke, V. (2006) Using Thematic Analysis in Psychology. *Qualitative Research in Psychology* 3: 77–101.

Brewis, J. (1999) How Does It Feel? Women Managers, Embodiment and Changing Public Sector Cultures. In Whitehead, S. and Moodley, R. (eds) *Transforming Managers: Gendering Change in the Public Sector.* London: Routledge.

Brewis, J. (2005) Signing My Life Away? Researching Sexuality and Organization. *Organization* 12(40): 493–510.

Brewis, J. and Linstead, S. (2000) *Sex, Work and Sex Work. Eroticizing Organization.* London: Routledge.

Brooks, J. (1996) The Sad and Tragic Life of Typhoid Mary. *Canadian Medical Association Journal* 154(6): 915–916.

Bruni, A., Gherardi, S. and Poggio, B. (2004a) Doing Gender, Doing Entrepreneurship: An Ethnographic Account of Intertwined Practices. *Gender, Work and Organization* 11(4): 406–429.

Bruni, A., Gherardi, S. and Poggio, B. (2004b) Entrepreneur-Mentality, Gender and the Study of Women as Entrepreneurs. *Journal of Organizational Change Management* 17(3): 256–268.

Bruni, A., Gherardi, S. and Poggio, B. (2005) *Gender and Entrepreneurship: An Ethnographic Approach.* London: Routledge.

Brush, C.G., Bruin, A. de and Welter, F. (2009) A Gender-Aware Framework for Women's Entrepreneurship. *International Journal of Gender and Entrepreneurship* 1(1): 8–24.

Bryans, P. and Mavin, S. (2003) Women Learning to Become Managers: Learning to Fit In or to Play a Different Game? *Management Learning* 34(1): 111–134.

Butler, J. (1988) Performative Acts and Gender Constitution: An Essay in Phenomenology and Feminist Theory. *Theater Journal* 49(1): 519–531.

Butler, J. (2000 [1990]) *Gender Trouble.* London: Routledge.

Butler, J. (2004) *Undoing Gender.* London: Routledge.

Calhoun, C. (2003) Pierre Bourdieu. In Ritzer, G. (ed.) *The Blackwell Companion to Major Contemporary Social Theorists.* Oxford: Blackwell Publishing.

Callon, M. (1986) Some Elements of a Sociology of Translation: Domestication of the Scallops and the Fishermen of St Brieuc Bay. In Law, J. (ed.) *Power, Action and Belief: A New Sociology of Knowledge.* London: Routledge & Kegan Paul.

Canetti, E. (1962 [1960]) *Crowds and Power.* London: Gollancz.

Canguilhem, G. (1989 [1966]) *The Normal and the Pathological* (Trans. C. R. Fawcett). Massachussetts: Zone Books.

Canosa, R. and Colonnello, I. (1989) *Storia Della Prostituzione in Italia Dal Quattrocento Alla Fine Del Settecento.* Roma: Sapere.

Chakraborty, A. (2006) The End of Medicine as a Profession. *British Medical Journal* 332: 51.

Charles-Jones, H., Latimer, J. and May, C. (2003) Transforming General Practice: The Redistribution of Medical Work in Primary Care. *Sociology of Health & Illness* 25(1): 71–92.

Chiappetta-Swanson, C. (2005) Dignity and Dirty Work: Nurses' Experiences in Managing Genetic Termination for Fetal Anomaly. *Qualitative Sociology* 28(1): 93–116.

Chung, Y. B. and Harmon, L. W. (1994) The Career Interests and Aspirations of Gay Men: How Sex-Role Orientation is Related. *Journal of Vocational Behaviour* 45(2): 223–239.

Churchill, L. (1990) AIDS and 'Dirt': Reflections on the Ethics of Ritual Cleanliness. *Theoretical Medicine and Bioethics* 3: 185–192.

Clarke, A. (2005) *Situational Analysis: Grounded Theory after the Postmodern Turn.* California: Sage.

Clayman, S. E. (1992) Footing in the Achievement of Neutrality: The Case of News-Interview Discourse. In Drew, P. and Heritage, J. (eds) *Talk at Work: Interaction in Institutional Settings.* Cambridge: Cambridge University Press.

Collins, A. (2004) Sexual Dissidence, Enterprise and Assimilation: Bedfellows in Urban Regeneration. *Urban Studies* 41(9): 789–806.

Connell, R. (2000) *The Men and the Boys*. Cambridge: Polity Press.

Connell, R. and Messerschmidt, J. (2005) Hegemonic Masculinity: Rethinking the Concept. *Gender and Society* 16(6): 829–859.

Connell, R. W. (2005) *Masculinities*. Sydney: Allen & Unwin.

Connellan, K. (2007) White Skins, White Surfaces: The Politics of Domesticity in South African Homes from 1920–1950. In Riggs, Damien (ed.) *Taking Up the Challenge: Critical Race and Whiteness Studies in a Postcolonising Nation*. Adelaide: Crawford House, pp. 248–259.

Cook, A. C. H. (2008) *A Study of Identity Formation in the London Investment Banking Sector*, PhD thesis, Department of Industrial Relations and Organizational Behaviour, Warwick Business School, University of Warwick, Warwick.

Coombes, R. (2008) Dr Nurse Will See You Now. *British Medical Journal* 337: 660–662.

Cooper, R. C. (1990) Canetti's Sting. *Scos Notework* 9(2/3): 45–53.

Cornell, D. (1995) What Is Ethical Feminism? In Benhabib, S., Butler, J., Cornell, D. and Fraser, N. (eds) *Feminist Contentions – A Philosophical Exchange*. London: Routledge.

Coser, L. A. (1994) *Everett C. Hughes on Work, Race and Sociological Imagination*. Chicago: University Of Chicago Press.

Costea, B., Crump, N. and Holm, J. (2005) Dionysus at Work? The Ethos of Play and the Ethos of Management. *Culture and Organization* 11(2): 139–151.

Coull, R. (2006) The Death of Nursing, the Dumbing Down of Medicine. *British Medical Journal* 332: 51.

Coulmont, B. and Hubbard, P. (2010) Consuming Sex: Socio-Legal Shifts in the Space and Place of Sex Shops. *Journal of Law and Society* 37(1): 189–209.

Cox, C. (2001) Advanced Nurse Practitioners and the Physician Assistant: What Is the Difference? Comparing the USA and UK. *Hospital Medicine* 62: 169–171.

Creed, B. (1993) *The Monstrous Feminine – Film, Feminism, Psychoanalysis*. London: Routledge.

Crisp, Q. (2007 [1968]) *The Naked Civil Servant*. London: Harper Perennial.

Crompton, R. (2008) *Class and Stratification*. Oxford: Polity.

Crossley, N. (1996) Body-Subject/Body-Power: Agency, Inscription and Control in Foucault and Merleau-Ponty. *Body and Society* 2(2): 99–116.

Currie, G., Finn, R. and Martin, G. (2008) Accounting for the 'Dark Side' of New Organizational Forms: The Case of Health Care Professions. *Human Relations* 61: 539–564.

Dahle, R. (2005) Men, Bodies and Nursing. In Morgan, D., Brandth, B. and Kvande, E. (eds) *Gender, Bodies and Work*. Aldershot, Hampshire, England: Ashgate, pp. 127–139.

Daily Mail Website (No Date) 'Spanish Eggs Blamed for Two Salmonella Deaths', Article and Comments, available at: http://www.dailymail.co.uk/news/article-1232196/spanish-eggs-blamed-salmonella-deaths.html.

Daly, W. and Carnwell, R. (2003) Nursing Roles and Levels of Practice: A Framework for Differentiating between Elementary, Specialist and Advancing Nursing Practice. *Journal of Clinical Nursing* 12: 158–167.

Dant, T. and Bowles, D. (2003) Dealing with Dirt: Servicing and Repairing Cars. *Sociological Research Online* 8(2), available at: http://www.socresonline.org.uk/8/2/dant.html.

Davidoff, L. (1973) Domestic Service and the Working-Class Life-Cycle. *Bulletin of the Society for the Study of Labour History* 26: 10–12.

Davies, B. and Harré, R. (1990) Positioning: The Discursive Production of Selves. *Journal for the Theory of Social Behaviour* 20: 43–65.

Davies, C. (1995) *Gender and the Professional Predicament in Nursing*. Buckingham: Open University Press.

Davies, C. (1996) The Sociology of the Professions and the Professions of Gender. *Sociology* 30(4): 661–678.

Day, S. (2007) *On the Game: Women and Sex Work*. London: Pluto Press.

De Clercq, D. and Voronov, M. (2009) Toward a Practice Perspective of Entrepreneurship: Entrepreneurial Legitimacy as Habitus. *International Small Business Journal* 27(4): 395–419.

Deal, T. E. and Kennedy, A. A. (1982) *Corporate Cultures: The Rites and Rituals of Corporate Life*. Massachusetts: Addison-Wesley.

Deleuze, G. and Guattari, F. (1987) *A Thousand Plateaus: Capitalism and Schizophrenia*. London: Continuum.

Delin, J. (2000) *The Language of Everyday Life*. London: Sage.

Demarest, J. and Garner, J. (1992) The Representation of Women's Roles in Women's Magazines over the Past 30 Years. *Journal of Psychology* 126(4): 357–69.

Derrida, J. (1976[1967]) *Of Grammatology* (Trans. G. C. Spivak). Baltimore: John Hopkins University Press.

Derrida, J. (1984 [1972]) Difference. In *Margins of Philosophy* (Trans. A. Bass). Chicago: University of Chicago Press.

Dick, P. (2005) Dirty Work Designations: How Police Officers Account for their Use of Coercive Force. *Human Relations* 58(11): 1363–1390.

Dick, P. (2008) Resistance, Gender, and Bourdieu's Notion of Field. *Management Communication Quarterly* 21(3): 327–343.

Dickerson, P. (1997) 'It's not just me who's saying this...' The Deployment of Cited Others in Televised Political Discourse. *British Journal of Social Psychology* 36: 33–48.

Diderot, D. (1949 [1773]) *Le Paradoxe Sur Le Comedien Avec Recueilles Presentees Par Marc Blanquet*. Paris: Editions Nord-Sud.

Diderot, D. (1985 [1773]) The Paradox of Acting. In Roach, J. R. (ed.) *'The Paradox of Acting' and 'Masks or Faces?'* London: Associated University Press.

Dillabough, J. (2004) Class, Culture and the 'Predicaments of Masculine Domination': Encountering Pierre Bourdieu. *British Journal of Sociology of Education* 25(4): 489–506.

Dingwall, R. (2008) *Essays on Professions*. Aldershot: Ashgate Publishing Limited.

Diprose, R. (1994) *The Bodies of Women – Ethics, Embodiment and Sexual Difference*. London: Routledge.

Diprose, R. (2002) *Corporeal Generosity – On Giving with Nietzsche, Merleau-Ponty and Lévinas*. New York: State University of New York Press.

Diprose, R. and Ferrell, R. (eds) (1991) *Cartographies – Poststructuralism and the Mapping of Bodies and Spaces*. St Leonards: Allen and Unwin.

Douglas, M. (2002 [1966]) *Purity and Danger: An Analysis of Concepts of Pollution and Taboo*. London: Routledge and Kegan Paul.

Douglas, M. and Mars, G. (2003) Terrorism: A Positive Feedback Game. *Human Relations* 56: 763–786.

Dressel, P. L. and Petersen, D. M. (1982) Becoming a Male Stripper: Recruitment, Socialization and Ideological Development. *Work and Occupations* 9: 387–406.

Drew, S. K., Mills, M. and Gassaway, B. M. (2007) *Dirty Work: The Social Construction of Taint.* Waco, Texas: Bailor University Press.

Du Gay, P. (1996) *Consumption and Identity at Work.* London: Sage.

Duffield, C., Gardner, G., Chang, A. and Catling-Paull, C. (2009) Advanced Nursing Practice: A Global Perspective. *Collegian* 16: 55–62.

Duffy, M. (2007) Doing the Dirty Work: Gender, Race, and Reproductive Labor in Historical Perspective. *Gender and Society* 21(3): 313–336.

Durkheim, E. (1982 [1895]) *The Rules of Sociological Methods* (Trans. W. D. Halls). New York: Free Press.

Dyer, R. (2004) *Heavenly Bodies: Film Stars and Society.* London: Routledge.

Edwards, M. (2010) Gender, Social Disorganization Theory and the Locations of Sexuality Orientated Businesses. *Deviant Behaviour* 31: 135–158.

Ehrenreich, B. and Hochschild, A. (2003) *Global Woman.* New York: Metropolitan Press.

Eisenhardt, K. M. (1989) Building Theories from Case Study Research. *Academy of Management Review* 14(4): 532–550.

Eisner, M. D. (1997) Infectious Complications of Pulmonary Artery Catheters. In Matthay, M. A. and Schwartz, D. E. (eds) *Complications in the Intensive Care Unit: Recognition, Prevention and Management.* New York: Chapman & Hall.

Emerson, R. M. and Pollner, M. (1975) Dirty Work Designations: Their Features and Consequences in a Psychiatric Setting. *Social Problems* 23(3): 243–254.

Entwistle, J. (2000) *The Fashioned Body: Fashion, Dress, and Modern Social Theory.* London: Wiley.

Essed, P. (2002) Everyday Racism: A New Approach to the Study of Racism. In Essed, P. and Goldberg, D. T. (eds) *Race Critical Theories: Text and Context.* Malden, MA: Basil Blackwell.

Evans, J. (1997) Men in Nursing: Issues of Gender Segregation and Hidden Advantage. *Journal of Advanced Nursing* 26: 226–231.

Evans, J. (2002) Cautious Caregivers: Gender Stereotypes and the Sexualisation of Men Nurses' Touch. *Journal of Advanced Nursing* 40(4): 441–448.

Feather, N. T. (1994) Attitudes towards High Achievers and Reactions to their Fall. *Advances in Experimental Social Psychology* 26: 1–73.

Feather, N. T. (1999) *Values, Achievements and Justice: Studies in the Psychology of Deservingness.* New York: Kluwer.

Feather, N. T. and Sherman, R. (2002) Envy, Resentment, Schadenfreude, and Sympathy: Reactions to Deserved and Undeserved Achievement and Subsequent Failure. *Personality and Social Psychology Bulletin* 28: 953–961.

Featherstone, M., Hepworth, M. and Turner, B. S. (eds) (1991) *The Body – Social Process and Cultural Theory.* London: Sage.

Ferguson, J. (2006) *Global Shadows: Africa in the Neoliberal World Order.* Durham, NC: Duke University Press.

Filby, M. (1992) The Figures, The Personality and The Bums: Service Work and Sexuality. *Work, Employment and Society* 6(1): 23–42.

Fleming, P. and Sewell, G. (2002) Looking for 'The Good Soldier Svejk': Alternative Modalities of Resistance in the Contemporary Workplace. *Sociology* 36(4): 857–873.

Fleming, P. and Spicer, A. (2007) *Contesting the Corporation*. Cambridge: Cambridge University Press.

Fleming, P. and Spicer, A. (2008) Beyond Power and Resistance: New Approaches to Organizational Politics. *Management Communication Quarterly* 21(3): 301–309.

Flowers, R. and Swan, E. (2011) *Eating at Us: Food Knowledge and Learning in Food Social Movements*, working paper, UTS, Sydney.

Forseth, U. (2005) Gender Matters? Exploring How Gender Is Negotiated in Service Encounters. *Gender, Work and Organization* 12(5): 440–459.

Foucault, M. (1989 [1973]). *The Birth of the Clinic: An Archaeology of Medical Perception* (Translated by A. M. Sheridan). London: Routledge.

Foucault, M. (2002 [1972]) *The Archaeology of Knowledge*. London: Routledge.

Fox, N. J. (1992) *The Social Meaning of Surgery*. Buckingham: Open University Press.

Frank, K. (2002) *G-Strings and Sympathy: Strip Club Regulators and Male Desire*. Durham: Duke University Press.

Freidson, E. (2001) *Professionalism: The Third Logic*. London: Polity Press.

Fry, S. (2008) Foreword. In Katz, B. (ed.) *Soho Society*. London: Quartet Books.

Furlong, E. and Smith, R. (2005) Advanced Nursing Practice: Policy, Education and Role Development. *Journal of Clinical Nursing* 14: 1059–1066.

FYEO (2004) *Pole and Tableside Dancing School Manual*. Available at http://www.fyeo.co.uk/

FYEO (2005) *For Your Eyes Only*, available at: www.fyeo.co.uk (accessed 4 May 2005).

Gallop, J. (1997) *Feminist Accused of Sexual Harassment*. Durham, NC and New York: Duke University Press.

Garfinkel, H. (1967) Studies of the Routine Grounds of Everyday Activities. In Garfinkel, Harold (eds) *Studies in Ethnomethodology*. Cambridge: Polity.

Garfinkel, H. and Sacks, H. (1970) On Formal Structures of Practical Actions. In McKinney, J. C. (ed.) *Theoretical Sociology: Perspectives and Developments*. New York: Appleton Crofts.

Gastelaars, M. (2010) What Do Buildings Do? In Van Marrewijk, A. and Yanow, D. (eds) *Organizational Spaces, Rematerializing the Workaday World*. Cheltenham: Edward Elgar.

Gatrell, C. and Swan, E. (2008) *Gender and Diversity in Management*. London: Sage.

Geertz, C. (1970) The Impact of the Concept of Culture on the Concept of Man. In Hammel, E. A. and Simmons, W. S. (eds) *Man Makes Sense: A Reader in Modern Cultural Anthopology*. Boston: Little, Brown & Co.

Geertz, C. (1973). *The Interpretation of Cultures*. New York: Basic Books.

Geertz, C. (1985). *Local Knowledge: Further Essays in Interpretive Anthropology*. New York: Basic Books.

Gendron, Y. and Spira, L. F. (2010) Identity Narratives under Threat: A Study of Former Members of Arthur Andersen. *Accounting Organizations and Society* 35(3): 275–300.

Ger, G. and Yenicioglu, B. (2004) Clean and Dirty: Playing with Boundaries of Consumers' Safe Havens. *Advances in Consumer Research* 31: 1181–1189.

Gibson, S. and Hamilton, L. (2011) The Rhetorical Construction of Polity Membership: Identity, Culture and Citizenship in Young People's Discussions of

Immigration in Northern England. *Journal of Community and Applied Social Psychology* 21(3): 228–242.

Gill, A. and Whedbee, K. (1997) Rhetoric. In Van Dijk, T. (ed.) *Discourse as Structure*. London: Sage, pp. 157–184.

Gill, R. (2007) Postfeminist Media Culture: Elements of a Sensibility. *European Journal of Cultural Studies* 10(2): 147–166.

Gillespie, S. and Bamford, K. (2000) *Medical Microbiology and Infection at a Glance*. Oxford: Blackwell.

Glenn, J. (1992) From Servitude to Service Work: Historical Continuities in the Racial Division of Paid Reproductive Labour. *Signs* 18(1): 1–43.

Glover, D. (2008) Advanced Practitioner Roles Have Failed to Benefit the Nursing Profession as a Whole. *Nursing Times*, 29 July.

Godin, P. (2000) A Dirty Business Caring for People Who Are a Nuisance or a Danger. *Journal of Advanced Nursing* 32(6): 1396–1402.

Godwin, L. N., Stevens, C. E. and Brenner, N. L. (2006) Forced to Play by the Rules? Theorizing How Mixed-Sex Founding Teams Benefit Women Entrepreneurs in Male-Dominated Contexts. *Entrepreneurship Theory and Practice* 30(5): 623–642.

Goffman, E. (1963) *Behavior in Public Places*. New York: Free Press.

Goffman, E. (1986 [1963]) *Stigma – Notes on the Management of Spoiled Identity*. Harmondsworth: Penguin Books.

Goffman, E. (1983) Felicity's Condition. *American Journal of Sociology* 89(1): 1–53.

Goffman, E. (1990 [1959]) *The Presentation of Self in Everyday Life*. Harmondsworth: Penguin.

Goffman, E. (1991 [1961]) *Asylums: Essays on the Social Situation of Mental Patients and Other Inmates*. Harmondsworth: Penguin.

Goffman, E. (1997 [1963]) The Stigmatized Self. In Lemert, C. and Branaman, A. (eds) *The Goffman Reader*. London: Blackwell.

Good, B. J. (1993). *Medicine, Rationality and Experience: An Anthropological Perspective*. New York: Cambridge University Press.

Gouldner, A. (1969) The Unemployed Self. In Fraser, R. (ed.) *Work*, Volume II. Harmondsworth: Penguin.

Gouldner, A. (1971) *The Coming Crisis of Western Sociology*. London: Heinemann.

Graham, A. and Regulska, J. (1997) Expanding Political Space for Women in Poland. *Communist and Post-Communist Studies* 30(1): 65–82.

Grandy, G. (2006) *Theorizing Identity at Work: Exotic Dancing as a Site for Organizational and Occupational Research*. PhD thesis, School of Business, University of Northumbria, Newcastle, p. 382.

Grandy, G. (2008) Managing Spoilt Identities: Dirty Workers' Struggle for a Favourable Sense of Self. *Qualitative Research in Organizations and Management: An International Journal* 3(3): 176–198.

Gray, A. (2003) Enterprising Femininity: New Modes of Work and Subjectivity. *European Journal of Cultural Studies* 6(4): 489–506.

Gregg, M. (2010) The Normalisation of Flexible Female Labour in the Information Economy. *Feminist Media Studies* 8(3): 285–299.

Gregg, P. and Wadsworth, J. (2003) Labour Market Prospects for Less Skilled Workers over the Recovery. In Dickens, R., Gregg, P. and Wadsworth, J. (eds) *The Labour Market under New Labour: The State of Working Britain*. Basingstoke: Palgrave Macmillan.

Gregson, N. and Lowe, M. (1994) *Servicing the Middle Classes: Class, Gender and Waged Domestic Labour in Contemporary Britain*. London: Psychology Press.

Grosz, E. (1994) *Volatile Bodies: Toward a Corporeal Feminism*. Indiana: Indiana University Press.

Guy, M. and Newman, M. (2004) Women's Jobs, Men's Jobs: Sex Segregation and Emotional Labour. *Public Administration Review* 64(3): 289–298.

Haas, J. (1977) Learning Real Feelings: A Study of High Steel Ironworkers' Reactions to Fear and Danger. *Work and Occupations* 4(2): 147–170.

Hamilton, E. (2006) Whose Story Is It Anyway? Narrative Accounts of the Role of Women in Founding and Establishing Family Businesses. *International Small Business Journal* 24(3): 253–271.

Hamilton, E. (2010) The Discourse of Entrepreneurial Masculinities (and Femininities). *Entrepreneurship and Regional Development* (submitted 30 August 2010).

Hamilton, F. (2009) Clean-Up Campaign Aims to Take the Sin Out of Soho in Time for Olympics. *The Times*, 14 March.

Hamilton, L. (2007) Muck and Magic: Cultural Transformations in the World of Farm Animal Veterinary Surgeons. *Ethnography* 8(4): 485–501.

Hancock, P. and Spicer, A. (2011) Academic Architecture and the Constitution of the New Model Worker. *Culture and Organization* 17(2): 91–105.

Hancock, P. and Tyler, M. (2000) Working Bodies. In Hancock, P., Hughes, B., Jagger, E., Patterson, K. and Russel, R. (eds) *The Body, Culture and Society*. Buckingham: Open University Press.

Harris, M. (2009) Injecting, Infection, Illness: Abjection and Hepatitis C Stigma. *Body and Society* 15(4): 33–51.

Hassard, J., Holliday, R. and Willmott, H. (eds) (2000) *Body and Organization*. London: Sage.

Haynes, K. (2008) (Re)Figuring Accounting and Maternal Bodies: The Gendered Embodiment of Accounting Professionals. *Accounting, Organizations and Society* 33(4–5): 328–348.

Heidegger, M. (1993) The Question Concerning Technology. In Krell, D. F. (ed.) *Martin Heidegger: Basic Writings*. London: Routledge.

Heikes, J. (1991) When Men Are in the Minority: The Case of Men in Nursing. *Sociological Quarterly* 32(3): 389–401.

Hetherington, K. and Munro, R. (1997) *Ideas of Difference*. Oxford: Blackwell.

Hillman, A., Latimer, J. and White, P. (2010) Accessing Care: Technology and the Management of the Clinic. In Schillmeier, M. and Domènech, M. (eds) *New Technologies and Emerging Spaces of Care*. Surrey: Ashgate.

Hobbs, D. (2003) *Bouncers: Violence and Governance in the Night Time Economy*. Oxford: Oxford University Press.

Hochschild, A. (1983) *The Managed Heart: The Commercialisation of Human Feeling*. Berkeley: University Of California Press.

Høigård, C. and Finstad, L. (1992) *Backstreets: Prostitution, Money and Love*. Cambridge: Polity Press.

Holgate, J. (2005) Organizing Migrant Workers: A Case Study of Working Conditions and Unionization in a London Sandwich Factory. *Work, Employment and Society* 19(3): 463–480.

Holliday, M. and Parker, E. (1997) Florence Nightingale, Feminism and Nursing. *Journal of Advanced Nursing* 26: 483–488.

Holliday, R. and Hassard, J. (eds) (2001) *Contested Bodies*. London: Routledge.

Hollway, W. (1989) *Subjectivity and Method in Psychology: Gender, Meaning and Science*. London: Sage Publications Ltd.

Holmes, D. and Gastaldo, D. (2004) Rhizomatic Thought in Nursing: An Alternative Path of the Development of the Discipline. *Nursing Philosophy* 5: 258–267.

Holmes, L. (2002) 'Can Only Managers (Learn to) Manage? Management, Practice and Trajectories of Emergent Identity', paper presented at the Third International Conference Connecting Learning and Critique, Cambridge University, Cambridge, UK.

Hood, J. C. (1988) From Night to Day: Timing and the Management of Custodial Work. *Journal of Contemporary Ethnography* 17(1): 96–116.

Höpfl, H. (2000) The Suffering Mother and Miserable Son: Organizing Women and Organizing Women's Writing. *Gender, Work and Organisation* 7(2): 98–105.

Höpfl, H. (2010) A Question of Membership. In Lewis, P. and Simpson, R. (eds) *Revealing and Concealing Gender – Issues of Visibility in Organizations*. New York: Palgrave Macmillan.

Höpfl, H. and Kostera, M. (2003) Introduction. In Höpfl, H. and Kostera, M. (eds) *Interpreting the Maternal Organisation*. London: Routledge.

Höpfl, H. J. (2004) The Hymn to Demeter. In Gabriel, Y. (ed.) *Myths, Stories and Organisations*. Oxford: Oxford University Press.

Houlbrook, M. (2005) *Queer London*. Chicago, IL: Chicago University Press.

Hoy, S. (1995) *Chasing Dirt: The American Pursuit of Cleanliness*. Oxford: Oxford University Press.

Hubbard, P. (2000) Desire/Disgust: Mapping the Moral Contours of Heterosexuality. *Progress in Human Geography* 24(2): 191–217.

Hubbard, P. and Sanders, T. (2003) Making Space for Sex Work: Female Street Prostitution and the Production of Urban Space. *International Journal of Urban and Regional Research* 27(1): 73–87.

Hubbard, P., Matthews, R. and Scoular, J. (2009) Legal Geographies – Controlling Sexually Oriented Businesses: Law, Licensing and the Geographies of a Controversial Land Use. *Urban Geography* 30(2): 185–205.

Hughes, E. C. (1946) Race Relations in Industry. In Whyte, W. F. (ed.) *Industry and Society*. New York: McGraw Hill.

Hughes, E. C. (1951) Work and the Self. In Rohrer, J. H. and Sherif, M. (eds) *Social Psychology at the Crossroads*. New York: Harper and Brothers.

Hughes, E. C. (1958) *Men and their Work*. Glencoe, IL: Free Press.

Hughes, E. C. (1962) Good People and Dirty Work. *Social Problems* 10(1): 3–11.

Hughes, E. C. (1974) 'Comments on Honor in Dirty Work', *Sociology of Work and Occupations* 1: 284–287.

Hughes, E. C. (1984) *The Sociological Eye*. New York: Transaction Publishers.

Hunter, S. (2010) What a White Shame: Race, Gender and White Shame in the Relational Economy of Primary Health Care Organisations in England. *Social Politics, Special Issue on Reproducing and Resisting Whiteness in Organisations, Policies and Places* 17(4): 450–476.

Irigaray, L. (1985) *Speculum of the Other Woman*. New York: Cornell University Press.

Irigaray, L. (1993) *An Ethics of Sexual Difference*. London: Athlone.

Isaksen, L. W. (2002) Toward a Sociology of (Gendered) Disgust. *Journal of Family Issues* 23(7): 791–811.

Isaksen, L. W. (2005) Gender and Care: The Role of Cultural Ideas of Dirt and Disgust. In Morgan, D., Brandth, B. and Kvande, E. (eds) *Gender, Bodies and Work*. Aldershot, Hampshire, England: Ashgate, pp. 115–127.

Jacobowitz, F. and Lippe, R. (1992) Empowering Glamour. *Cineaction* 26/27, Winter: 2–11.

James, N. (1992) Care = Organisation + Physical Labour + Emotional Labour. *Sociology of Health and Illness* 14(4): 488–509.

Jeffreys, S. (1997) *The Idea of Prostitution*. Melbourne: Spinifex Press.

Jervis, L. (2001) The Pollution of Incontinence and the Dirty Work of Care Giving in a US Nursing Home. *Medical Anthropology Quarterly* 15(1): 84–99.

Jinks, A. and Bradley, E. (2004) Angel, Handmaiden, Battleaxe or Whore? A Study Which Examines Changes in Newly Recruited Student Nurses' Attitudes to Gender and Nursing Stereotypes. *Nursing Education Today* 24: 121–127.

Johnson, P., Buehring, A., Cassell, C. and Symon, G. (2006) Evaluating Qualitative Research: Towards a Contingent Criteriology. *International Journal of Management Reviews* 8(3): 131–156.

Johnston, D. and Swanson, D. (2003) Invisible Mothers: A Content Analysis of Motherhood Ideologies and Myths in Magazines. *Sex Roles* 49(1): 21–33.

Jost, J. T. and Banaji, M. R. (1994) The Role of Stereotyping in System-Justification and the Production of False Consciousness. *British Journal of Social Psychology* 33: 1–27.

Jost, J. T. and Burgess, D. (2000) Attitudinal Ambivalence and the Conflict between Group and System Justification Motives in Low States Groups. *Personality and Social Psychology Bulletin* 26: 293–305.

Jost, J. T., Banaji, M. R. and Nosek, B. A. (2004) A Decade of System Justification Theory: Accumulated Evidence of Conscious and Unconscious Bolstering of the Status Quo. *Political Psychology* 25(6): 881–919.

Just, S. N. (2006) Embattled Agencies – How Mass Media Comparisons of Lynndie England and Jessica Lynch Affect the Identity Positions Available to Female Soldiers in the US Army. *Scandinavian Journal of Management* 22: 99–119.

Karrenman, D. and Alvesson, M. (2001) Making Newsmakers: Conversational Identity at Work. *Organization Studies* 22(1): 59–89.

Katz, F. (1969) Nurses. In Etzioni, A. (ed.) *The Semi-Professions and their Organization*. London: The Free Press, pp. 54–81.

Kempadoo, K. (ed.) (1999) *Sun, Sex, and Gold: Tourism and Sex Work in the Caribbean*. Lahnam: Rowman and Littlefield Publisher.

Kent, T. and Berman Brown, R. (2006) Erotic Retailing in the UK (1963–2003): The View from the Marketing Mix. *Journal of Management History* 12(2): 199–211.

Kerfoot, D. (1999) Body Work: Estrangement, Disembodiment and the Organisational 'Other'. In Hassard, J., Holliday, R. and Willmott, H. (eds) *Body and Organization*. London: Sage.

Kinnersley, P., Anderson, E., Parry, K., Clement, J., Archard, L., Turton, P., Stainthorpe, A., Fraser, A., Butler, C. and Rogers, C. (2000) Randomised Controlled Trial of Nurse Practitioner Care for Patients Requesting 'Same Day' Consultations in Primary Care. *British Medical Journal* 320: 1043–1048.

Kirkpatrick, I., Ackroyd, S. and Walker, R. (2005) *The New Managerialism and Public Service Professions*. London: Palgrave.

Kohonen, E. (2005) Learning through Narratives about the Impact of International Assignments on Identity. *International Studies of Management and Organization* 34(3): 27–45.

Komesaroff, P. A. (ed.) (1995) *Troubled Bodies – Critical Perspectives on Postmodernism, Medical Ethics and the Body*. Durham: Duke University Press.

Kong, T. S. K. (2003) 'What It Feels Like for a Whore: The Body Politics of Women Performing Erotic Labour in Hong Kong', paper presented at the Gender, Work and Organisation Conference, Keele University, Keele, UK.

Kreiner, G. E., Ashforth, B., Blake, E. and Sluss, D. M. (2006) Identity Dynamics in Occupational Dirty Work: Integrating Social Identity and System Justification Perspectives. *Organization Science* 17(5): 619–636.

Kristeva, J. (1982) *Powers of Horror: An Essay on Abjection*. New York: Columbia University Press.

Kristeva, J. (1987) *Tales of Love* (Trans. L. Roudiez). New York: Columbia University Press.

Kundera, M. (1996) *Testaments Betrayed*. London: Faber and Faber.

Lakhani, S. R., Dilly, S. A. and Finlayson, C. J. (1993) *Basic Pathology – An Introduction to the Mechanisms of Disease*. London: Edward Arnold.

Larkin, G. (1981) Professional Autonomy and the Ophthalmic Optician. *Sociology of Health and Illness* 3: 15–30.

Latimer, J. and Munro, R. (2006) Driving the Social. In Böhm, S., Jones, C., Land, C. and Paterson, M. (eds) *Against Automobility*. Oxford: Blackwell.

Latimer, J. E. (1993) *Writing Patients, Writing Nursing: The Social Construction of Nursing Assessment of Elderly Patients in an Acute Medical Unit*, unpublished PhD thesis, University of Edinburgh, Edinburgh, UK.

Latour, B. (1987) *Science in Action*. Massachusetts: Harvard University Press.

Law, J. (1994). *Organising Modernity*. Oxford: Blackwell.

Law, J. (2004) *After Method: Mess in Social Science Research*. London: Routledge.

Lawler, J. (1991) *Behind the Screens: Nursing, Somology and the Problem of the Body*. Melbourne: Churchill Livingstone.

Lawler, S. (1999) Getting Out and Getting Away: Women's Narratives of Class Mobility. *Feminist Review* 63(1): 3–24.

Lawler, S. (2002) Mobs and Monsters: Independent Man Meets Paulsgrove Woman. *Feminist Theory* 3(1): 103–113.

Lawler, S. (2005) Disgusted Subjects: The Making of Middle-Class Identities. *Sociological Review* 53(3): 429–446.

Lawton, J. (1998) Contemporary Hospice Care: The Sequestration of the Unbounded Body and 'Dirty Dying'. *Sociology of Health and Illness* 20(2): 121–143.

Lechte, J. (1990) *Julia Kristeva*. London: Routledge.

Leder, D. (1990) *The Absent Body*. Chicago: Chicago University Press.

Lee-Treweek, G. (1997) Women, Resistance and Care: An Ethnographic Study of Nursing Auxiliary Work. *Work, Employment and Society* 11(1): 47–63.

Lee-Treweek, G. (2010) 'Be Tough, Never Let Them See What It Does to You': Towards an Understanding of the Emotional Lives of Economic Migrants. *International Journal of Work Organization and Emotion* 3(2): 206–226.

Lee-Treweek, G. and Gorna, B. (2008) *Community Perceptions of Economic Migration in Northton.* Manchester Metropolitan University, unpublished report for Higher Education Funding Council for England (HEFCE).

Lewin, K. Z. (1946) Action Research and Minority Problems. *Journal of Social Issues* 2(4): 34–46.

Lewis, P. (2006) The Quest for Invisibility: Female Entrepreneurs and the Masculine Norm of Entrepreneurship. *Gender, Work and Organization* 13(5): 453–469.

Lewis, P. (2010) 'Mumpreneurs': Revealing the Post-Feminist Entrepreneur. In Lewis, P. and Simpson, R. (eds) *Revealing and Concealing Gender: Issues of Visibility in Organizations.* Basingstoke: Palgrave Macmillan.

Lewis, P. and Simpson, R. (2007) *Gendering Emotions in Organizations.* London: Palgrave.

Lewis, R. (2001) *Nurse-Led Primary Care: Learning from PMS Pilots.* London: King's Fund.

Linstead, S. (2000) Dangerous Fluids and the Organization-Without-Organs. In Hassard, J., Holliday, R. and Willmott, H. (eds) *Body and Organization.* London: Sage.

Linstead, S. A. (1997) Resistance and Return: Power, Command and Change Management. *Culture and Organization* 3(1): 67–89.

Linstead, S. A. and Chan, A. (1994) The Sting of Organization: Command, Reciprocity and Change Management. *Journal of Organizational Change Management* 7(5): 4–19.

Loe, M. (1999) Feminism for Sale: Case Study of a Pro-Sex Feminist Business. *Gender and Society* 13(6): 705–732.

Lohman, J. (1964) Violence in the Streets: Its Context and Meaning. *Notre Dame Law Review* 40: 517–530.

Lowendahl, B. (1997) *Strategic Management of Professional Service Firms.* Copenhagen: Handleshøjskolens Forlag.

Luke, C. (1996) *Feminisms and Pedagogies of Everyday Life.* New York: State University of New York Press.

Lunt, P. and Lewis, T. (2008) Oprah.com: Lifestyle Expertise and the Politics of Recognition. *Women & Performance: A Journal of Feminist Theory* 18(1): 9.

Lupton, B. (1999) Maintaining Masculinity: Men Who Do Women's Work. *British Journal of Management* 11: S33–S48.

Lynch, M. (1991) Method: Measurement – Ordinary and Scientific Measure as Ethnomethodological Phenomena. In Button, G. (ed.) *Ethnomethodology and the Human Sciences.* Cambridge: Cambridge University Press.

Lyotard, J. (1986) *The Postmodern Condition: A Report on Knowledge* (Trans. G. Bennington and B. Massumi). Manchester: Manchester University Press.

Machin, D. and Leeuwen, T. van (2003) Global Schemas and Local Discourses in 'Cosmopolitan'. *Journal of Sociolinguistics* 7(4): 493–512.

Machin, D. and Leeuwen, T. van (2005) Language Style and Lifestyle: The Case of a Global Magazine. *Media, Culture & Society* 27(4): 577.

Malina, D. and Schmidt, R. (1997) It's Business Doing Pleasure with You: *Sh!* A Women's Sex Shop Case. *Marketing Intelligence and Planning* 15(7): 352–360.

Manchester, C. (1986) *Sex Shops and the Law.* London: Gower.

Mangan, P. (1994) Private Lives. *Nursing Times* 90(4): 60.

Marlow, S. (2002) Women and Self-Employment: A Part of or Apart from Theoretical Construct? *International Journal of Entrepreneurship and Innovation* 3(2): 83–91.

Martin, P. Y. (2006) Practising Gender at Work: Further Thoughts on Reflexivity. *Gender, Work and Organization* 13(3): 254–276.

Maslow, A. H. (1943) A Theory of Human Motivation. *Psychological Review* 50(4): 370–396.

Maslow, A. H. (1982 [1968]) *Toward a Psychology of Being* (Second Edition). London: Van Nostrand Reinhold.

Mason, J. (2002) *Qualitative Researching* (Second Edition). London: Sage Publications Ltd.

Massey, A. (2000) *Hollywood beyond the Screen: Design and Material Culture*. Oxford: Berg.

Massey, D.B. (2005) *For Space*. London: Sage.

Massuni, K. (2004) Modeling Work. *Gender & Society* 18/1: 47.

McCleary, R. and Tewksbury, R. (2010) Female Patrons of Porn. *Deviant Behaviour* 31: 208–223.

McClintock, A. (1995) *Imperial Leather: Race, Gender, and Sexuality in the Colonial Contest*. New York: Routledge.

McCracken, G. (1988) *The Long Interview*. Newbury Park, CA: Sage Publications Ltd.

McIntyre, A. (2007) *Participatory Action Research*. London: Sage.

McMahon, C. (1998) Dirty Hands. *The Furrow* 49 (7/8): 402–407.

McMurray, R. (2006) Field Notes – GP Surgery.

McMurray, R. (2010a) Tracing Experiences of NHS Change in England: A Process Philosophy Perspective. *Public Administration* 88 (3): 724–740.

McMurray, R. (2010b) Living with Neophilia: Case Notes from the New NHS. *Culture & Organization* 16 (1): 55–71.

McMurray, R. (2011) The Struggle to Professionalize: An Ethnographic Account of the Occupational Position of Advanced Nurse Practitioners. *Human Relations* 64 (6): 801–822.

McMurray, R. and Pullen, A. (2008) Boundary Management, Interplexity & Nostalgia: Managing Marginal Identities in Public Health Working. *International Journal of Public Administration* 31 (9): 1058–1078.

McNay, L. (1999) Gender, Habitus and the Field. *Theory, Culture & Society* 16(1): 95–117.

McPhee, S. J., Lingappa, V. R., Ganong, W. F. and Lange, J. D. (1995) *Pathophysiology of Disease – An Introduction to Clinical Medicine*. Stamford: Appleton and Lange.

McRobbie, A. (2004) Post Feminism and Popular Culture. *Feminist Media Studies* 4(3): 255–264.

McWilliams, E. and Jones, A. (1996) Eros and Pedagogical Bodies: The State of (Non)Affairs. In McWilliam, E. and Taylor, P. F. (eds) *Pedagogy, Technology and The Body*. New York: Peter Lang.

Meara, H. (1974) Honor in Dirty Work: The Case of American Meat Cutters and Turkish Butchers. *Sociology of Work and Occupations* 1: 259–283.

Meisenbach, R. (2010) Stigma Management Communication: A Theory and Agenda for Applied Research on How Individuals Manage Moments of Stigmatised Identity. *Journal of Applied Communication Research* 38(3): 268–292.

Merleau-Ponty, M. (1968) *The Visible and the Invisible*. Evanston: Northwestern University Press.

Merleau-Ponty, M. (1989[1962]) *Phenomenology of Perception* (Trans. C. Smith). London: Routledge.

Miller, W. (1997) *The Anatomy of Disgust*. Cambridge, MA: Harvard University Press.

Moi, T. (ed.) (1986) *The Kristeva Reader*. Oxford: Blackwell.

Mol, A. and Law, J. (1994) Regions, Networks and Fluids: Anaemia and Social Topology. *Social Studies of Science* 24: 641–671.

Moll, A. (2002) *The Body Multiple: Ontology in Medical Practice*. London: Duke University Press.

Moll, A. (2003) *The Body Multiple*. London: Duke University Press.

Monteiro, L. (1985) Florence Nightingale on Public Health Nursing. *American Journal of Public Health* 75(2): 181–186.

Morgan, D. (1992) *Discovering Men*. London: Routledge.

Morgan, G. and Knights, D. (1991) Gendering Jobs: Corporate Strategy, Managerial Control and the Dynamics of Job Segregation. *Work, Employment and Society* 5(2): 181–200.

Morgan, P. I. and Ogbonna, E. (2008) Subcultural Dynamics in Transformation: A Multi-Perspective Study of Health Care Professionals. *Human Relations* 61: 39–65.

Mort, F. (1998) Cityscapes: Consumption, Masculinities and the Mapping of London. *Urban Studies* 35(5–6): 889–907.

Munro, R. (1997) Ideas of Difference: Stability, Social Spaces and the Labour of Division. In Hetherington, K. and Munro, R. (eds) *Ideas of Difference*. Oxford: Blackwell.

Munro, R. (2001) Disposal of the Body: Upending Postmodernism. *Ephemera* 1(2): 108–130.

Munro, R. (2005) Partial Organization: Marilyn Strathern and the Elicitation of Relations. *Sociological Review* 53(1): 245–266.

Murphy, B. (1994) Women's Magazines: Confusing Differences. In Turner, L. and Sterk, H. (eds) *Differences That Make a Difference: Examining the Assumptions of Gender Research*. Thousand Oaks, CA: Sage, pp. 119–127.

Murray, S. (1996) 'We all love Charles': Men in Childcare and the Social Construction of Gender. *Gender and Society* 10(4): 368–385.

Nancarrow, S. A. and Borthwick, A. M. (2005) Dynamic Professional Boundaries in the Health Care Workforce. *Sociology of Health and Illness* 27(7): 897–919.

Nead, L. (1988) *Myths of Sexuality*. Oxford: Basil Blackwell.

Negra, D. (2009) *What a Girl Wants: Fantasizing the Reclamation of Self in Postmodernism*. London: Routledge.

Nelson, S. and Gordon, S. (2004) The Rhetoric of Rupture: Nursing as a Practice with a History. *Nursing Outlook*, 52(5): 255–261.

Newman, K. (1999) *No Shame in My Game: The Working Poor in the Inner City*. New York: Vintage.

Ng, R. and Höpfl, H. J. (2011) Objects in Exile: The Intimate Structures of Resistance and Consolation. *Journal of Organizational Change Management* 24(6): 751–766.

Ngai, S. (2005) *Ugly Feelings*. Cambridge, MA: Harvard University Press.

Nietzsche, F. (1974 [1887]) *The Gay Science: With a Prelude in Rhymes and an Appendix of Songs* (Trans. W. Kauffman). New York: Vintage.

Nightingale, F. (1860) *Notes on Nursing: What It Is and What It Is Not* (Kindle Edition). London: Harrison.

Nightingale, F. (1969) *Notes on Nursing*. London: Scutari.

Noon, M. and Blyton, P. (2007) *The Realities of Work: Experiencing Work and Employment in Contemporary Society*. Basingstoke: Palgrave Macmillan.

Nursing Times (2009) Doctors v Nurses: Blurring the Boundaries. *Nursing Times*, 29 September.

Nussbaum, M. C. (1999) Secret Sewers of Vice: Disgust, Bodies and the Law. In Bandes, S. A. (ed.) *The Passions of Law*. New York: New York University Press.

Oakley, A. (1993) *Essays on Women, Medicine and Health*. Edinburgh: Edinburgh University Press.

O'Connel Davidson, J. (2002) The Rights and Wrongs of Prostitution. *Hypatia* 17(2): 84–98.

Ogbor, J. O. (2000) Mythicizing and Reification in Entrepreneurial Discourse: Ideology-Critique of Entrepreneurial Studies. *Journal of Management Studies* 37(5): 605–635.

Overall, C. (1992) What's Wrong with Prostitution? Evaluating Sex Work. *Signs* 17(4): 705–724.

Oxford English Dictionary (2010) Online Edition. Oxford: Oxford University Press, available at: http://oed.com.

Paetzold, R. L., Dipboye, R. L. et al. (2008) A New Look at Stigmatization in and of Organizations. *Academy of Management Review* 33(1): 186–193.

Parker, R. and Aggleton, P. (2003) HIV and AIDS-Related Stigma and Discrimination: A Conceptual Framework and Implications for Action. *Social Science and Medicine* 57(1): 13–24.

Peckham, S. (2007) The New General Practice Contract and Reform of Primary Care in the United Kingdom. *Health Care Policy* 2: 34–48.

Penttinen, E. (2008) Imagined and Embodied Spaces in the Global Sex Industry. *Gender, Work and Organization* 17: 28–44.

Perriton, L. (1999) Paper Dolls: The Provocative and Evocative Gaze upon Women in Management Development. *Gender and Education* 11(3): 295–307.

Pheterson, G. (1996) *The Prostitution Prism*. Amsterdam: Amsterdam University Press.

Pheterson, G. (2009) Wards of the State: Pregnant and Prostitute Women. *Política Y Sociedad* 46(1): 97–106.

Pitt, M. (1998) A Tale of Two Gladiators: 'Reading' Entrepreneurs as Texts. *Organization Studies* 19(3): 387–414.

Place, B. (2000) Constructing the Bodies of Critically Ill Children: An Ethnography of Intensive Care. In Prout, A. (ed.) *The Body, Childhood and Society*. Basingstoke: Palgrave Macmillan.

Playfair, J. (1995) *Infection and Immunity*. Oxford: Oxford University Press.

Poggio, B. (2006) Outline of a Theory of Gender Practice. *Gender, Work and Organization* 13(3): 232–233.

Pollert, A. (2003) Women, Work and Equal Opportunities in Post-Communist Transition. *Work, Employment and Society* 17(2): 331–357.

Potter, J. (1996) *Representing Reality: Discourse, Rhetoric and Social Construction*. London: Sage.

Price, K. K. (2008) Stripping Work in the Lion's Den: Keeping the Dancers in Check. *Gender and Society* 22(2): 367–389.

Pullen, A. (2006a) Gendering the Research Self: Social Practice and Corporeal Multiplicity in the Writing of Organizational Research. *Gender, Work and Organization* 13(3): 277–298.

Pullen, A. (2006b) *Managing Identity*. London: Palgrave.

Pullen, A. and Knights, D. (2007) Editorial. Undoing Gender: Organizing and Disorganising. *Gender, Work and Organization* 14: 505–511.

Pullen, A. and Linstead, S. (2005) *Organization and Identity*. New York: Routledge.

Pullen, A. and Rhodes, C. (2008) Dirty Writing. *Culture and Organization* 14(3): 241–259.

Pullen, A. and Rhodes, C. (2010) Gender, Mask and the Face: Towards a Corporeal Ethics. In Lewis, P. and Simpson, R. (eds) *Revealing and Concealing Gender – Issues of Visibility in Organizations*. New York: Palgrave Macmillan.

Pullen, A. and Simpson, R. (2007) Managing Difference in Feminized Work: Men, Otherness and Social Practice. *Human Relations* 62(4): 561–587.

Radner, H. (1995) *Shopping Around: Feminine Culture and the Pursuit of Pleasure*. London: Routledge.

Raelin, J. (1985) *The Clash of Cultures: Managers and Professionals*. Boston: Harvard Business School Press.

RCN (2008) *Advanced Nurse Practitioners: An RCN Guide to the Advanced Nurse Practitioner Role, Competencies and Programme Accreditation*. London: RCN.

RCN (2009) Draft Policy Statement: RCN's Position on Advanced Nursing Practice. Online, available at: www.rcn.org.uk/__data/assets/pdf_file/0017/290231/RCN_position_on_advanced_nursing_pratice.pdf (accessed April 2010).

Rhodes, C. and Pullen, A. (2009) Organizational Moral Responsibility. In Clegg, S. R. and Cooper, C. (eds) *The Sage Handbook of Organizational Behaviour: Macro Approaches*. London: Sage.

Richardson, N. (2000) *Dog Days in Soho: One Man's Adventures in 1950s Bohemia*. London: Phoenix.

Ridgeway, C. L. (1997) Interaction and the Conservation of Gender Inequality: Considering Employment. *American Sociological Review* 62(2): 218–235.

Riessmann, C. K. (2001) Analysis of Personal Narratives. In Gubrium, J. F. and Holstein, J. A. (eds) *Handbook of Interview Research: Context and Method*. Thousand Oaks, CA: Sage.

Rippin, A. (2007) The Economy of Magnificence: Organization, Excess and Legitimacy. *Culture and Organization* 2: 115–129.

Roach, J. R. (1985) *The Player's Passion, Studies in the Science of Acting*. Newark, DE: University of Delaware Press.

Roberts, M. and Turner, C. (2005) Conflicts of Liveability in the 24-Hour City: Learning from 48 Hours in the Life of London's Soho. *Journal of Urban Design* 10(2): 171–193.

Rollins, J. (1985) *Between Women: Domestics and their Employers*. Philadelphia: Temple University Press.

Ronai, C. R. and Ellis, C. (1989) Turn-Ons for Money: Interactional Strategies of the Table Dancer. *Journal of Contemporary Ethnography* 18(3): 271–298.

Rorty, R. (1979) *Philosophy and the Mirror of Nature*. New Jersey: Princeton University Press.

Rubin, G. S. (1993) Thinking Sex: Notes for a Radical Theory of Politics of Sexuality. In Abelove, H., Barale, M. A. and Haplerin, D. M. (eds) *The Lesbian and Gay Studies Reader*. London: Routledge.

Ryder, A. (2004) The Changing Nature of Adult Entertainment Districts: Between a Rock and a Hard Place or Going from Strength to Strength? *Urban Studies* 41(9): 1659–1686.

Safilios-Rothschild, C. (1977) *Love, Sex and Sex Roles*. Englewood Cliffs, NJ: Prentice Hall.

Salisbury, C., Manku-Cott, T., Moore, L., Chalder, M. and Sharp, D. (2002) Questionnaire Survey of Users in NHS Walk-In Centres: Observational Study. *British Journal of General Practice* 52: 554–560.

Salutin, M. (1971) Stripper Morality. *Transaction* 8: 12–22.

Sanders, T. (2005a) 'It's Just Acting': Sex Workers' Strategies for Capitalizing on Sexuality. *Gender, Work and Organization* 12(4): 319–342.

Sanders, T. (2005b) *Sex Work: A Risky Business*. Cullompton: Willan.

Sanders, T. (2008a) *Paying for Pleasure*. Cullompton: Willan.

Sanders, T. (2008b) Selling Sex in the Shadow Economy. *International Journal of Social Economics* 35(10): 704–716.

Schmied, V. and Lupton, D. (2010) Blurring the Boundaries: Breastfeeding and Maternal Subjectivity. In Rudge, T. and Holmes, D. (eds) *Abjectly Boundless – Boundaries, Bodies and Health Work*. Surrey: Ashgate Publishing.

Science Daily (2002) Inspections Sharply Reduce Diarrhoea Outbreaks on Cruise Ships, 18 December. Center for the Advancement of Health.

Science Daily (2011) Cruise Ship Norovirus Outbreak Highlights How Infections Spread, 25 March. Infectious Diseases Society of America.

Scott, W. R. (2008) Lords of the Dance: Professionals as Institutional Agents. *Organization Studies* 29: 219–238.

Selanders, L. (1998) Florence Nightingale: The Evolution and Social Impact of Feminist Values in Nursing. *Journal of Holistic Nursing* 16(2): 227–243.

Shildrick, M. (1997) *Leaky Bodies and Boundaries: Feminism, Postmodernism and (Bio)Ethics*. London: Routledge.

Shildrick, M. (2002) *Embodying the Monsters: Encounters with the Vulnerable Self*. London: Sage.

Shilling, C. (2003) *The Body and Social Theory* (Second Edition). London: Sage.

Shove, E. (2003) *Comfort, Cleanliness and Convenience: The Social Organization of Normality*. Oxford: Berg.

Sievers, Burkard (2000) AIDS and the Organization: A Consultant's View of the Coming Plague. In Klein, Edward B., Gabelnick, F. and Herr, P. (eds) *Dynamic Consultation in a Changing Workplace*. Madison, CT: Psychosocial Press.

Sillince, J. A. A. and Brown, A. D. (2009) Multiple Organizational Identities and Legitimacy: The Rhetoric of Police Websites. *Human Relations* 62(12): 1829–1856.

Simmel, G. (2004) *The Philosophy of Money* (Third Edition). New York: Routledge.

Simpson, R. (2005) Men in Non-traditional Occupations: Career Entry, Career Orientation and Experience of Role Strain. *Gender, Work and Organization* 12 (4): 363–380.

Simpson, R. (2009) *Men in Caring Occupations: Doing Gender Differently*. Basingstoke: Palgrave MacMillan.

Simpson, R. (2010) A Reversal of the Gaze: Men's Experiences of Visibility in Non-Traditional Occupations. In Lewis, P. and Simpson, R. (eds) *Revealing and Concealing Gender – Issues of Visibility in Organizations*. New York: Palgrave Macmillan.

Skeggs, B. (1997) *Formations of Class and Gender: Becoming Respectable*. London: Sage.

Skeggs, B. (2004) *Class, Self, Culture*. London: Routledge.

Skeggs, B. (2005) The Making of Class and Gender through Visualizing Moral Subject Formation. *Sociology* 39(5): 965–982.

Slutskaya, N., Simpson, R. and Hughes, J. (2009) Men Managing Taint in the Meat Trade, paper presented at the Gender, Work and Organization Conference, Keele, July.

Smith, B. and Sparkes, A. (2008) Contrasting Perspectives on Narrating Selves and Identities: An Invitation to Dialogue. *Qualitative Research* 8(5): 5–35.

Smith, C. (2007) Designed for Pleasure: Style, Indulgence and Accessorized Sex. *European Journal of Cultural Studies* 10(2): 167–184.

Somers, M. (1994) The Narrative Constitution of Identity: A Relational and Network Approach. *Theory and Society* 23(5): 605–649.

Sotirin, P. and Gottfried, H. (1999) The Ambivalent Dynamics of Secretarial 'Bitching': Control, Resistance, and the Construction of Identity. *Organization* 6(1): 57–80.

Sparkes, A. C. and Smith, B. (2008) Narrative Constructionist Inquiry. In Holstein, J. A. and Gubrium, J. F. (eds) *Handbook of Constructionist Research*. New York: Guildford Press.

Spradley, J. P. (1979) *Ethnographic Interview*. Orlando: Harcourt Brace Jonanovich College Publishers.

Stacey, C. (2005) Finding Dignity in Dirty Work: The Constraints and Rewards of Low-Wage Home Care Labour. *Sociology of Health and Illness* 27(6): 831–854.

Stake, R. E. (1994) Case Studies. In Denzin, N. K. and Lincoln, Y. S. (eds) *Handbook of Qualitative Research*. London: Sage.

Stallybrass, P. and White, A. (1986) *The Politics and Poetics of Transgression*. New York: Cornell University Press.

Stannard, C. (1973) Old Folks and Dirty Work: The Social Conditions for Patient Abuse in a Nursing Home. *Social Problems* 20(3): 329–342.

Stein, M. (1990) *An Ethnography of an Adult Bookstore: Private Scenes, Public Places*. Lewiston, NY: Edwin Mellen Press.

Stenross, B. and Kleinman, S. (1989) The Highs and Lows of Emotional Labor: Detectives' Encounters with Criminals and Victims. *Journal of Contemporary Ethnography* 17: 435–452.

Stenvoll, D. (2002) Newspaper Coverage of Cross-Border Prostitution in Northern Norway, 1990–2001. *European Journal of Women's Studies* 9(2): 143–162.

Stephens, P. (2009) Shoot the Bankers, Nationalise the Banks. *The Financial Times*. London.

Stiernstedt, F. and Jakobsson, P. (2009) Total Decentring, Total Community: The Googleplex and Informational Culture, paper presented at the Annual Meeting of the International Communication Association, Marriott, Chicago, IL, 20 May.

Storr, M. (2003) *Latex and Lingerie: Shopping for Pleasure at Ann Summers Parties*. Oxford: Berg.

Strathern, M. (2004) *Partial Connections – Updated Edition*. California: Alta Mira.

Street, A. (2009) Failed Recipients: Extracting Blood in a Papua New Guinean Hospital. *Body and Society* 15(2): 193–215.

Strong, P. M. (1979) *The Ceremonial Order of the Clinic*. London: Routledge Kegan Paul.

Suddaby, R. and Greenwood, R. (2005) Rhetorical Strategies of Legitimacy. *Administrative Science Quarterly* 50: 35–67.

Summers, J. (1989) *Soho: A History of London's Most Colourful Neighbourhood*. London: Bloomsbury.

Swan, E. (2010) A Testing Time, Full of Potential?: Gender in Management, Histories and Futures. *Journal of European Industrial Training* 25(8): 661–675.

Swan, E. and Wray-Bliss, E. (2010) *The Good Life? Transnational Global Elite and Public Pedagogy*, proposal for UTS Research Grant, UTS, Sydney.

Symon, G. (2000) Everyday Rhetoric: Argument and Persuasion in Everyday Life. *European Journal of Work and Organizational Psychology* 9(4): 477–488.

Symon, G. (2005) Exploring Resistance from a Rhetorical Perspective. *Organization Studies* 26(11): 1641–1663.

Symon, G. (2008) Developing the Political Perspective on Technological Change through Rhetorical Analysis. *Management Communication Quarterly* 22(1): 74–98.

Symon, G., Buerhring, A., et al. (2008) Positioning Qualitative Research as Resistance to the Institutionalization of the Academic Labour Process. *Organization Studies* 29(10): 1315–1336.

Tajfel, H. and Turner, J. (1985) The Social Identity Theory of Intergroup Behaviour. In Worchel, S. and Austin, W. (eds) *Psychology of Intergroup Relations* (Second Edition). Chicago: Nelson Hall.

Talbot, M. (2000) Strange Bedfellows: Feminism in Advertising. In Andrews, M. and Talbot, M. (eds) *All the World and Her Husband: Women and Consumption in the Twentieth Century*. London: Cassell, pp. 177–191.

Tate, B. (2010) *West End Girls*. London: Orion.

Taylor, S. and Bogdan, R. (1984) *Introduction to Qualitative Research Methods: The Search for Meanings*. New York: Wiley.

Taylor, S. and Tyler, M. (2000) Emotional Labour and Sexual Difference in the Airline Industry. *Work Employment and Society* 14(1): 77–95.

Tewksbury, R. (1990) Patrons of Porn: Research Notes on the Clientele of Adult Bookstores. *Deviant Behaviour* 11: 259–271.

Tewksbury, R. (1993) Peep Shows and Perverts: Men and Masculinity in an Adult Bookstore. *Journal of Men's Studies* 2(1): 53–70.

Thanem, T. (2006) Living on the Edge: Towards a Monstrous Organization Theory. *Organization* 13(2): 163–193.

Thiel, D. (2007) Class In Construction: London Building Workers, Dirty Work and Physical Cultures. *British Journal of Sociology* 58(2): 227–251.

Thomas, R. and Davies, A. (2005) Theorizing the Micro-Politics of Resistance: New Public Management and Managerial Identities in the UK Public Services. *Organization Studies* 26(5): 683–706.

Thomas, R. and Linstead, A. (2002) Losing the Plot? Middle Managers and Identity. *Organization* 9(1): 71–93.

Thompson, W. E. (1983) Hanging Tongues: A Sociological Encounter with the Assembly Line. *Qualitative Sociology* 6(3): 215–237.

Törrönen, J. (2001) The Concept of Subject Position in Empirical Social Research. *Journal for the Theory of Social Behaviour* 31: 313–329.

Tovey, P. and Adams, J. (2001) Primary Care as Intersecting Social Worlds. *Social Science and Medicine* 52: 695–706.

Tracy, S. and Scott, C. (2006) Sexuality, Masculinity and Taint Management among Firefighters and Correctional Officers: Getting Down and Dirty with 'America's Heroes' and the 'Scum of Law Enforcement'. *Management Communication Quarterly* 20(1): 6–38.

Tracy, S. J., Myers, K. K. and Scott, C. W. (2006) Cracking Jokes and Crafting Selves: Sensemaking and Identity Management among Human Service Workers. *Communication Monograms* 73(3): 283–308.

Trethewey, A. (1999) Disciplined Bodies: Women's Embodied Identities at Work. *Organization Studies* 20(3): 423–450.

Tronto, J. (2002) The 'Nanny' Question in Feminism. *Hypatia* 17(2): 34–51.

Twigg, J. (2000) Care Work as a Form of Body Work. *Ageing and Society* 20: 389–411.

Twigg, J. (2006) *The Body in Health and Social Care*. New York: Palgrave Macmillan.

Vachhani, S. J. (2009) Vagina Dentata and the Demonological Body – Explorations of the Feminine Demon in Organisation. In Pullen, A. and Rhodes, C. (eds) *Bits of Organization*. Copenhagen: Liber Press.

Van Den Brink, M. and Stobbe, L. (2009) Doing Gender in Academic Education: The Paradox of Visibility. *Gender, Work and Organization* 16(4): 451–470.

Van Dongen, E. and Elema, R. (2001) The Art of Touching: The Culture of Body Work in Nursing. *Anthropology and Medicine* 8: 149–162.

Velena, H. (2003) La prostituzione virtuale. In *Porneia. voci es guardi sulla prostituzione*. Padova: Il Poligrafo.

Venning, P., Durie, A., Roland, M., Roberts, C. and Leese, B. (2000) Randomised Controlled Trial Comparing Cost Effectiveness of General Practitioners and Nurse Practitioners in Primary Care. *British Medical Journal* 320: 1048–1053.

Walby, S. and Greenwell, J. (1994) *Medicine and Nursing: Profession in a Changing Health Service*. London: Sage.

Walkerdine, V. (2003) Reclassifying Upward Mobility: Femininity and the Neoliberal. *Gender and Education* 15(3): 237–248.

Warhurst, C. and Nickson, D. (2009) Who's Got the Look? Emotional Aesthetics and Sexualized Labour in Interactive Services. *Gender, Work and Organization* 16(3): 385–404.

Watson, T. J., and Harris, D. (1999) *The Emergent Manager*. London: Sage Publications Ltd.

Weber, M. (1992 [1968]) *Economy and Society* (Trans. G. Roth and C. Wittich). California: University of California Press.

Wegar, K. (1993) Conclusions. In Riska, E. and Wegar, K. (eds) *Gender, Work and Medicine*. London: Sage.

Weiss, G. and Haber, H. (eds) (1999) *Perspectives on Embodiment – The Intersections of Nature and Culture*. London: Routledge.

Weitzer, R. (2000) Why We Need More Research on Sex Work. In Weitzer, R. (ed.) *Sex for Sale. Prostitution, Pornography and the Sex Industry*. New York: Routledge.

West, C. and Zimmerman, D. H. (1987) Doing Gender. *Gender and Society* 1: 125–151.

West, J. and Austrin, T. (2002) From Work as Sex to Sex as Work: Networks, 'Others' and Occupations in the Analysis of Work. *Gender, Work and Organization* 9(5): 482–503.

Whimster, S. (1992) Yuppies: A Keyword of the 1980s. In Budd, L. and Whimster, S. (eds) *Global Finance and Urban Living: A Study of Metropolitan Change*. London: Routledge.

White, P. J. (2008) *On Producing and Reproducing Intensive Care: The Place of the Patient, The Place of the Other*, Unpublished PhD thesis, School of Social Sciences, Cardiff University, Wales.

White, P. J. (2009) Knowing Body, Knowing Other: Cultural Materials and Intensive Care. *Sociological Review* 56(s2): 117–137.

White, P. J., Hillman, A. and Latimer, J. E. (2012) Ordering, Enrolling and Dismissing: Moments of Access across Hospital Spaces. *Environment and Planning D: Space and Culture*.

Whitford, M. (1991) *Luce Irigaray – Philosophy in the Feminine*. London: Routledge.

Wiesenfeld, B. M., Wurthmann, K. A. et al. (2008) The Stigmatization and Devaluation of Elites Associated with Corporate Failures: A Process Model. *Academy of Management Review* 33(1): 231–251.

Williams, C. (ed.) (1993) *Doing Women's Work: Men in Non-Traditional Occupations*. London: Sage.

Williams, Claire (2003) Sky Service: The Demands of Emotional Labour in the Airline Industry. *Gender, Work and Organization* 10(5): 513–550.

Williams, D. (2004) The Effects of Childcare Activities on the Duration of Self-Employment in Europe. *Entrepreneurship: Theory and Practice* 28(3): 467–485.

Witz, A. (1992) *Professions and Patriarchy*. London: Routledge.

Wolf, Z. (1988) *Nurses' Work: The Sacred and the Profane: Studies in Health, Illness and Caregiving*. Pennsylvania: University of Pennsylvania Press.

Wolkowicz, C. (2003) The Social Relations of Body Work. *Work, Employment and Society* 16 (3): 497–510.

Wolkowitz, C. (2006) *Bodies at Work*. London: Sage Publications.

Woodroffe, E. (2006) Nurse-Led General Practice: The Changing Face of General Practice? *British Journal of General Practice* 56 (529): 632–633.

Woolgar, S. and Pawluch, D. (1985) Ontological Gerry-Mandering: The Anatomy of Social Problems Explanations. *Social Problems* 32: 214–227.

Zoonen, L. van (1994) *Feminist Media Studies*. Thousand Oaks, CA: Sage.

Zussman, R. (1992) *Intensive Care: Medical Ethics and the Medical Profession*. Chicago: University of Chicago Press.

Index